Visual Basic® .NET

PROGRAMMER'S REFERENCE

Dan Rahmel

D0368440

McGraw-Hill/Osborne

New York   Chicago   San Francisco
Lisbon   London   Madrid   Mexico City   Milan
New Delhi   San Juan   Seoul   Singapore   Sydney   Toronto

McGraw-Hill/Osborne
2600 Tenth Street
Berkeley, California 94710
U.S.A.

To arrange bulk purchase discounts for sales promotions, premiums, or
fund-raisers, please contact McGraw-Hill/Osborne at the above address. For
information on translations or book distributors outside the U.S.A., please
see the International Contact Information page immediately following the
index of this book.

Visual Basic® .NET Programmer's Reference

Publisher   Brandon A. Nordin
Vice President & Associate Publisher   Scott Rogers
Acquisitions Editor   Jim Schachterle
Project Editor   Laura Stone
Acquisitions Coordinator   Timothy Madrid
Technical Editor   Greg Guntle
Copy Editors   Richard H. Adin and Robert Campbell
Proofreader   Karen Mead
Indexer   Rebecca Plunkett
Computer Designers   Carie Abrew and George Toma Charbak
Illustrators   Michael Mueller and Lyssa Wald
Series Design   Peter F. Hancik

1234567890 DOC DOC 01987654321

ISBN 0-07-219534-7

This book was composed with Corel VENTURA™ Publisher.

In the wake of the September 11th attacks, I would like to dedicate this book to all the people who use their passion and energy to create rather than to destroy—and to the survivors who must find the courage to build again.

About the Author

Dan Rahmel is a Windows programmer with over 14 years of experience designing and implementing information systems and deploying mid-sized client/server solutions using Visual Basic, ASP, C++, and SQL Server. He has authored numerous books including the *Visual Basic Programmer's Reference*, first and second editions; *Building Web Database Applications with Visual Studio*; *Teach Yourself Database Programming in 24 Hours*; and *Developing Client-Server Applications with Visual Basic*. He is a contributor to *DBMS*, *Internet Advisor*, and *American Programmer* magazines.

CONTENTS @ A GLANCE

v

CONTENTS

viii   Contents

5   Extensible Markup Language 61

6   Language Reference 73

x Contents

9   Excel XP Object Model Diagrams 283

10   Word XP Object Model Diagrams 313

xvi Contents

Contents **xvii**

ACKNOWLEDGMENTS

It was a pleasure to work with the people at Osborne again on this new edition. Combining the creation of the book with the superior Osborne staff often made the difficult seem easy. I'd like to thank the people with whom I often interacted (Jim Schachterle, Tim Madrid, Laura Stone, Greg Guntle, Richard Adin, and Robert Campbell), and all the others who had to work tirelessly in production and editing to produce this book.

I'd like to thank my parents (Ron and Marie), siblings (David and Darlene), and friends (David Rahmel, Don Murphy, Greg Mickey, John Taylor, Juan Leonffu, Ed Gildred, and Weld O'Connor) for their unconditional support. To David Rahmel, who made fantastic suggestions on how to improve the book and actively took part in shaping the new edition, my many thanks.

Most of all, I'd like to thank the readers. By buying this book, you make it possible for all of us in the book industry to labor to produce good work. I'd like to say a special thanks to Christopher Lopez and Simon Walke, who sent me suggestions and pointed out errors in the previous edition. When pulling the long hours to complete a book, knowing that every little improvement will help the development community is what really makes the difference. Thanks.

INTRODUCTION

Welcome to the new edition of the *Visual Basic.NET Programmer's Reference*. Writing this book has been a pleasure because of its longevity. Years ago, when the Osborne staff initially contacted me about writing the first edition, I questioned the need for such a book. With all of the online help included with VB, who needed a reference? We worked together to refine a concept of the book that would add a good deal of value to the existing VB information. By including code samples, object diagrams, how-to examples, key code charts, and cross-references in a small and convenient book size, the value of such a book was obvious. Over the years the VB system has become more complicated and the people at Osborne and I have endeavored to keep this reference book as up-to-date and useful as possible.

Who Is This Book For?

With the whole new world that Visual Basic .NET represents, I hope this book will help ease you into using the new Visual Basic .NET system. I've also written a sister volume, the *.NET Programmer's Reference* (ISBN 0-07-219466-9), which holds reference information for the class libraries included in the .NET Framework. If you find this volume useful, you may find the companion book helpful in programming the vast .NET Framework.

The book you hold in your hands contains reference information for the Visual Basic/VBA/VBScript family of products. The book generally assumes some programming experience, but if you're new to programming, you will most likely find this book invaluable. I have tried to provide extensive cross-references within the book.

How to Read This Book

I have written this book with the idea of making it instantly usable for programming projects. All of the functions and statements for VB.NET are listed alphabetically in Chapter 6 for quick reference. If you know the general type of functionality you need, you can most likely look up a function you already know and follow the **See Also** references or other aids in the text to lead you to your exact topic.

If you're a programmer who has experience with earlier versions of VB, be sure to look through Chapter 1. It explains many of the changes in the new .NET version of Visual Basic, including some changes that, although present in the programming system, were not listed in the What's New section of the actual documentation.

Special Features and Tools

Perhaps the most useful feature of this book are the code samples (included in the **Immediate Window Sample**, **Code Sample**, and **HTML Code Sample** sections) provided with each reference command. Seldom does a programmer seek to learn about a Visual Basic command out of random curiosity. I wanted a book that shows exactly how to use each VB command, so I constructed this book with that philosophy in mind. With each language term is a simple example that can be entered and executed immediately.

This concept is augmented in the **How-To** sections you'll find in Chapter 4. These show step-by-step examples of common operations that you frequently need to perform, but may not always quite remember the exact method of implementation. Now you can just jump to the proper section and see the framework.

Another great feature of the book is the inclusion of **Object Diagrams** in Chapters 7–13. The object diagrams provided by Microsoft and replicated in most other books show a jumble of objects and collections. It is often difficult to tell which shape in the diagram denotes a single object versus a collection. Not so in my diagrams. Each diagram shows only a single level of the object model. Collections are obvious both by their appearance (like a deck of stacked cards) and the listing of the plural collection name followed by the singular object name shown below in parentheses.

I hope that you find these object models an invaluable reference when creating Visual Basic/VBA projects. Object models are becoming almost more important to a project than the actual programming language, as you may have noticed with the adoption of the .NET Framework. For this reason, any improvements that can be made in understanding and referencing the object model (whether it's for Excel, PowerPoint, or any system) should be embraced.

Everyone looks up topics in a different way. If you don't find something listed under the heading you expected, please make a note of it and send us the information. That way, the next revision of the book can be even better.

I hope you find this book as useful as the people at Coherent Data (www.coherentdata.com) already have. I also hope you'll provide feedback with any suggestions you have or mistakes you find. A page devoted to this book is located on the Coherent Data site. Please stop by.

Chapter 1
Visual Basic .NET Features

The changes that have occurred to transform the previous version of Visual Basic (VB) into VB.NET are too substantial to fully cover in a reference book. The entire development system has evolved from its runtime and native compiler-based foundation to a virtual machine (Microsoft Intermediate Language or MSIL) Just-In-Time (JIT) compiler-based system. Visual Basic has also been incorporated into a unified Integrated Development Environment (IDE) with the other Visual Studio languages.

For these reasons, the descriptions of changes in this book reflect the principal changes that a developer will encounter when upgrading to VB.NET. They do not, however, cover the core deployment challenges that will be faced by adopting this new system. Be aware that the entire .NET Framework system has been integrated into the Visual Studio.NET environment. To take full advantage of .NET features will require a developer to approach VB.NET as an entirely new system rather than as an evolutionary update to Visual Basic.

New VB.NET Elements

VB.NET is a substantial departure from previous versions of Visual Basic. Primary changes include

- **Integration into the Visual Studio IDE**   Like the other languages included in Visual Studio, Visual Basic has been integrated into a single common development environment. Whether you develop in C#, C++, or VB, the same windows, menus, and controls are available (see the "Integrated Development Environment" section later in the chapter).

- **Compilation of code into MSIL**   Unlike previous VB versions, no project type compiles into native machine code or interpreted token code. All source code is compiled into a metalanguage called MSIL that functions similarly to Java Virtual Machine bytecode. At the time of execution, MSIL application code is converted to native code by a JIT compiler.

1

- **Addition of .NET Framework access**   All routines of the Windows system are available through an advanced object framework known as the .NET Framework. Use of the system objects in the .NET Framework supersedes previous VB elements (such as forms and controls), calls to the Win32 Application Programming Interface (API), or object creation through the Microsoft Foundation Classes (MFC).

- **Alterations to the VB language**   Slight additions to keywords and functions have been made to the VB language (see the "Language Changes" section later in the chapter).

- **Extension of data types**   Data types such as Integer and Long have been augmented and other type refinements have been made (see the "Data Variable Types" section later in the chapter).

- **Extension of object-oriented features**   The three cornerstones of full object-oriented programming (inheritance, overloading, and polymorphism) are now available for programming from Visual Basic (see the "Object-Oriented Concepts" section later in the chapter).

- **Addition of multithreading capabilities**   VB.NET now supports complete multithreading with thread creation, management, and priority options.

- **Creation of console applications**   Command-line programs can now be created within Visual Basic. These applications can be run from the console, MS-DOS prompt, or command prompt, and require no user interface.

- **Creation of Windows NT services**   Long the domain of C++, VB can now be used to create NT services. Services are routines that execute in the background of an operating system (OS) to perform a variety of functions, from monitoring portable battery usage to providing FTP server services. An NT service can execute on NT 4, Windows 2000, and Windows XP.

- **Addition of Web services**   Like an NT service, a Web service can actively run on a server machine in the background. Web services, however, are tailored to enable communication through standard Internet protocols. A Web service may be called remotely via a standard uniform resource locator (URL).

- **Support of ADO.NET**   ADO.NET provides an upgrade to the features of ActiveX Data Objects (ADO) including full support of extensible markup language (XML), disconnected data sets, and XML schemas.

1

- **Inclusion of structured error handling**   Long supported by other languages such as C++, structured handling has now been added to VB.NET in the form of an advanced implementation of the Try...Catch mechanism (see the "Error Handling" section later in the chapter).

- **Creation of server controls**   VB can be used to create a server control that executes on the Internet Information Server (IIS). The control executes on the Web server and returns rendered hypertext markup language (HTML) that can be inserted into a Web page that will be sent to the browser.

- **Extension of data binding to the Web**   Although VB has supported data binding on controls on a VB form since version 3, VB.NET augments this capability by creating the features to let Web forms include bound controls.

Language Changes

In terms of actual commands, the Visual Basic language has altered less than 5 percent. Most of the common keywords, statements, and functions are still available, although there are new prescribed ways of using certain capabilities (such as using the MessageBox.Show() method instead of the MsgBox() function).

The primary languages changes include

- **Atn, Sgn, and Sqr have been eliminated**   They have been replaced by the methods Atan, Sign, and Sqrt, respectively, which are found in the System.Math class.

- **Circle and Line functions have been eliminated**   They have been replaced by the methods DrawEllipse and DrawLine, respectively, which are found in the System .Drawing.Graphics class.

- **Date and Time have been eliminated**   They have been replaced by the properties Today and TimeOfDay, respectively, which can be used just as Date and Time were used.

- **Date$ and Time$ have been eliminated**   They have been replaced by the properties DateString and TimeString, respectively, which can be used just as Date$ and Time$ were used.

- **Debug.Print has been eliminated**   It has been replaced by the methods Write, WriteIf, WriteLine, and WriteLineIf, which are found in the System.Diagnostics.Debug class. Typically, the command Console.WriteLine(myStr) would be used instead of the command Debug.Print(myStr).

- **Def functions are no longer supported**   The functions DefBool, DefByte, DefCur, DefDate, DefDbl, DefDec, DefInt, DefLng, DefObj, DefSng, DefStr, and DefVar are not supported in VB.NET.

- **DoEvents has been eliminated**   It has been replaced by the method DoEvents found in the System.Windows.Forms.Application class.

- **Empty and Null have been eliminated**   Both should be replaced by the Nothing setting.

- **GoSub has been eliminated.**

- **IsEmpty has been eliminated.** It has been replaced by the IsNothing function.

- **IsMissing has been eliminated**   In VB.NET, every optional argument in a procedural definition must have a default value setting, making the IsMissing function that used to determine whether an argument was supplied unnecessary.

- **IsNull and IsObject have been eliminated**   They have been replaced by the methods IsDBNull and IsReference, respectively, that are found in the Microsoft.VisualBasic.Information class.

- **LSet and RSet have been eliminated**   They have been replaced by the methods PadRight and PadLeft, respectively, which are found in the System.String class.

- **PSet and Scale have been eliminated**   No direct equivalent exists in VB.NET.

- **Rnd and Round have been eliminated**   They have been replaced by the methods Rnd and Round, respectively, that are found in the System.Math class.

- **Set statement**   Object references can now be copied directly with the equal (=) operator.

- **Type has been eliminated**   The Type command was used to define a user-defined data type (UDT). The keyword Structure should now be used in its place.

- **Wend has been eliminated**   Wend was used as a control flow statement to end a While loop; it has been replaced by the End While statement.

- **Property Get, Property Let, and Property Set have been eliminated**   These commands have been replaced by the Property...End Property definition structure.

- **Open #, Close #, Put, Set, and Width have been eliminated**   They have been replaced by the functions FileOpen, FileClose, FilePut, FileSet, and FileWidth, respectively.

- **Name has been eliminated**   It has been replaced by the Rename function.

- **AndAlso and OrElse statements added**   These additional statements are all conditional functions with short-circuiting.

Data Variable Types

The data types available for variable and property declaration have not changed dramatically from Visual Basic 6 to VB.NET. The most complicated change is the alteration in the sizes of the Integer and Long variable types (their sizes have been doubled). These types have been expanded to accommodate the significant increases in the microprocessor architecture power that has occurred over the last decade.

Other changes to data type handling from Visual Basic 6 include

- **Array bounds**   Although arrays had a default lower bound of 0 in VB 6, this bound could be changed by using the Option Base keywords. In VB.NET, all arrays start at a lower bound of 0 and it cannot be changed.

- **Elimination of Variant data type**   The Variant type has been eliminated and the default for an undeclared type is now Object. Functionally, this change doesn't substantially affect coding procedures.

- **Multiple variable declaration added**   Now multiple variables of the same type (that is, Dim i, j, k As Integer) don't require separate data type listings

The following table shows the entire set of core VB.NET data types as well as the characteristics of each type. These characteristics include the Common Language Runtime (CLR) type that indicates where the type is located in the .NET namespace and the size of the type in bytes. Also included is a column that indicates how the current type relates to the previous version of Visual Basic.

VB.NET Type	CLR Type	Size (Bytes)	VB 6 Type	Notes
Boolean	System.Boolean	2	Boolean	Boolean value of True or False.
Byte	System.Byte	1	Byte	Individual bytes most often used for binary data or file data access. Range: 0–255 (unsigned).
Char	System.Char	2	N/A	Unicode character. Range: 0–65535 (unsigned).
N/A	N/A	8	Currency	The Currency type has been eliminated in VB.NET. Use the Decimal type instead.
Date	System.DateTime	8	N/A	Holds a date value that may be between January 1, 0001 and December 31, 9999. VB 6 used the Double type to hold a DateTime. To convert a VB 6 date/time value stored in a double data type, use the ToDouble() and FromOADate() methods in the DateTime class.
Decimal	System.Decimal	16	Decimal	In VB.NET, the Decimal type has increased in size from 14 bytes to 16 bytes. It should be used as a replacement for Currency variable types in previous VB versions. Range: +/–79,228,162, 514,264,337,593,543,950, 335 with no decimal point; +/–7.922816251 4264337593543950335 with 28 places to the right of the decimal.

VB.NET Type	CLR Type	Size (Bytes)	VB 6 Type	Notes
Double	System.Double	8	Double	Holds a double-precision floating-point value. Range: Negative values between −1.7976931 3486231E+308 and −4.94065645841247E−324; positive values between 4.940656458 41247E−324 and 1.797 69313486231E+308.
Integer	System.Int32	4	Long	In VB.NET, the Integer type has increased in size from 2 to 4 bytes. Range: Between −2,147,483,648 and 2,147,483,647.
Long	System.Int64	8	N/A	In VB.NET, the Long type has increased in size from 4 to 8 bytes. Range: Between −9,223,372,036,854,775,808 and 9,223,372,036,854,775,807.
Object	System.Object	4	Object	Holds an object reference.
Short	System.Int16	2	Integer	In VB.NET, the Short type represents the same size as the previous version of Integer. Range: Between −32,768 and 32,767.
Single	System.Single	4	Single	Holds a single-precision floating-point value. Range: Negative values between −3.402823E+38 and −1.401298E−45; positive values between 1.401298E−45 and 3.402823E+38.

VB.NET Type	CLR Type	Size (Bytes)	VB 6 Type	Notes
String	System.String	Variable	String	Fixed length strings are no longer supported in VB.NET. Use an array of BYTEs or CHARs for limited string definition. Range: Between 0 and 2 billion Unicode characters.
N/A	N/A	Variable	Variant	Variant has been eliminated from VB.NET and Object is not the default type for an untyped variable.

VB.NET has also added a number of new operators that act on variables and values for specific bitwise operations. While And, Or, Xor, and Not were previously used for both Boolean and bitwise operations, now there are a number of new commands that are only available for bitwise expressions. The following table contains the new operators and the equivalent operators of ones that have been replaced.

VB.NET	Visual Basic 6
BitAnd (for bitwise operations)	And
BitOr (for bitwise operations)	Or
BitXor (for bitwise operations)	Xor
BitNot (for bitwise operations)	Not
=	Eqv
Not and Or (that is, (Not A) Or B)	Imp

Integrated Development Environment

The new Integrated Development Environment (IDE) of Visual Studio has allowed all of the languages in Visual Studio to be united under a common interface. Figure 1-1 shows the common presentation of a Windows application in the IDE. Each section of the screen is divided into a number of panes. These panes can be resized and every pane can contain multiple windows, each one displayed as a named tab.

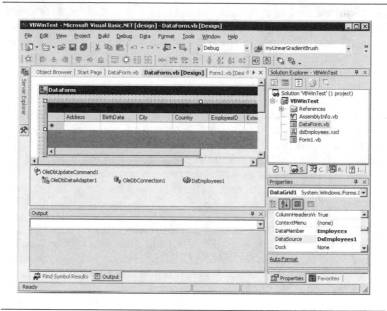

Figure 1-1.   The unified IDE for all of the Visual Studio
programming languages

For reference, the screen is divided into the following general parts:

- **Left Side**   Along the left side are pop-out menus of the Server
  Explorer and the Toolbox. The Server Explorer is used for
  selection of data sources and data adapters. The Toolbox
  contains all standard UI controls (check box, button, and so on)
  that can be dragged on dropped on the displayed form. If
  visible, the Document Outline is also displayed here.

- **Center**   The center pane of the window displays the selected
  document. This document may be a form, a code page, a Web
  page, the object browser, or the display of a help topic.

- **Bottom**   Directly under the document window, a number of
  available panes are displayed as tabs in the window. Some of
  these include Output window, Debugging window, Dynamic
  help search results, Command Window, Find Symbol Results,
  and Breakpoints.

- **Right side** The right side of the window contains two different panes. The lower pane holds the Property window or the Favorites selection. The upper pane has many possible options available through a tabbed window, some of which include the Solution Explorer, Class View, Resource View, Macro Explorer, and Dynamic Help index.

The variety of options available in the toolbar has grown extensively. One of the most important is the Solution Configurations combo box, shown in Figure 1-2. Through it, a developer can select what will occur when the Start button is pressed. For example, when Release is selected, the build that occurs on execution will be precisely that—an EXE or component that will be generated by the final build. This means no debugging information is included.

NOTE: If you execute an application and debugging options are not available, be sure to check the Solution Configurations combo box. It may be confusing when the setting has been left on Release because any attempt to activate debugging is ignored while executing in this mode although Visual Basic does not indicate why.

Through the Solution Configurations combo box, access to the Configuration Manager is available for creating custom settings. Settings such as debugging options, target platform, and determining whether a build takes place on execution are available options.

Object Browser

The Object Browser is provided as part of the Visual Basic.NET environment. It can be used to examine the members of any object model installed on the system (including any of the .NET Framework libraries) that arc imported into the current project.

Figure 1-3 shows the Object Browser that is available through the View | Other Windows menu, from an icon on the toolbar, or by

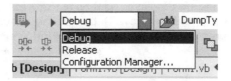

Figure 1-2.   This combo box displays the available solution configurations

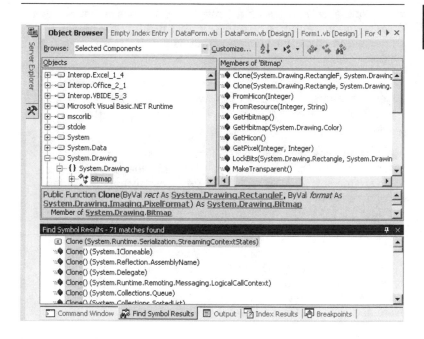

Figure 1-3.   The Object Browser displaying the members of a class

pressing F2. The Object Browser contains three panes, the Objects pane, the Members pane, and the Search pane. The Browse combo box shows what current libraries are being shown in the various panes.

The *Objects* pane displays an alphabetical list of all the available objects and collections. In Chapters 7 through 13 of this book, you will find the complete Object Model diagrams for all of the Office applications as well as other components. Using these diagrams in conjunction with the Object Browser should enable you to create nearly any object-based solution. Clicking on an object or collection in the Objects pane will automatically change the members shown in the Members pane.

The *Members* pane contains all of the properties, fields, events, and methods for an object class (object or collection) selected in the Objects pane. Methods have an icon that looks like a speeding box. Properties have the traditional icon (hand pointing to a box) that represents properties. Clicking on a particular member will fill the bottom of the dialog box with the calling conventions of that member. If the member is a property, it will detail the data type held in that property. A method will show any values that it requires to be passed as arguments and any values it will return.

The *Find* pane is hidden until you activate a search, and then it appears underneath the Object Browser window. You can execute a search by clicking on the Find button (the button with the binoculars icon).

All of the objects shown in the Object Browser are the object libraries assigned to the current project. This does not mean that these are the only libraries registered with your system. For example, Excel defaults to adding the Excel object libraries to the project, but doesn't add the Word libraries, because most people will have no use for them in an Excel project.

To add other libraries to the project, select the Project | Add Reference menu option. Depending on the application you are using, this will appear on different menus. Any object libraries references added to the project will become available for examination in the Object Browser.

Menu Shortcuts

Although some of the menu options will change depending on the language that you will be developing in, most of the commands will remain the same. Here is a list of shortcut keys for the most common menu commands.

Shortcut	Description
ALT-F12	Find symbol
ALT-SHIFT-A	Add existing item
CTRL-A	Select All
CTRL-ALT-P	Examine debug processes
CTRL-B	Add new breakpoint
CTRL-F	Find
CTRL-F1	Dynamic help
CTRL-F5	Start execution without debugging
CTRL-G	Goto (line number)
CTRL-H	Replace
CTRL-N	New File
CTRL-O	Open File

Shortcut	Description
CTRL-P	Print
CTRL-S	Save Item
CTRL-SHIFT-A	Add new item
CTRL-SHIFT-B	Build current project
CTRL-SHIFT-F	Find in Files
CTRL-SHIFT-F9	Clear all breakpoints
CTRL-SHIFT-H	Replace in Files
CTRL-SHIFT-N	New Project
CTRL-SHIFT-O	Open Project
CTRL-SHIFT-S	Save All
CTRL-SHIFT-U	Make uppercase
CTRL-U	Make lowercase
CTRL-Y	Redo
CTRL-Z	Undo
F1	Help
F3	Find again
F4	Properties window
F5	Start execution
F7	View code
F9	Set breakpoint
F10	Step over
F11	Step into
SHIFT-ALT-ENTER	Display in full screen mode

Object-Oriented Concepts

The addition of complete object-oriented features to the latest version of Visual Basic is significant. These new capabilities make Visual Basic programming more like other languages such as C++ and Java. As an object-oriented system with hierarchical class navigation and definition capabilities, Visual Basic enjoys access to the complete functionality of the .NET Framework.

The new object-oriented capabilities are far more substantial than those of the previous Visual Basic version that only provided for the creation and management of Component Object Model (COM) component objects. The foundations of traditional object-oriented programming are now part of the new VB.

The three cornerstones of full object-oriented programming (inheritance, polymorphism, and overloading) are implemented at the class level of scope for all Visual Studio languages. Therefore, most of the implementation of these features within a project occurs in the definition portions of the class and its members. For example, when a class is set to inherit from another class, the parent class is specified using the Inherits keyword in the class header.

Inheritance

A *class* is a collection of data and the methods and events related to it. With inheritance, a class may become a child of other classes. A child class is said to *inherit* the functionality of the parent class. The new class may contain all of the members of the parent class, including properties, methods, fields, and events. In this example, a new class called NewChildClass has inherited the members of the parent ParentClass but overridden and created its own myDraw method:

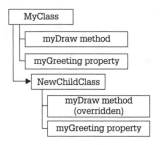

Inheritance allows existing program logic to be reused without any reprogramming. The new class may be extended to include new members and it can also be adapted to other needs as any inherited member of the parent class can be overridden or disabled. There is the flexibility to mirror an existing class and add a few new features or completely redefine the functionality that is provided by the parent class.

As a simple example of the advantages of inheritance, you could create a rectangle class that would initialize, move, and draw a rectangle on the screen. Next you could create a rounded rectangle class that inherits behaviors from the rectangle parent class for actions such as moving and resizing. The new class could override the constructor methods (to accept the corner rounding arguments), the drawing method (to draw a rounded rectangle), and add new properties to accept the measures for rounding.

Because the rounded rectangle class is subclassed to the rectangle class, any objects created with it can also be passed to a method that expects a rectangle object as an argument. The additional information of the extended rectangle class is simply ignored by the method and the object is treated as a rectangle. This enables a programmer to make a child of an existing class, add additional data or methods, and yet continue to use this object with older routines that accept object types of the parent class.

In Visual Basic, defining a new class to extend an existing class uses the Inherits keyword like this:

```
Public Class myComponent
    Inherits System.ComponentModel.Component
```

This definition creates a new component that inherits all of the existing properties, methods, events, and fields of the existing class System.ComponentModel.Component. The component is then expected to extend this generic foundation class in order to provide the desired functionality for this custom component.

Not all classes provide inheritance features in the same way. In VB.NET there are a number of different class types and each has restrictions on how the child class may inherit from a parent. The three primary types of classes that affect inheritance are

- **Standard** Provides inheritance for all of its members.
- **Abstract (MustInherit modifier)** An abstract class cannot be instantiated itself, but instead can be used as a parent class for another class or provides basic utility methods without instantiation. Members of an abstract class are often defined but not implemented because no standard implementation is possible. The class that inherits from the abstract class is expected to implement definitions for these members. An abstract class may include the modifier MustInherit that causes it to be used only as a parent class.
- **Concrete (NotInheritable modifier)** This type of class must be used as it is and cannot be extended with child classes.

When a new class is created, the choice of the type of class is specified in the definition. There are three modifier sets that can be used.

- **Public or Private or Protected or Friend or Protected Friend**   Any one of these modifiers may be used, but only one per class. The Public modifier makes the class visible to classes outside the assembly, whereas Private keeps it invisible. Protected makes a class visible to classes within the assembly and those in a derived class. Friend indicates that the class is visible only within the program that contains the declaration, and Protected Friend grants access of both the Protected and Friend modifiers.

- **Shadows**   Sets the class to shadow an already existing class in that namespace. Essentially, shadowing performs the act of overloading (see the "Overloading" section later in the chapter) but operates on a class instead of a method, property, or other member.

- **MustInherit or NotInheritable**   MustInherit makes the class so it cannot be instantiated and the creation of a child class is required to use its functionality. NotInheritable prohibits the class from being used for further inheritance.

Only one member of each modifier set may be used in a definition (that is, the MustInherit and NotInheritable modifiers can't both be used in the same definition). Each of these modifiers is used to describe the inheritance features and the available scope of the new class.

Within a class, members can also exist that modify the effect of inheritance. For example, virtual members are method, properties, or events that exist in a class or interface that is not directly up the inheritance chain from the current class. You may notice a number of objects in the .NET Framework that have a hierarchy with a root object defined as Object.MarshalByRefObject. These classes are located somewhere in the class hierarchy apart from where they draw their members. The virtual members reference the origination point.

NOTE: In the .NET documentation, there are often references to C# notation that are not explicitly cited as from that language. One example is the frequent use of the modifier **sealed** (that has the same effect of the **NotInheritable** modifier in VB) in the text descriptions related to class definition. This problem even occurs in parts of the .NET system (such as System.Reflection) that return information in C# definition format regardless of the language (such as VB) that accesses these routines. Therefore, if you can't find a reference to a particular statement or keyword in the VB manual, check the C# documentation.

All nonabstract classes must have at least one constructor. In many cases, the constructor of the child class is required to call the constructor of the parent class within its definition. If you look in the code automatically generated in VB for a new form, you will often see a statement such as this:

```
Public Sub New()
 MyBase.New()
```

As part of the constructor method, the constructor of the base/foundation/parent class is called so proper initialization can occur. If a new class is defined to inherit from a parent class but a constructor isn't defined, VB.NET implicitly activates the constructor of the parent class to be invoked when a new instance is created.

Polymorphism

Polymorphism enables multiple classes, named differently, to be called with the same methods and properties. For example, a rectangle, an oval, and a rounded rectangle may all have the method Draw() that draws them to the screen. A routine could be written that accepts an object of any of these types and executes the Draw() method on it without concerning itself with the actual type of object. Here you can see the same myDraw() method being sent to three different objects created with three different classes:

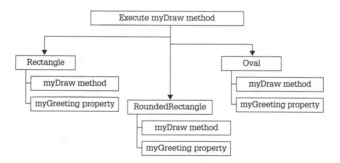

In previous versions of Visual Basic, polymorphism could be simulated through the use of interfaces. In VB.NET, full inheritance-based polymorphism is also supported. Either inheritance or interfaces can be used for polymorphism. As a general rule, make a selection on whether to use inheritance or an interface based on these two guidelines:

- Use inheritance to extend base classes.

- Use interfaces for multiple implementations that don't have much in common.

Inheritance-Based Polymorphism   Inheritance-based polymorphism occurs when several different classes inherit from the same parent class and each child class contains either the inherited version or an overridden version of the primary methods and properties. A class can only inherit from a single base class. Often an abstract class can be used in the same functional role as an interface. An abstract class can partially or fully implement the functionality of the class. Use an abstract class when

- **Multiple versions of a component are needed**   Each class is provided with complete versioning control through the assembly structure.

- **Large functional units are needed**   Because an abstract class can include at least a partial implementation of some of the programming logic, it is more useful than an interface for large structures.

Interface-Based Polymorphism   An interface can be constructed that represents the members of one or more classes. Several interfaces can be created that feature the same foundation members that can be used in a polymorphic system. The previous version of Visual Basic could address interfaces, whereas VB.NET provides complete definition capabilities for new interfaces.

An interface inherits all of the members of its base class. You should use interface-based polymorphism instead of inheritance-based when

- **Post-publishing flexibility is needed**   Although interfaces cannot be changed, interface updates are possible that would prevent code based on interfaces from failing. With inheritance, changes to the base class could cause unwanted problems for all of the classes inherited from the base class.

- **Unrelated object types are needed**   When a mongrel class is being created from many different and unrelated class types, an interface is more effective.

- **No implementation** Use interfaces where there is no need to inherit implementations from a base class.

- **When using structures** Structures cannot inherit from a class but they can implement an interface.

An interface is never directly created; instead it is a representation of a class or class members. Interfaces cannot be changed once they've been published and should be implemented by a class with every feature exactly as specified by the designer. An interface can be considered a contract between the interface publisher (who agrees not to change the interface) and the user (who should implement the interface completely).

Interfaces are defined with the Interface keyword and included in another class or interface with either the Inherits or Implements keywords. Although a class can only inherit from a single base class, it can implement many different interfaces. An interface acts much like an abstract class. Single polymorphism is implemented like this:

```
Public Class myCursor
 Inherits Cursor
 ' Add code to override,overload, or extend members
 ' inherited from the base class
 [variable, property, method and event declarations]
End Class
```

To implement multiple interfaces, you would use a statement like this:

```
Interface myComboBoxI
 Inherits myTextBoxI, myListBoxI
End Interface
```

Overloading

Overloading allows multiple methods to have the same name. However, each method has different arguments and is useful in different circumstances. Whenever multiple methods have the same name, as long as each method has different arguments or a different return type, the compiler will automatically compile each method as an overloaded method. In the following model, you can see a class that contains four overloaded definitions of the method myDraw.

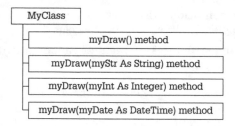

Overloading is used primarily with constructors where multiple ways of instantiating an object can be useful. For example, the class Cursor in the .NET Framework has four constructors:

```
// Constructor
public Cursor(System.String fileName)
public Cursor(System.IntPtr handle)
public Cursor(System.IO.Stream stream)
public Cursor(System.Type type, _
   System.String resource)
```

Each constructor of the class represents a slightly different method of specifying the location of the new mouse cursor bitmap. In spite of the differences in arguments, all of these methods perform exactly the same function: each initializes the mouse cursor with a bitmap.

Overloading can simplify a class by allowing a single method name to represent a particular type of functionality. At the same time, overloading helps a developer avoid creating numerous separate methods that perform the same function but only vary in their initialization parameters.

Primary Framework Assemblies

The .NET Framework is a large collection of routines that govern every aspect of the Windows operating system and application execution. Routines are grouped together in files known as *assemblies*. Visual Studio stores the assemblies of the .NET Framework in roughly 30 dynamic link library (DLL) files. These files can be found in the .NET directory of your system directory. On a Windows 2000 machine, for example, the path may be

```
c:\WinNT\Microsoft.NET\Framework\v1.0.2914
```

The final directory name will address the current version of the .NET Framework stored on your machine. In that directory, you will find the following .NET assembly files:

- Microsoft.JScript.dll
- Microsoft.Jscript.resources.dll
- Microsoft.VisualBasic.dll
- Microsoft.VisualBasic.Compatibility.dll
- Microsoft.VisualBasic.Compatibility.Data.dll
- Microsoft.VisualBasic.Vsa.dll
- Microsoft.VisualC.dll
- Microsoft.VisualStudio.VSHelp.dll
- Microsoft.Vsa.dll
- System.dll
- System.Configuration.Install.dll
- System.Data.dll
- System.Design.dll
- System.DirectoryServices.dll
- System.Drawing.dll
- System.Drawing.Design.dll
- System.EnterpriseServices.dll
- System.EnterpriseServices.Thunk.dll
- System.Management.dll
- System.Runtime.Remoting.Serialization.Formatters.Soap.dll
- System.Security.dll
- System.ServiceProcess.dll
- System.Web.dll
- System.Web.RegularExpressions.dll
- System.Web.Services.dll
- System.Windows.Forms.dll
- System.XML.dll

Each of these files contains a number of classes for the framework. You can examine the namespaces of these files using the MSIL

Disassembler. The Disassembler will convert the namespace of a designation file into a hierarchical outline similar to the one used for the standard file Explorer interface. For example, to examine the class System.Windows.Forms, you would use the following instruction at the MS-DOS command line or command prompt to execute the Disassembler:

```
ildasm
```

After the Disassembler is activated, you can open any of the assembly files. You can double-click on the entry for the Manifest of the assembly and it will be displayed in the Notepad application. The core assembly library used by the .NET Framework has the filename of *mscorlib.dll* and can be found in the \Framework folder:

```
C:\WinNT\Microsoft.NET\Framework\v1.0.2914\mscorlib.dll
```

Global class libraries can be registered with the system for use by multiple applications. All of the global assemblies are located in the \Assembly directory:

```
C:\WinNT\Assembly
```

Libraries for use with ASP.NET should be located in the \bin directory in the application directory that will use it. For example:

```
C:\inetpub\wwwroot\HelloNetWorld\bin
```

Project Types

Visual Basic.NET features far more application types than previous versions of VB. These additions have raised the total available VB.NET project types to eight:

- **Windows Application** A standard Windows application with forms, modules, and dialog boxes.

- **Class Library** A new class may be created to extend an existing class in the .NET library or create a custom class that can be used by other programs.

- **Windows Control Library** A Windows control or component may be created with a user interface that will be available for use within an ActiveX- or OLE Control-capable development environment such as the Visual Studio IDE or the Excel VBA environment.

- **ASP.NET Web Application**   This project will contain a set of Active Server Pages.NET (ASPX) pages and their matched code that provide a full-function and HTML-compatible (hence browser-independent) application.

- **ASP.NET Web Service**   A service that supports Internet protocols that can be activated or accessed through HTTP requests.

- **Web Control Library**   A Web control that runs on the server and presents a user interface and other functionality. A single Web page may be saved as a reusable Web control.

- **Console Application**   A standard command-line application that can be activated from the console. Any switch settings passed by the user at the command line are sent to the application as an array of string arguments.

- **Windows Service**   Creation of a Windows NT Service that can run in the background on a server executing any of the following operating systems: Windows NT, Windows 2000, or Windows XP.

There are also two other projects—Empty Project and Empty Web Project—that are available for starting completely blank project shells. These project types include no default documents (such as a blank form or code template) and no default class library references. They are especially useful if you need to convert an existing project (such as an application) into another type (such as a class library). The exact needs of the new class library can be specified in the empty project.

Selecting a Project Type

The number of available project types has made choosing the most appropriate type of solution a difficult decision. Even more challenging is that after the design choices are made, it is often complicated to make a change to the project foundation. Because of the difficulties involved, the better the choices made in the beginning, the more likely a project will be completed on schedule and budget.

Any medium- to large-size project will most likely require several different project types. A standard e-commerce solution, for example, would likely use Web controls, Web services, and ASP.NET application technology. Selecting how the various project pieces fit together are decisions that must be made based on the needs of the individual project. However, each piece should be chosen because it best fulfills the role that fits its need.

The table below provides some project characteristics that can help you narrow the choices for your project type. By examining what functions are needed for the completion of a project against this table, a preferable selection can be made.

Type	UI?	Standalone?	Web?	98 & ME Compatible?	Extensible?
Windows Application	Yes	Yes	No	Yes	No
Class Library	No	No	Yes	Yes	Yes
Windows Control Library	Yes	No	Yes	Yes	Yes
ASP.NET Web Application	Yes	No	Yes	No	No
ASP.NET Web Service	No	No	Yes	No	Yes
Web Control Library	Yes	No	Yes	No	Yes
Console Application	No	Yes	No	Yes	No
Windows Service	No	Yes	No	No	Yes

Error Handling

Although Visual Basic.NET preserves the error-trapping capabilities of previous versions (On Error Resume Next, and so on), it also introduces a new and more precise method of managing exceptions. Known as structured error handling, error management is localized to a particular block of code such as a file writing routine. Structured handling can also target particular error types and execute code appropriate to them.

When an error occurs, the system propagates execution up the call stack until an error routine is encountered. If your program has provided no error routines at all, the VB system itself receives the error and the user is prompted to quit the application because of a fault in its execution. To prevent complete program shutdown, accurate error handling is critical to any application, service, or component.

There are three types of errors every programmer encounters: syntax, runtime, and logic errors. Syntax errors are caused by mistyped elements (such as keywords or variable names) or by improper statement construction. These are the most common types of errors and they prevent the compiler from completing a build. Because they occur before execution can begin, they can't be managed by error-handling code.

There are two types of errors that can be trapped by an error-handling routine:

- **Runtime errors**   These errors are usually caused by mistakes in addressing resources such as attempts to access missing files, passing an uninitialized object to a method as an argument, reading past the bounds of an array or collection, and so on.

- **Logic errors**   These exceptions are generated primarily by the accumulation of user actions. A series of actions in an unintended sequence produces the logic fault. For example, if the user entered the number 0 for a value in one window and that value elsewhere as a denominator in a division calculation, an error will occur. These errors are often the most difficult to find and the use of error logging in a handling routine can greatly aid a developer.

Unstructured error handling can catch either of these two error types and prevent the program from unceremoniously exiting. However, by using structured exception handling, specific errors (such as file not found or division by zero) can be managed and the program can recover from the exception gracefully.

Structured Exception Handling

The *Try...Catch...Finally* control structure is at the heart of the new structured error handling. It has been long supported in other languages, including C++. VB.NET supports an advanced version of this structure that allows a program to intercept multiple error types as well as perform conditional execution based on an expression.

In its simplest form, the Catch keyword can be used by itself without any processing code to simply ignore the error. For example:

```
Dim a, b, c As Integer
a = 100
b = 0
Try
  c = a / b
Catch
End Try
```

Without the Try code, a message box would display an error message such as "An unhandled exception of type 'System.OverflowException' occurred in VBWinTest.exe" and the program would exit. To implement an error handler, the Try, Catch, and Finally clauses must contain code that reacts to the error that's generated.

Blocks of Code   A structured handling routine encapsulates a block of code in a way similar in appearance to an If...Then...Else structure. To begin adding actual error handling, you need to receive the information provided by the exception:

```
Dim a, b, c As Integer
a = 100
b = 0
Try
  c = a / b
Catch myEx As Exception
  MessageBox.Show(myEx.ToString())
Finally
  MessageBox.Show("Execution complete.")
End Try
```

The properties (such as the Message property) of myEx object can be examined in order to determine the exact nature of the error. Any code located in the Finally clause will execute regardless of whether an error occurred in execution or not. Code in this clause is typically used to close files, to flush unsaved changes, or to eliminate objects.

NOTE: Exceptions of type IOException and EndOfStreamException are automatically seized by the system for handling first. All other error types are passed directly to the custom error handlers first without any preprocessing.

If the exception has been identified and proper handling is impossible, the Exit Try keyword can be used within the Catch clause to end execution of the Try statement. Using Exit Try will skip execution of any code contained in the Finally clause.

Using Filters   In the general use of the Catch keyword, an Exception object is passed to receive the information about the given error. However, it is also possible within the Catch statement to specify a particular error to watch for and detect.

To implement error filtering, the When keyword may be used. This keyword only allows the code block that follows the Catch statement to execute when the specific error type has been encountered. The When keyword accepts any expression that returns a Boolean value, although the expression most commonly checks for specific error types. Because multiple Catch statements can be contained in a single Try structure, an error handler can filter out specific types of errors for handling and, lastly, can provide a general error-handling routine. For example:

```
Dim a, b, c As Integer
a = 100
b = 0
Try
  c = a / b
Catch myEx As Exception When b = 0
  MessageBox.Show("Divide by zero error")
Catch myEx As Exception
  MessageBox.Show(myEx.ToString())
Finally
  MessageBox.Show("Execution complete.")
End Try
```

Multiple handlers are searched in the order specified in the handler definition and are included simply by adding additional Catch statements to the error control structure.

Exception Class   Like the Err object of unstructured exception handling, objects created from the Exception class contain information about the error that occurred. Within the Exception object is information describing the location in the code where the error occurred, the error type, and the causes of the exception.

The Exception object includes the following properties:

Property	Description
HelpLink	Contains a link to the help file associated with the current error.
HResult	A unique numeric value assigned to this exception.
Message	Holds the text message of the error.
Source	Holds the name of the object or assembly in which the error occurred.
StackTrace	Contains the list of methods on the call stack showing the method calls that lead to the error.
TargetSite	Contains the method that caused the exception. If the call stack is available, this method name will match the name listed on the top of the stack.

In the Catch statement, the object that accepts the exception information must be either based on the Exception class or on a class that inherits from it. There are a number of derived classes included in the .NET Framework available to capture situation-specific information including ApplicationException; CodeDomSerializerException; InvalidPrinterException; IOException; IsolatedStorageException; PathTooLongException; CookieException; ProtocolViolationException; WebException; MissingManifestResourceException; SUDSGeneratorException; SUDSParserException; SystemException; UriFormatException; and SoapException.

Unstructured Exception Handling

The unstructured exception handling available through the On Error keywords is still active in VB.NET and can be used. However, there is a performance and resource usage penalty for implementing unstructured handling instead of structured error catching.

Unstructured handling is best used as a safety net for a program designed using structured error handling. Any errors that are not picked up by the structured handlers will be intercepted by the unstructured handlers without the whole program faulting and requiring the application or component to quit.

While a method or subroutine can contain a structured or unstructured error-trapping routine, it cannot have both. Therefore, it is usually easier to put the unstructured routine high in the call hierarchy and structured routines lower. That way, any errors that get past the method-specific error-trapping routines will be caught by a higher-level unstructured routine.

On Error Command	Description
On Error Goto *destination*	When an error occurs, execution will skip to the line specified by the destination argument.
On Error Goto –1 *or* On Error Goto 0	Disables any unstructured exception handler in the current routine.
On Error Resume Next	When an error occurs, skip the statement line where the execution faulted and continue executing on the line following it.

Error Chart

Visual Basic allows you to identify and trap most of the errors that could occur in your program. Technical support calls are difficult to handle without a clear understanding of which error actually occurred.

The following chart lists all the trappable errors and the descriptions that will be returned by the ErrorToString() function. You can use the ErrorToString() function in a message box or log file within your program to provide a description of the error that occurs.

Error Number	Description
3	Return without GoSub
5	Invalid procedure call or argument
6	Overflow
7	Out of memory
9	Subscript out of range
10	This array is fixed or temporarily locked
11	Division by zero
13	Type mismatch
14	Out of string space
16	Expression too complex

Error Number	Description
17	Can't perform requested operation
18	User interrupt occurred
20	Resume without error
28	Out of stack space
35	Sub or Function not defined
47	Too many DLL application clients
48	Error in loading DLL
49	Bad DLL calling convention
51	Internal error
52	Bad filename or number
53	File not found
54	Bad file mode
55	File already open
57	Device I/O error
58	File already exists
59	Bad record length
61	Disk full
62	Input past end of file
63	Bad record number
67	Too many files
68	Device unavailable
70	Permission denied
71	Disk not ready
74	Can't rename with different drive
75	Path/File access error
76	Path not found
91	Object variable or With block variable not set
92	For loop not initialized
93	Invalid pattern string
94	Invalid use of Null
96	Unable to sink events of object because the object is already firing events to the maximum number of event receivers that it supports
97	Cannot call Friend function on object that is not an instance of defining class
321	Invalid file format
322	Can't create necessary temporary file
325	Invalid format in resource file

Error Number	Description
380	Invalid property value
381	Invalid property array index
382	Set not supported at runtime
383	Set not supported (read-only property)
385	Need property array index
387	Set not permitted
393	Get not supported at runtime
394	Get not supported (write-only property)
422	Property not found
423	Property or method not found
424	Object required
429	ActiveX component can't create object
430	Class doesn't support Automation
432	Filename or class name not found during Automation operation
438	Object doesn't support this property or method
440	Automation error
442	Connection to type library or object library for remote process has been lost. Press OK for dialog box to remove reference
443	Automation object does not have a default value
445	Object doesn't support this action
446	Object doesn't support named arguments
447	Object doesn't support current locale setting
448	Named argument not found
449	Argument not optional
450	Wrong number of arguments or invalid property assignment
451	Object not a collection
452	Invalid ordinal
453	Specified DLL function not found
454	Code resource not found
455	Code resource lock error
457	This key is already associated with an element of this collection
458	Variable uses an Automation type not supported in Visual Basic
459	Object or class does not support the set of events
460	Invalid clipboard format

Error Number	Description
481	Invalid picture
482	Printer error
735	Can't save file to TEMP
744	Search text not found
746	Replacements too long
31001	Out of memory
31004	No object
31018	Class is not set
31027	Unable to activate object
31032	Unable to create embedded object
31036	Error saving to file
31037	Error loading from file

Binding

When a compiler processes an object reference to determine the target object, it is known as *binding*. Traditionally, the binding occurs at compile time and this is known as *early* or *static* binding. Any code that creates an object with the New keyword followed by the class type uses early binding.

NOTE: Including the Option Strict keyword in the header of an application or component will prevent any late binding from occurring. With this option set, late binding statements will generate an error at compile time.

If the process of binding is deferred until runtime, it is known as *late* or *dynamic* binding because the object reference type to be contained in a variable is not known until execution. Late binding can be useful because the object does not have to be determined until runtime, so a different version or a not-yet-installed object can be addressed. However, late binding also has two disadvantages: poor performance and lack of type checking.

Late binding occurs when the CreateObject() method is used to generate the object references. All variables to hold references to late bound objects must be set to type Object (System.Object). Any property, method, field, or event reference that is coded for such an object also won't be bound until runtime.

NOTE: In ASP.NET, late binding can also be used by creating objects with the Server.CreateObject() method. In Active Server

Pages (ASP), the same performance penalties and error-checking restrictions apply.

Because the object name and type is not known to the VB system at compile time, the compiler cannot perform data type checking. This verification process performed by the compiler decreases the chances of runtime errors and also speeds performance because it is unnecessary to check for these errors just prior to execution.

Note that late binding has also changed in the new version of Visual Basic. In VB 6, the Set function was required to assign an object to a variable like this:

```
Set myObj = CreateObject("Excel.Application")
```

That same operation can now be performed with the standard equal operator:

```
myObj = CreateObject("Excel.Application")
```

Late binding may be performed only on classes, not interfaces.

Command Groups

Finding the correct command or group of commands to accomplish a particular task is often very difficult. To aid you in finding the functions that you need, here is a reference that provides groupings into the following common areas: Financial, Disk Access, Mathematical, Date and Time, and Strings. After you have located one of the commands you need, the See Also references included with each command will guide you to similar commands.

Financial

Visual Basic's financial commands are

DDB	FV	NPer	PV
FormatCurrency	IPmt	NPV	Rate
FormatNumber	IRR	PMT	SLN
FormatPercent	MIRR	PPmt	SYD

Disk Access

Visual Basic's disk-access commands are

ChDir	FileDateTime	InputString	Rename
ChDrive	FileGet	Kill	Reset
CurDir	FileLen	LineInput	RmDir
Dir	FileOpen	Loc	Seek
Environ	FilePut	Lock...Unlock	SetAttr
EOF	FileWidth	LOF	Shell
FileAttr	FreeFile	MkDir	Spc
FileClose	GetAttr	Print	Write
FileCopy	Input	PrintLine	WriteLine

Mathematical

Visual Basic's mathematical commands are

*	+=	Cos	Not
+	−=	CSng	Oct
−	/=	Exp	Or
/	\=	False	OrElse
<=	Abs	Fix	Randomize
<>	And	FormatNumber	Rnd
=	AndAlso	FormatPercentage	Round
>	Atan	Hex	Sign
>=	CDbl	Int	Sin
\	CDec	IsNumeric	Sqrt
^	CInt	Log	Tan
*=	CLng	Mod	XOR

Date and Time

Visual Basic's commands related to date and time are

CVDate	Hour	TimeSerial
DateAdd	IsDate	TimeString
DateDiff	Minute	TimeValue
DatePart	Month	Today
DateSerial	MonthName	WeekDay
DateString	Now	WeekdayName
DateValue	Second	Year
Day	TimeOfDay	
FormatDateTime	Timer	

Strings

Visual Basic's commands pertaining to strings are

&	InStr	Option Compare	StrConv
&=	InStrRev	Replace	StrDup
+	Join	Right	StrReverse
Chr	LCase	RTrim	Tab
ChrW	Left	Space	Trim
CStr	Len	Split	UCase
Filter	LTrim	Str	Val
Format	Mid	StrComp	

Chapter 2
ASCII/Unicode Chart

When working on a complex programming project, you will often need to directly access characters in the format in which the computer stores them. ASCII is the standard for the relation between a numeric value and a character type. The capital letter A, for example, is stored as a numeric value of 65. In ASCII, each character is stored as a single byte, or 8 bits.

Within the newer Unicode standard, the values of the first 255 characters are identical to those in the ASCII standard. Unicode represents each character as two bytes (16 bits) to accommodate the numerous extra characters of various non-English alphabets.

The following ASCII chart shows the values of all the characters between 0 and 255. The chart includes the decimal and hexadecimal values of the characters, as well as a basic character name. Some of the characters cannot be displayed as characters (such as those below the ASCII value of 8), but are instead used as control characters. In these cases, the character Char column remains empty.

Additionally, within the HTTP standard for URLs, there are a number of characters (such as spaces and quotes) that must be encoded to be used. For example, a URL might appear like this: http://www.microsoft.com/myquery?Name=John%20Smith. The %20 specifies the hexadecimal value of a space (decimal 32). You can use the Hex column of this table to determine which characters are included in a URL or to manually encode your own.

Decimal	Char	Hex	Decimal	Char	Hex
0		/x00	9	(tab)	/x09
1		/x01	10	(linefeed)	/x0A
2		/x02	11	(carriage return)	/x0B
3		/x03	12		/x0C
4		/x04	13		/x0D
5		/x05	14		/x0E
6		/x06	15		/x0F
7		/x07	16		/x10
8	(backspace)	/x08	17		/x11

Decimal	Char	Hex	Decimal	Char	Hex
18		/x12	55	7	/x37
19		/x13	56	8	/x38
20		/x14	57	9	/x39
21		/x15	58	:	/x3A
22		/x16	59	;	/x3B
23		/x17	60	<	/x3C
24		/x18	61	=	/x3D
25		/x19	62	>	/x3E
26		/x1A	63	?	/x3F
27		/x1B	64	@	/x40
28		/x1C	65	A	/x41
29		/x1D	66	B	/x42
30		/x1E	67	C	/x43
31		/x1F	68	D	/x44
32	(space)	/x20	69	E	/x45
33	!	/x21	70	F	/x46
34	"	/x22	71	G	/x47
35	#	/x23	72	H	/x48
36	$	/x24	73	I	/x49
37	%	/x25	74	J	/x4A
38	&	/x26	75	K	/x4B
39	'	/x27	76	L	/x4C
40	(	/x28	77	M	/x4D
41	)	/x29	78	N	/x4E
42	*	/x2A	79	O	/x4F
43	+	/x2B	80	P	/x50
44	,	/x2C	81	Q	/x51
45	-	/x2D	82	R	/x52
46	.	/x2E	83	S	/x53
47	/	/x2F	84	T	/x54
48	0	/x30	85	U	/x55
49	1	/x31	86	V	/x56
50	2	/x32	87	W	/x57
51	3	/x33	88	X	/x58
52	4	/x34	89	Y	/x59
53	5	/x35	90	Z	/x5A
54	6	/x36	91	[	/x5B

2

Decimal	Char	Hex	Decimal	Char	Hex
92	\	/x5C	129	•	/x81
93	]	/x5D	130	,	/x82
94	^	/x5E	131	ƒ	/x83
95	_	/x5F	132	„	/x84
96	`	/x60	133	…	/x85
97	a	/x61	134	†	/x86
98	b	/x62	135	‡	/x87
99	c	/x63	136	ˆ	/x88
100	d	/x64	137	‰	/x89
101	e	/x65	138	Š	/x8A
102	f	/x66	139	‹	/x8B
103	g	/x67	140	Œ	/x8C
104	h	/x68	141	•	/x8D
105	i	/x69	142	•	/x8E
106	j	/x6A	143	•	/x8F
107	k	/x6B	144	•	/x90
108	l	/x6C	145	'	/x91
109	m	/x6D	146	'	/x92
110	n	/x6E	147	"	/x93
111	o	/x6F	148	"	/x94
112	p	/x70	149	•	/x95
113	q	/x71	150	–	/x96
114	r	/x72	151	—	/x97
115	s	/x73	152	˜	/x98
116	t	/x74	153	™	/x99
117	u	/x75	154	š	/x9A
118	v	/x76	155	›	/x9B
119	w	/x77	156	œ	/x9C
120	x	/x78	157	•	/x9D
121	y	/x79	158	•	/x9E
122	z	/x7A	159	Ÿ	/x9F
123	{	/x7B	160	(no-break space)	/xA0
124	|	/x7C	161	¡	/xA1
125	}	/x7D	162	¢	/xA2
126	~	/x7E	163	£	/xA3
127	•	/x7F	164	¤	/xA4
128	•	/x80	165	¥	/xA5

Decimal	Char	Hex	Decimal	Char	Hex
166	¦	/xA6	203	Ë	/xCB
167	§	/xA7	204	Ì	/xCC
168	¨	/xA8	205	Í	/xCD
169	©	/xA9	206	Î	/xCE
170	ª	/xAA	207	Ï	/xCF
171	«	/xAB	208	Ð	/xD0
172	¬	/xAC	209	Ñ	/xD1
173	–	/xAD	210	Ò	/xD2
174	®	/xAE	211	Ó	/xD3
175	¯	/xAF	212	Ô	/xD4
176	°	/xB0	213	Õ	/xD5
177	±	/xB1	214	Ö	/xD6
178	²	/xB2	215	×	/xD7
179	³	/xB3	216	Ø	/xD8
180	´	/xB4	217	Ù	/xD9
181	µ	/xB5	218	Ú	/xDA
182	¶	/xB6	219	Û	/xDB
183	·	/xB7	220	Ü	/xDC
184	¸	/xB8	221	Ý	/xDD
185	¹	/xB9	222	Þ	/xDE
186	º	/xBA	223	ß	/xDF
187	»	/xBB	224	à	/xE0
188	¼	/xBC	225	á	/xE1
189	½	/xBD	226	â	/xE2
190	¾	/xBE	227	ã	/xE3
191	¿	/xBF	228	ä	/xE4
192	À	/xC0	229	å	/xE5
193	Á	/xC1	230	æ	/xE6
194	Â	/xC2	231	ç	/xE7
195	Ã	/xC3	232	è	/xE8
196	Ä	/xC4	233	é	/xE9
197	Å	/xC5	234	ê	/xEA
198	Æ	/xC6	235	ë	/xEB
199	Ç	/xC7	236	ì	/xEC
200	È	/xC8	237	í	/xED
201	É	/xC9	238	î	/xEE
202	Ê	/xCA	239	ï	/xEF

Decimal	Char	Hex	Decimal	Char	Hex
240	ð	/xF0	248	ø	/xF8
241	ñ	/xF1	249	ù	/xF9
242	ò	/xF2	250	ú	/xFA
243	ó	/xF3	251	û	/xFB
244	ô	/xF4	252	ü	/xFC
245	õ	/xF5	253	ý	/xFD
246	ö	/xF6	254	þ	/xFE
247	÷	/xF7	255	ÿ	/xFF

2

Chapter 3
Hungarian Notation

Understanding complex code can be difficult, especially if it was written some time ago or by someone else. Any technique that clarifies code is a great help, particularly when you're attempting to debug an application.

A programmer by the name of Charles Simonyi invented a technique known as *Hungarian notation*. Hungarian notation simply specifies that a descriptive prefix be added to the names of variables and objects. This prefix denotes the type of variable or object being addressed. For example, the Name property of a form may use the standard three-character prefix *frm* followed by the capitalization of the first letter of the object name (that is, a form may be named frmMain). In code, when the programmer encounters text such as frmMain.Show(), there is no confusion about the type of object being addressed.

If applied consistently, Hungarian notation greatly increases the readability of your code. It also considerably simplifies team development. The following is a list of the prefixes for the most common user interface items and variables/structures. The prefix, usually three letters, is followed by a generic object name as an example.

User Interface Items	Sample Name
Animated Button	aniControl
Checkbox	chkControl
Class	clsClassname
ComboBox	cboControl
CommandButton	cmdControl
DataControl	datControl
DataGrid	grdMygrid
DirListBox	dlbControl
DriveListBox	drbControl
FileListBox	flbControl
Form	frmForm
Frame	fraControl
Hscrollbar	hsbControl

43

User Interface Items	Sample Name
Image	imgControl
Item	itmMyitem
Label	lblControl
Line	linControl
Listbox	lstControl
Listview	lsvControl
Menu	mnuFile
OLEControl	oleControl
OptionButton	optControl
PictureBox	pbxControl
Remote Data Control	rdcControl
Shape	shpControl
TextBox	txtControl
Timer	tmrControl
Treeview	trvControl
Vscrollbar	vsbControl

Variables and Structures	Sample Name
Byte	bNumber
Character string	strString
Constant	cName
Currency	curCurrency
Date/Time	dtDate
Decimal	decDecimal
Double	dNumber
Flag Long	flFlag
Flag Short	fsFlag
Integer	iNumber
Return code	rcReturnvalue
Single	sNumber

Chapter 4
How-To Code Examples

This How-To section provides some examples of problems commonly faced by programmers. By examining a simplified but complete example of a common function, you will be able to quickly construct the code that you need.

The following examples are as general as possible, so you can modify them to your particular circumstances. For brevity, most of the code does not include lengthy comments or remarks. Also, the event definitions are usually long and cumbersome (for example, Private Sub cmdReadFile_Click(ByVal sender As System.Object, ByVal e As System.EventArgs) Handles cmdReadFile.Click) so they have been abbreviated (for example, Sub cmdReadFile_Click()). Use the long headers automatically generated by VB rather than abbreviating them to match the code.

The examples include

- Reading a file into an array
- Adding data to an array from a database
- Filling a combo box from an array
- Drawing an analog clock
- Enabling user setting of the background color of the form
- Creating a browse file window and checking if the file exists
- Using the .NET library to draw on a picture
- Using the DirectSound system to play a sound file
- Sending e-mail through Outlook
- Centering a form
- Accepting EXE-passed parameters
- Displaying a list of fonts in a combo box

Reading a File into an Array

Reading data files of various formats is a common need for Visual Basic programs. VB has the built-in capability of reading text files line-by-line. After a line has been read, the Split() function can be used to parse the text based on any specified delimiter (for example, commas or tabs). Most spreadsheets can output a worksheet in common text file format with comma delimiters (typically with the CSV file extension).

1. Use a text editor such as Notepad to enter the following text and save it as a file named **vbr1.csv** in the root directory.

```
Joe,Girsh,10
John,Smith,11
Phil,Stewart,12
Dirk,Lumper,13
```

2. Create a new Windows application project in Visual Basic.

3. Add a command button and set the Name property of the button to **cmdReadFile.**

4. Enter the following code into the Click event of the button:

```
Sub cmdReadFile_Click()
   ' Open file stream to destination file
   Dim myFS As New IO.FileStream("c:\vbr1.csv", _
      IO.FileMode.Open, IO.FileAccess.Read)
   ' Open StreamReader for input
   Dim r As New IO.StreamReader(myFS)
   Dim i As Integer
   Dim myLine, tempStr As String
   ' Setup arrays to receive the text line
   ' and the data
   Dim myLineStr() As String, a$(100), b$(100)
   Dim c(100) As Integer
   i = 0
   myLine = r.ReadLine
   Do While Not (myLine Is Nothing)
     myLineStr = myLine.Split(",")
     a(i) = myLineStr(0) : b(i) = myLineStr(1)
     c(i) = Val(myLineStr(2))
     myLine = r.ReadLine
```

```
        i += 1
    Loop
End Sub
```

5. Execute the application.

When executing, the code loads the information from the text file into the three arrays. The example doesn't actually do anything with the data because data handling varies from project to project. Note that the third variable, *c,* uses the Val() function to load the value for that column into a typed field (in this case an Integer).

4

Adding Data to an Array from a Database

Accessing the data within a database through the query interface and bound controls can provide a powerful way of sorting or retrieving quantities of up-to-date information. Often, however, working with a small amount of data can be much more accessible if you read the data into a simple memory array. This example provides a self-expanding array that uses the ADO.NET objects to load information from the Northwind database.

The name of your Northwind database will vary depending on the applications you have installed. In this example, the database included with FrontPage (FPNWIND.MDB) is used. If you don't know where your Northwind database is located or what it is called (usually NWind.mdb), try searching for *NWIND.MDB to locate it.

1. Create a new Windows application project in Visual Basic.

2. In the header of the default form, enter the following:

```
Imports System.Data.OleDb
```

3. Add a command button and set the Name property of the button to **cmdReadDB.**

4. Enter the following code into the Click event of the button:

```
Sub cmdReadDB_Click()
    Dim myConn As OleDbConnection
```

```
Dim myCmd As OleDbCommand
Dim myReader As OleDbDataReader
Dim myConnStr As String
Dim myArray(0) As String
Dim i As Integer

myConnStr = "Provider=" & _
   "Microsoft.Jet.OLEDB.4.0;Password=;" & _
   "User ID=Admin;Data Source=" & _
   "C:\myData\FPNWIND.MDB;" & _
   "Mode=Share Deny None;"
myConn = New OleDbConnection(myConnStr)
myCmd = New OleDbCommand()
myCmd.CommandType = CommandType.Text
myCmd.CommandText = "Select * from Customers"
myCmd.Connection = myConn
myConn.Open()
myReader = myCmd.ExecuteReader()
Do While myReader.Read()
   myArray(i) = myReader!ContactName
   ReDim Preserve myArray(UBound(myArray) + 1)
   i += 1
Loop
MsgBox("Found " & i & " records")
myConn.Close()
End Sub
```

5. Execute the application.

Filling a Combo Box from an Array

Arrays are often used to hold a variety of information, particularly a list of items. VB programmers often have to transport array data into controls such as the ComboBox. The following project generates random text entries and places them in an array. This array data is then transferred to the combo box.

1. Create a new Windows application project in Visual Basic.

2. Add a ComboBox control to the form and set the Name property to **cboMyCombo.**

3. Add a command button and set the Name property of the button to **cmdMakeCombo.**

4. Enter the following code into the Click event of the button:

```
Sub MakeCombo_Click()
   Dim myArray(10) As String
   Dim i As Integer

   For i = 0 To 9
      myArray(i) = "ID: " & Rnd() * 100
   Next

   For i = 0 To UBound(myArray) - 1
      cboMyCombo.Items.Add(myArray(i))
   Next
End Sub
```

5. Execute the application.

Drawing an Analog Clock

The PictureBox control contains a complete drawing environment that can be used for graphic display. When used in conjunction with the .NET drawing capabilities, almost any graphic operation can be implemented. This clock example demonstrates programming graphic commands, using the timer, using trigonometric functions, and converting the hours/minutes/seconds to graphic coordinates. Note that the clock will not work properly if your system is set to display time in 24-hour mode (not A.M./P.M.).

1. Create a new Windows application project in Visual Basic.

2. Add a Timer control to the form.

3. Add a command button and set the Name property of the button to **cmdClock.**

4. Add a PictureBox control to the form and set the Name property to **pbxClock.**

5. Create a new procedure to the form called **DrawHand** and add
the following code:

```
Sub DrawHand(ByVal myGraphics As Graphics, _
  ByVal myPen As Pen, ByVal cx As Integer, _
  ByVal cy As Integer, ByVal num As Integer, _
  ByVal rad As Integer)
  Dim x, y As Integer

  x = rad * Math.Sin((num * Math.PI) / 30)
  y = rad * Math.Cos((num * Math.PI) / 30)
  myGraphics.DrawLine(myPen, cx, cy, cx + x, _
    cy - y)
End Sub
```

6. Enter the following code into the Tick event of the Timer
control:

```
Sub Timer1_Tick()
  Dim cx, cy, rad As Integer
  cx = 100 : cy = 100 : rad = 80
  Dim myGraphics As System.Drawing.Graphics

  myGraphics = pbxClock.CreateGraphics()
  myGraphics.FillEllipse(Brushes.White, _
    cx - rad, cy - rad, rad * 2, rad * 2)

  myGraphics.DrawEllipse(Pens.Yellow, _
    cx - rad, cy - rad, rad * 2, rad * 2)


  DrawHand(myGraphics, Pens.Red, cx, cy, _
    Hour(Now) * 5, rad * 0.6)
  DrawHand(myGraphics, Pens.Green, cx, cy, _
    Minute(Now), rad * 0.9)

  DrawHand(myGraphics, Pens.Blue, cx, cy, _
    Second(Now), rad)

  myGraphics.Dispose()
End Sub
```

7. Enter the following code into the Click event of the button:

```
Sub cmdClock_Click()
   Timer1.Enabled = True
End Sub
```

8. Set the Interval property of the Timer control to **1000** (so it will activate every second).

9. Execute the application.

Enabling User Setting of the Background Color

The common dialog boxes included in Visual Basic provide a number of widely used capabilities including color selection, file opening and saving, printing, and font selection. The color dialog box provides a complete color selection interface to return a color in RGB selected format. This example enables the user to select a color for the background color of the form.

1. Create a new Windows application project in Visual Basic.

2. Add a command button and set the Name property of the button to **cmdSelectColor.**

3. Enter the following code into the Click event of the button:

```
Sub cmdSelectColor_Click()
   Dim myColorDlog As New ColorDialog()
   Dim result As DialogResult
   ' Allow custom color setting
   myColorDlog.AllowFullOpen = True
   myColorDlog.Color = System.Drawing.Color.Blue
   result = myColorDlog.ShowDialog()
   If result = DialogResult.OK Then
      Form1.ActiveForm.BackColor = _
         myColorDlog.Color
            End If
End Sub
```

4. Execute the application and click the button.

After the user has selected a color and clicked the OK button, the background color of the form will change. Note that because the controls are children of the form, they will also show the selected color for their background.

Creating a Browse File

The common dialog box class has derived classes that allow the selection of files to open or save. This example uses the Open dialog box to allow the user to select a file, either showing all file types or filtering for those with the DAT extension. The nature of the Open file dialog box allows the user to enter a filename by hand as well.

After the file is selected and the user clicks the OK button, the program code checks whether the file actually exists and displays a dialog box to notify the user.

1. Create a new Windows application project in Visual Basic.

2. Add a TextBox control and set the Name property of the control to **txtFileName.**

3. Add a command button and set the Name property of the button to **cmdBrowse.**

4. Enter the following code into the Click event of the button:

```
Sub cmdBrowse_Click()
  Dim myFileDlog As New OpenFileDialog()

  myFileDlog.InitialDirectory = "c:\"
  myFileDlog.Filter = "All Files (*.*)|*.*" & _
    "|Data Files (*.dat)|*.dat"
  myFileDlog.FilterIndex = 2
  myFileDlog.RestoreDirectory = True

  If myFileDlog.ShowDialog() = _
    DialogResult.OK Then
```

```
        If Dir(myFileDlog.FileName) <> "" Then
          MsgBox("FileExists: " & _
            myFileDlog.FileName, _
            MsgBoxStyle.Information)
        Else
          MsgBox("File not found", _
            MsgBoxStyle.Critical)
        End If
      End If
    End Sub
```

5. Execute the application.

The common dialog boxes can be used to specify exactly the types of files to filter and allow for selection. There are also additional flags and the available constant parameter settings that are enumerated in the VB documentation.

Using .NET Graphics Functions with Pictures

This example uses an Image object to load a bitmap, rotate it 180 degrees, and save the modified bitmap in a different file type. It demonstrates that creating a graphic file modification utility is a fairly simple process.

1. Create a new Windows application project in Visual Basic.

2. Add a command button and set the Name property of the button to **cmdSimpleBitmap.**

3. Add a PictureBox control to the form and set the Name property to **pbxImage**.

4. Enter the following code into the Click event of the button:

```
Sub cmdSimpleBitmap_Click()
  Dim myImage As Image
```

```
Dim myGraphics As System.Drawing.Graphics

myGraphics = pbxSimpleBitmap.CreateGraphics()
myImage = Image.FromFile("c:\botticelli.jpg")
myImage.RotateFlip( _
  RotateFlipType.Rotate180FlipNone)
myGraphics.DrawImage(myImage, 0, 0)
myImage.Save("c:\botticelli.bmp")
End Sub
```

5. Execute the application.

This example expects a bitmap file named botticelli.jpg in the root directory. You can replace this reference with any qualified path to a bitmap, GIF, or JPEG file. The example writes the modified file to the root directory as a bitmap named botticelli.bmp.

Using the Windows API to Play a Sound

For user feedback or general background audio, playing a sound (WAV) file can be a very useful tool. The .NET framework only directly supports the Beep() function. However, through the COM library interface, an application has full access to the DirectSound audio system. DirectSound is only one of the DirectX technologies available for advanced multimedia applications. The DirectX areas include:

- **DirectDraw** Fast access to the video hardware system for games, multimedia, and animation.

- **Direct3D** Optimized routines that take advantage of available 3D hardware acceleration or use software to emulate functions to provide the same capabilities.

- **DirectSound** Plays synchronous and asynchronous sound files and includes the ability to mix multiple sound channels and add digital effects (reverb, chorus, and so on).

- **DirectMusic** Advanced support of MIDI and WAV sources in conjunction with chord progressions, styles, and other general musical structure data to allow music to be created dynamically.

- **DirectShow** Supports streaming media such as displaying ASF feeds or playing DVD content.

- **DirectPlay**   Network-based routines that allow creation of multiplayer applications including games over the network, modem, or Internet.

- **DirectInput**   Provides a general interface for input devices such as joysticks, as well as advanced, specific implementation for devices such as force feedback sticks.

The following example uses the DirectSound system to play a WAV file through the default audio system. You may notice that the code loads the sound file into the secondary buffer instead of the primary buffer (which is seldom used directly). The primary buffer is the mixing channel used for final output. While only a single primary buffer exists, as many secondary buffers may be created as available RAM and processor resources can allow. These buffers can then be freely mixed together for output on the primary channel.

4

Note that with each new version of DirectX, Microsoft has dramatically altered usage of many aspects of the interface. Therefore, this example has been tested to work with DirectX 8 and may not function properly with other versions of DirectX.

1. Create a new Windows application project in Visual Basic.

2. Under the Project menu, select the Add Reference item.

3. From the References dialog, select the COM tab and add the DirectX 8 for Visual Basic Type Library item to the project. If this is the first time you've accessed this library, a dialog will appear asking whether a wrapper should be created for this library. Click Yes to create the .NET-to-COM wrapper.

4. In the General Declarations area of the main form, enter the following code:

```
Imports DxVBLibA
```

5. Add a command button and set the Name property of the button to **cmdPlaySound.**

6. Enter the following code into the Click event of the button:

```
Private Sub cmdPlaySound_Click()
    Dim myDSound As DirectSound8
    Dim myBufDesc As New DSBUFFERDESC()
    Dim D8 As New DirectX8()
    Dim myBuffer As DirectSoundSecondaryBuffer8
```

```
mybufdesc.guid3DAlgorithm = _
   AUDIOCONSTANTS.GUID_DS3DALG_DEFAULT
myDSound = D8.DirectSoundCreate(vbNullString)
myBuffer=myDSound.CreateSoundBufferFromFile( _
   "c:\winnt\media\Windows Logon Sound.wav", _
mybufdesc)
   ' The cooperative level must be set for the
   ' current window before a sound can be played.
   myDSound.SetCooperativeLevel( _
      Me.Handle.ToInt32, _
      CONST_DSSCLFLAGS.DSSCL_NORMAL)
   myBuffer.Play( _
      CONST_DSBPLAYFLAGS.DSBPLAY_DEFAULT)
End Sub
```

7. Execute the application.

Because this code example expects a specific sound file in the Media folder, you may need to change the coded path to point to a WAV file available on your system.

Sending E-Mail Through Outlook

It is often useful to send e-mail from within Visual Basic. Although the Messaging API (MAPI) enables you to program the transmission of any type of message, the programming is fairly complicated. Sending an e-mail through Outlook is simple, and mail items created this way can be added to the Sent Items folder if you wish to track the mail sent.

1. Create a new Windows application project in Visual Basic.

2. Set the Add References dialog box, under the COM tab, to include the latest version of the Microsoft Outlook Object Model.

3. Add the following code to the header of the default project form:

```
Imports Outlook
```

4. Add a command button and set the Name property of the button to **cmdOutlookMail.**

5. Enter the following code into the Click event of the button:

```
Sub cmdOutlookMail_Click()
   Dim objOutlook As New Outlook.Application()
   Dim objItem As MailItem

   objItem = objOutlook.CreateItem( _
     OlItemType.olMailItem)
   With objItem
     .Subject = "VB.NET Prog Ref"
     .To = "danr@cvisual.com"
     .CC = "danr@coherentdata.com"
     .Body = "I found this book useful."
     .Attachments.Add("c:\autoexec.bat")
     .Send()
   End With
   MsgBox("Mail sent.")
End Sub
```

6. Execute the application.

This example does not provide error detection, and it also assumes a file named autoexec.bat is located in the root directory on the C: drive. The addresses in the example are in Internet address format. However, you can use standard names, such as "John Doe," from the address book, just as you do when manually sending Outlook mail.

4

Centering a Form

A common need for central dialog windows or splash screens is to center the form within the current screen. This example retrieves the size of the screen from the Windows system and moves the current form to the appropriate location.

1. Create a new Windows application project in Visual Basic.

2. Add a command button and set the Name property of the button to **cmdCenterForm.**

3. Enter the following code into the Click event of the button:

```
Private Sub cmdCenterForm_Click()
    Dim screenRect, formRect As Rectangle
    Dim cx, cy As Integer
    Dim sx, sy As Integer

    screenRect = Screen.PrimaryScreen.Bounds()
    formRect = Form1.ActiveForm.Bounds
    ' Get centerpoint of screen
    sx = screenRect.Width / 2
    sy = screenRect.Height / 2
    ' Get centerpoint of form
    cx = (formRect.Width / 2) + formRect.Left
    cy = (formRect.Height / 2) + formRect.Top
    ' Offset the difference
    formRect.Offset(sx - cx, sy - cy)
    Form1.ActiveForm.SetBounds(formRect.Left, _
        formRect.Top, formRect.Width, formRect.Height)

End Sub
```

4. Execute the application.

Accepting EXE-Passed Parameters

When programs are launched from the Windows environment, they may include command-line parameters or the names of files that have been dragged and dropped onto the EXE icon. Reading the passed string enables you to access user input to the application before the complete environment execution has begun. The Command() function returns a string of the commands sent to the EXE. The following code uses the Split() function to parse the commands into an array and displays a message box with the number of items received.

1. Create a new Windows application project in Visual Basic.

2. Enter the following code into the Load event of the main form:

```
Private Sub Form_Load()
  Dim fieldDelim As String = " "
  Dim myCommands As String
  Dim myArgs() As String
  myCommands = Command()
  myArgs = myCommands.Split( _
    fieldDelim.ToCharArray)
  MsgBox("There were " & UBound(myArgs) & _
    " argument(s) passed to the EXE")
End Sub
```

4

3. Use the Build option under the Build menu to create an executable.

4. From the Windows system, drag and drop a file onto the EXE.

When execution occurs, the program checks whether any parameters have been passed to the application. If parameters are present, the number of parameters is displayed in a message box.

Displaying a List of Available Fonts

It is possible to determine which fonts are available on a display device by addressing the InstalledFontCollection property. In this example, the fonts for the screen device are detected and added as items for selection in a combo box.

1. Create a new Windows application project in Visual Basic.

2. Add a ComboBox control to the form and set the Name property to **cboMyCombo**.

3. Add a command button and set the Name property of the button to **cmdListFonts**.

4. Enter the following code into the Click event of the button:

```
Sub cmdListFonts_Click()
   Dim myInstalledFonts As New _
      System.Drawing.Text.InstalledFontCollection()
   Dim i As Integer

   For i = 0 To _
      myInstalledFonts.Families.Length - 1
   cboMyCombo.Items.Add( _
      myInstalledFonts.Families(i).GetName(1))
   Next
End Sub
```

5. Execute the application.

Chapter 5
Extensible Markup Language

The Extensible Markup Language (XML) is a format for storing typed data in a machine-independent structured data format. The standard was created by the World Wide Web Consortium (W3C) to allow for easy information exchange. Microsoft has embraced XML in almost all areas of Visual Studio development. The new ADO.NET technology actually uses XML as the middleware format for exchanging data sets between a data provider and a data consumer. XML is also the storage format for disconnected data sets and any XML data source can be used as a data provider.

To the Visual Basic developer, the adoption of XML is a godsend. Through the functionality that is included with the Microsoft XML parser, a human-readable hierarchical data file can be easily read, written, or modified. That means that any application can use an XML-based file for a standard document storage format instead of adopting an unwieldy custom-structured binary or text file.

Because XML, like HTML, is human readable, you can open, examine, and edit files with a standard text editor. This chapter provides an overview of the XML format so that inspection of an XML file will be understandable. The general conventions of XML are also provided as a starting point for constructing a formatted file from scratch.

Here is an example of an extremely simple XML document:

```
<?xml version="1.0"?>
<Team>
  <Player Name="Kurt Trout" Position="LB">
    <Nickname>Eyes and Ears</Nickname>
    <JerseyNumber>52</JerseyNumber>
  </Player>
  <Player Name="George Zip" Position="QB">
    <Nickname>Zippy</Nickname>
    <JerseyNumber>7</JerseyNumber>
  </Player>
</Team>
```

The first line identifies this file as an XML document and states the version of the standard used to build it. Following this header is

61

the first element, which provides the root for the entire document: <Team>. Contained within this element are two other elements, which represent the data for separate players. As you can see, this file generally resembles a file stored in HTML format.

As a beginning point, this chapter assumes that you have a working familiarity with the current HTML standard. Because XML and HTML are closely related, many of the concepts learned by a developer (including general structure, layout, element definition, and the like) are easily translated to apply to an XML document.

Differences Between XML and HTML

XML files use many of the same conventions as HTML files. In fact, if the need arose, an HTML file could be converted to XML without much work. Despite their similarity, an XML file differs from an HTML file in these significant ways:

- **All tags must be matched** Some HTML tags, such as <P>, don't need to be explicitly closed with an end tag (that is, </P>). In XML, all tags must be explicitly opened and closed.

- **A header should be included** In XML, a document header should appear at the beginning of the document to indicate the schema that will be used for the data contained in the file. This header is known as a Document Type Definition (DTD) and may be included in the file itself or provided as a reference to an external DTD.

- **All attributes must appear within quotes** In HTML, placing quotes around attribute values is optional (for example, IMG SRC=MyPict.GIF), but XML requires these quotes (for example, IMG SRC="MyPict.GIF").

- **External resources must be referenced as entities** In HTML, an external resource (such as the IMG SRC tag for a GIF file) may be included anywhere in the document. XML requires references to files to be declared as separate entities at the beginning of the document. When this external resource is needed later in the XML document, the entity reference name is used instead of a URL (as in HTML).

NOTE: Although every tag requires an opening and closing tag, there is a special tag form to indicate empty content for a field while minimizing the memory space taken up by the item. The name of the tag is simply followed by a forward slash character (/) like this: <Name/>. This indicates that the Name element is present, but empty.

XML Capabilities

Despite the similarity to HTML, XML serves a completely different purpose. Although nearly every HTML document is meant to be displayed (as a Web page or frame construct), XML is a structured data file. This data file can be either displayed in a custom manner or used as a data provider.

5

As a data exchange format, XML has these advantages:

- **Shared protocol with HTML**   XML files are, by default, sent and received via the same HTTP protocol used for standard HTML files. The use of the HTTP protocol allows XML data exchange to transfer data easily through firewall-protected networks.

- **Partial loading capabilities based on target notation**   In HTML, to jump directly to a place in a larger document, a target may be specified with the pound sign (#). Regardless of the size of the target requested, the entire HTML document must be loaded. In XML, a selective load may be requested that sends only the referenced part of the file.

- **Interoperability with SGML**   SGML is the parent standard from which HTML was originally created. A document, if fully compliant with the XML standard, will also be in compliance with the SGML standard and can be used by most SGML-based programs.

- **Free XML Parser**   The Microsoft XML parser is available through the .NET framework and is also available as a separate ActiveX control. Using this parser makes implementing XML file access within nearly any program a simple process.

- **Support within ADO.NET**   In addition to the other XML features, ADO.NET provides a mechanism to export any data set as a formatted XML file.

- **XML Style Sheets**   XML supports a new type of style sheet known as XS. XS is far more powerful than the HTML standard known as Cascading Style Sheets, level 1 or CSS1.

- **Unicode is the standard for XML**   Although XML still supports the 8-bit ASCII file format for documents, Unicode is the recommended standard. By embracing Unicode, XML files can be used for applications requiring data to be stored with international character sets.

- **Structured data query**   Because the entire document is organized as structured data, filters may be applied based on fields or data type criteria. A search may be filtered to examine only data with the specified attributes.

XML Document Structure

XML documents may be stored as one of three file types: Unicode text file (default), ASCII text file, or a binary file. Binary files are most often used to store binary data such as images, non-differentiated data, or unstructured information. The actual structure of a formatted XML document can be divided into three parts:

- **Header**   The header indicates that the document is an XML type file and specifies the version of XML compliance. It may also contain settings that specify the DTD, cultural characteristics, and other setup information.

- **Document element**   There may be only one root element known as the *document element*. It is an element formatted like any other element (with begin and end tags), but it must be used to encapsulate all the other data elements in the document.

- **Body elements**   The body elements comprise the meat of the actual document. Within the body elements, all of the data for the XML file is contained.

The XML header indicates the type of document and the document's standards compliance. If the document uses XML standard formatting, this header can be placed at the beginning of the file:

```
<?XML version="1.0"?>
```

XML divides a document into a number of *elements*. For example, an element that represents a nickname might look like this:

```
<Nickname>Eyes and Ears</Nickname>
```

An XML document can contain only one root level element. Therefore, this simple XML file is improper:

```
<?XML version="1.0"?>
<Node>My 1st heading.</Node>
<Node>My another heading.</Node>
```

However, the file may have an unlimited number of nodes under the root element. In this case, both of the heading nodes are encapsulated in a primary root element:

```
<?XML version="1.0"?>
<Node>
<Node>My 1st heading.</Node>
<Node>My another heading.</Node>
</Node>
```

You are probably already familiar with this root element formatting convention from HTML documents. Everything in a standard Web file must be encapsulated by one, and only one, set of <HTML></HTML> tags.

In addition to elements that delineate the fields of data, there are a number of tags and attributes that the XML standard defines for special treatment within an XML document.

Character Data Tags

The CDATA tag can be used to incorporate a section of raw character data. This data can include character items such as quote marks without requiring specific XML escape characters. For example:

```
<![CDATA[<p>Testing of "character data" system. ]]>
```

White Space Attributes

White space may be specifically delineated with the XML-SPACE attribute. Activating the Preserve setting will include white space in the final document. This example demonstrates setting and eliminating observance of white space:

```
<L>     This element ignores the beginning spaces.</L>
<L XML-SPACE="PRESERVE">    This element doesn't.</L>
<L XML-SPACE="DEFAULT">    This ignores the spaces.</L>
```

XML-Link Tags

The linking capabilities of XML are far more robust than those found in HTML. In addition to normal hyperlink functionality, an XML-Link may be used for two-way links (which may be followed in either direction) or for multidirectional links (which connect two or more targets).

In XML, links are divided into two separate types:

- **Simple**   A simple link is the type used as a standard HTML hyperlink.
- **Extended**   The extended link is far more powerful because it allows multiple targets, multiple sources, and link associations that can be located outside of the source document. By placing the links in a separate file, it makes lists of links such as link pages easier to manage.

A simple link may be used much like a traditional HTML link:

```
<A XML-LINK="SIMPLE"
   HREF="http://www.w3c.org/XML">myLink</A>
```

This same link can instead be used with the **XML LINK** keyword:

```
<LINK="SIMPLE"
   HREF="http://www.w3c.org/XML">myLink</LINK>
```

An extended link can separate the link itself from the location within the document. For example, a two-paragraph link can allow a link to be followed either way:

```
<LINK="EXTENDED" ROLE="sibling">
<LOCATOR HREF="#firstPara" TITLE="Number1" />
<LOCATOR HREF="#secondPara" TITLE="Number2" />
</LINK>
```

Then, in the actual body of the XML document, these targets would be identified using the ID attribute:

```
<P ID="firstPara">This is the start.</P>
<P ID="secondPara">This is the end.</P>
```

Comments Tags

Comments are used the same way in XML as they are in HTML. However, be wary of using comments instead of simply including that same information in a data field that is ignored. Comments are not required as information to be rewritten by most XML parsers. Therefore, if an XML file is read and parsed by a program and then written to a different location, the comments are likely to be lost. This is an example of using a comment:

```
<!-- This is my comment. -->
```

5

Document Type Definition (DTD)

In HTML, the rules for the format of the document are defined in the HTML standard created by the W3C. In XML, definitions must be available for the creation and adoption of a wider range of possible uses. For this reason, the rules for the structure, syntax, variable types, and other attributes can be defined within the file itself or referenced to an external definition file.

The rules for a particular file type are held in a DTD. A DTD sets up the rules against which an XML file is verified for formatting compliance. DTD formatting may be included within the XML file itself, or the XML may reference an external DTD file.

There are two basic levels of compliance with the XML standard:

- **Well-formed documents**   These documents are structured properly (with matching open and close tags, and the like). However, a well-formed document may appear to be correct, but actually violates attribute settings or conditionals that are stored in a DTD.

- **Valid documents**   This type of document conforms to the DTD. For a server to validate a document according to the specified DTD, resources are required that may make the cost of validity checking outweigh the potential benefits. If a file fully complies with the rules defined in the DTD, it is said to be a *valid* document.

NOTE: The declarations of a DTD occur in a language very similar to a programming language known as Scheme, invented at MIT in the 1970s. Although Scheme does not have the user base or popularity of languages such as VB or C++, it is a Lisp-dialect that promotes small, clean code. That makes it the perfect code type to provide logic for data files.

The XML file can be set to use a specific DTD with the DOCTYPE element. Here is a simple example of setting up an internal DTD that accepts character data into a node element field:

```
<?XML version="1.0"?>
<!DOCTYPE Node [ <!ELEMENT Node (#PCDATA)> ]>
<Node>My 1st heading.</Node>
```

To load an external DTD, code similar to this can be used:

```
<?XML version="1.0"?>
<!DOCTYPE Node SYSTEM "MyNodeStyle.DTD"
<Node>My 1st heading.</Node>
```

Accessing XML Through the .NET Framework

Microsoft has devoted an entire namespace within the .NET framework to XML functionality. All of the XML classes are found under the System.XML path. The main XML classes that you are likely to use are:

- **XmlDeclaration class** Contains the XML declaration node that must occur at the start of each XML document in the form of *<?xml version='1.0' ?>* followed by any specified attributes.

- **XmlDocument class** Provides the foundation for an XML document. Some of the most commonly used methods available for this class are: CreateComment(data As String); CreateAttribute(name As String); CreateElement(name As String); CreateNode(nodeTypeString As String, name As

String, namespaceURI As String); CreateTextNode(text As
String); Load(filename As String); LoadXml(xml As String);
and Save(filename As String).

- **XmlElement class**   Provides a representation of an XML
  element.

- **XmlEntity class**   Provides a representation of an entity
  created by the XML syntax <*!ENTITY name* >. An entity
  may be an image (for example, <!ENTITY myPict SYSTEM
  "myPicture.GIF" NDATA BMP>), text file (for example,
  <!ENTITY myDoc SYSTEM "myDocument.txt">), or other
  resource used within the XML document . The entity is
  referenced within XML by the name assigned to it in the
  declaration.

- **XmlText class**   Provides a representation of the text held in
  an element or attribute.

- **XmlTextReader class**   Provides a class for fast, forward-only
  read-only access to XML data. This class enforces XML
  well-formed rules (for example, matching open and close
  tags) for the document, DocumentType nodes, and entity
  declarations. This class does not provide data validation
  and also does not expand default attributes. For full data
  validation, use the XmlValidatingReader class.

- **XmlTextWriter class**   Provides a class for fast, forward-only
  write access of an XML file that conforms to the W3C XML
  specification. Note, if the encoding argument in the constructor
  is passed as a null reference (Nothing in VB), the file will be
  written in ASCII UTF-8 format.

- **XmlValidatingReader class**   Provides a class for reading
  XML data while validating that it conforms to the DTD,
  XDR, XSD schema, and well-formed conventions of an XML
  document. This class also enforces XML well-formed rules
  (for example, matching open and close tags) for the document,
  DocumentType nodes, and entity declarations. Specify the
  schema files to use from an XmlSchemaCollection with the
  Schemas property. Specify the validation type with the
  ValidationType property.

Writing an XML File

The class XMLTextWriter contains all of the necessary routines
to easily write XML formatted files. This class will automatically

handle all of the necessary housekeeping to ensure that the file written is a well-formed XML document.

To use the XMLTextWriter class, follow these five steps:

1. Create a new XML stream and use the WriteStartDocument() method. This method will write the proper XML declaration to the file.

2. Write the root data element with the WriteStartElement() method.

3. Write additional elements into the file.

4. Close the final element with WriteEndElement() method.

5. Finalize the XML data with the WriteEndDocument() method. It is very important to call this method because it will close any elements or other structures that have not been properly closed. This ensures that the document is properly formatted so that no parser will fault reading the file.

By using a series of nested WriteStartElement() calls, a hierarchical data file can be created.

NOTE: In Chapter 8, there are two examples that demonstrate how to communicate between XML data files and ADO. Look under the WriteXML entry for an example of writing a DataSet into a file. The GetXML entry shows how to read from an XML file into a DataSet.

To create a sample project that will write an XML file, first start a new VB Windows application project. Add this header to the very beginning of a form file:

```
Imports System.Xml
```

Now place the following code in the Click event of a button:

```
Sub cmdXMLWrite_Click()
    ' For testing, you can use this line instead:
    ' Dim myTW As New XmlTextWriter(Console.Out)
    Dim myTW As New XmlTextWriter("C:\myTeam.xml", _
        Nothing)
    ' Inset the <?xml > version header
    myTW.WriteStartDocument()
    myTW.Formatting = Formatting.Indented
```

```
' Open the root node
myTW.WriteStartElement("Team")
' Open a data node
myTW.WriteStartElement("Player")
myTW.WriteAttributeString("Name", "George Zip")
myTW.WriteAttributeString("Position", "QB")
myTW.WriteElementString("Nickname", "Zippy")
myTW.WriteElementString("JerseyNumber", _
    XmlConvert.ToString(7))
' Close the data node
myTW.WriteEndElement()
' Close the root node
myTW.WriteEndElement()
myTW.WriteEndDocument()
myTW.Close()
End Sub
```

5

The simplest XML file should have the XML header and a single root node that encompasses all of the other data. Executing the application and clicking the button will output the structure of the well-formed XML data file example shown at the beginning of this chapter.

Reading an XML File

To read from an XML file is as easy as writing it. The parser automatically processes the XML entries and determines what type of element or document item is being addressed. In the following simple example, an XML file is read element by element and displayed in the Output window of the Visual Basic IDE.

Place the following code in another button on the form for the project you just created. This code uses the XmlTextReader class to read the contents of the myTeam XML file and displays each item to the Output window:

```
Sub cmdXMLRead_Click()
    Dim myTR As New XmlTextReader("c:\myTeam.xml")
    Dim myAttr As String
    While myTR.Read()
        If myTR.NodeType = XmlNodeType.Element Then
            Console.Write(myTR.Name & "")
            ' Check for any attributes
            myAttr = "<"
            While myTR.MoveToNextAttribute()
```

```vb
            myAttr = myAttr & " " & myTR.Name & _
               "='" & myTR.Value & "'"
         End While
         ' If there were attributes, display them
         If myAttr.Length > 1 Then
            Console.WriteLine(myAttr & "> ")
         Else
            Console.WriteLine("")
         End If
         If myTR.IsEmptyElement = True Then
            Console.Write("-- Empty element --")
         End If
      ElseIf myTR.NodeType = XmlNodeType.Text Then
         Console.WriteLine("   " & myTR.Value)
      End If
   End While
End Sub
```

Chapter 6
Language Reference

!

Database field operator.

Description   Using the exclamation command (!) allows access to a single database field while bypassing a complete database field object reference (using the Fields collection). The code sample requires a recordset created with the name "myRS" pointing at a data source that contains a column (field) named "LastName."

Syntax
```
recordset!field
```

Parameters

recordset   Required. Recordset of dynaset, table, or snapshot type.

field   Required. Field contained in the recordset.

Returns   N/A

Code Sample
```
Console.WriteLine(myRS!LastName)
```

See Also   &, IsDbNull

#

Double operator.

Description   This operator will set the variable to be a Double type.

Syntax
```
a#
```

Parameters

a   Any permitted variable name.

Returns   N/A

Code Sample
```
Dim a# = 56
```

See Also   CDbl, CType

Used to enclose a Date type.

Description   Surrounding a Date or Time value with the # sign will generate a proper Date value.

Syntax
```
#date#
```

Parameters

date   Required. Any valid date or time.

Returns   Object type

Code Sample
```
Console.WriteLine(#11/2/01#)
```

See Also   CDate, CType

#Const

Conditional compile constant.

Description   This operator creates a private constant in a module. These constants can be used only by other conditional operators (#if, #else, etc.) and are not seen by normal programming operators.

Syntax

```
#Const constname = expression
```

Parameters

constname   Any permitted variable name.

expression   Can include an operator (except Is) or a numeric value.

Returns   N/A

Code Sample

```
#Const conDemoApp = True
#If conDemoApp = False Then
    ' Include saving & printing routines
#End If
```

See Also   #if...#else...#endif, Const

#if...#else...#endif

Conditional compilation of a section of code.

Description   The conditional compile operator adds the encapsulated code only if the condition is True. This can be used to include or exclude demo code, to set up multiple deployment versions, or to make other final application changes.

Syntax

```
#if condition-1 Then
    [actions-1]
[#ElseIf condition-2 Then] : [actions-2]
[#ElseIf condition-n Then] : [actions-n]
[#Else] : [else-actions] : #End If
```

Parameters

conditions   Required. Boolean expressions.

Returns   N/A

Code Sample

```
#Const conVal = 1
#If conVal = 1 Then
```

```
   Dim astr As Object
#Else
   Dim astr As String
#End If
```

See Also   #Const

#Region

Groups a series of source code lines.

Description   This directive will begin a grouped section of lines that may be collapsed and hidden (an outlining feature) in the Visual Basic.NET source code window. Regions may not begin or end inside the body of a method. By default, when opening a file with a region, it will be collapsed.

Syntax
```
#Region "titleString"
   [codeLines]
#End Region
```

Parameters
titleString   Title text shown for the section when collapsed.

Returns   N/A

Code Sample
```
#Region "MyNoiseRoutine"
Sub myBeep()
   Beep()
End Sub
#End Region
```

See Also   #if...#else...#endif

 $

Sets the data type of the variable to a string.

Description This string operator serves the same function as defining a variable with the "Dim a As String" command. Once the operator is used in a definition, the variable name without the operator can be used to access the same variable (that is, myString$ and myString address the same variable).

Syntax

```
a$
```

Parameters

a Any permitted variable name.

Returns N/A

Code Sample

```
Dim a$ = "Hello" & 2
Console.WriteLine(a$)
Console.WriteLine(a)
```

See Also CStr, CType, Dim

6

%

Sets the data type of the variable to an integer.

Description This operator serves the same function as defining a variable with the "Dim a As Integer" command. Once the operator is used in a definition, the variable name without the operator accesses the same variable.

Syntax

```
a%
```

Parameters

a Any permitted variable name.

Returns N/A

Code Sample

```
Dim a% = 5.14
Console.WriteLine(a%)
Console.WriteLine(a)
```

78 &

See Also CInt, CType

String combining or concatenation operator.

Description This operator is extremely powerful, because it automatically converts between types as it combines or concatenates into a resultant string. Therefore, it can be used to combine several different variable types into a string without any explicit conversion.

Syntax
```
a & b
```

Parameters

a, b Any Object or data types.

Returns Object

Code Sample
```
Console.WriteLine("a" & 12 & 1.22 & #11/2/01#)
```

See Also &=, !, +, CStr

String and string variable combining or concatenation operator.

Description This operator is extremely powerful, because it automatically converts between types as it combines or concatenates into a resultant string. It adds a passed string to the string stored in a variable and places the combined string into the variable.

Syntax
```
a &= b
```

Parameters

a A string variable.

b Any Object or data types.

Returns   N/A

Code Sample

```
Dim myStr1 As String = "This is a"
Dim myStr2 As String = " stickup!"
myStr1 &= myStr2
Console.WriteLine(myStr1)
```

See Also   !, &, +, +=, CStr

'

Remark command.

Description   The apostrophe (') command can be used to mark code as a remark. The text that follows the apostrophe (until a carriage return is reached) will be ignored by the compiler. In the Immediate window, Visual Basic will ignore any command that follows this character.

6

Syntax

```
' comment
```

Parameters

comment   Any text.

Returns   N/A

Code Sample

```
' Console.WriteLine("1")
```

See Also   Rem

*

Multiplication operator.

Description   This operator multiplies one number by another and provides the result.

Syntax

```
a * b
```

Parameters

a, b   Required. Any valid numeric expression.

Returns   Object

Code Sample

```
Console.WriteLine(2.12 * 3.14)
```

See Also   +, −, /, ^, { ... }, Mod

Variable multiplication assignment operator.

Description   This operator multiplies a number by the value in a variable and stores the result in that variable.

Syntax

```
a *= b
```

Parameters

a   Required. A numeric variable.

b   Required. Any valid numeric expression.

Returns   N/A

Code Sample

```
Dim a As Integer = 10
a *= 2
Console.WriteLine(a)
```

See Also   +=, −=, /=, \=

Addition operator.

Description   This operator adds one number to another and
provides the result.

Syntax

```
a + b
```

Parameters

a, **b**   Required. Any valid numeric expression.

Returns   Object

Code Sample

```
Console.WriteLine(2.12 + 3.14)
```

See Also   *, −, /, ^, Mod

+

6

String addition operator.

Description   The + operator can be used many times within a
single line to create a large combination of strings. Unlike when
using the & operator, if you try to create a string using the +
operator with multiple variable types (such as String type + Single
type), a "Type Mismatch" error will occur. Use the & operator to
avoid the error.

Syntax

```
a + b
```

Parameters

a, **b**   Required. Any valid expression.

Returns   Object

Code Sample

```
Console.WriteLine("U.S. economy..." + _
  "Status: " + "solid.")
```

See Also   &, &=, CStr

Variable addition assignment operator.

Description   This operator adds a number to the value in a variable and stores the result in that variable.

Syntax

```
a += b
```

Parameters

a   Required. A numeric variable.

b   Required. Any valid numeric expression.

Returns   N/A

Code Sample

```
Dim a As Integer = 10
a += 2
Console.WriteLine(a)
```

See Also   *=, –=, /=, \=

Subtraction or negation operator.

Description   This operator subtracts one number from another and provides the result.

Syntax

```
a - b
```

Parameters

a, b   Required. Any valid numeric expression.

Returns   Object

Code Sample

```
Console.WriteLine(-1)
Console.WriteLine(5 - 3)
Console.WriteLine(3 - 5)
```

See Also   −=, *, +, /, ^, Mod

−=

Variable subtraction assignment operator

Description   This operator subtracts a number from the value in a variable and stores the result in that variable.

Syntax

```
a -= b
```

Parameters

a   Required. A numeric variable.

b   Required. Any valid numeric expression.

Returns   N/A

Code Sample

```
Dim a As Integer = 10
a -= 2
Console.WriteLine(a)
```

See Also   −, *=, +=, /=, \=

/

Division operator.

Description   This operator divides one number by another and provides the result. The result of the division will be returned in the data type appropriate to the result (that is, 10 / 3 will be returned as a Single). Use the \ operator to force the return of an

---

integer. Use the Mod operator to return the remainder that results in an integer division.

Syntax

```
a / b
```

Parameters

a, b   Required. Any valid numeric expression.

Returns   Object

Code Sample

```
Console.WriteLine(9/3)
Console.WriteLine(9/2)
```

See Also   /=, *, +, −, ^, Mod

/=

Variable division assignment operator.

Description   This operator divides a number by the value in a variable and stores the result in that variable.

Syntax

```
a /= b
```

Parameters

a   Required. A numeric variable.

b   Required. Any valid numeric expression.

Returns   N/A

Code Sample

```
Dim a As Integer = 10
a /= 2
Console.WriteLine(a)
```

See Also   /, *=, +=, −=, \=

<

Less-than operator.

Description Using the less-than operator compares two numeric values and returns a Boolean True or False value depending on the result. If this operator is passed nonnumeric values such as strings, they will be evaluated by their alphabetical values, including case sensitivity. Some of the code sample operators demonstrate these nonintuitive results.

Syntax

```
a < b
```

Parameters

a, b Required. Any valid numeric expression.

6

Returns Object

Code Sample

```
Console.WriteLine(3 < 5)
Console.WriteLine(3 < 2)
Console.WriteLine("a" < "z")
Console.WriteLine("z" < "a")
Console.WriteLine("A" < "a")
Console.WriteLine("21" < "200")
```

See Also <=, <>, =, >, >=, And, Like, Not

<=

Less-than or equal-to operator.

Description This operator compares two values for a less-than or equivalent condition.

Syntax

```
a <= b
```

Parameters

a, b   Required. Any valid numeric expression.

Returns   Object

Code Sample

```
Console.WriteLine(1 <= 2)
Console.WriteLine(2 <= 1)
```

See Also   <, <>, =, >, >=, And, Like, Not

<>

Nonequality operator.

Description   This operator compares two values for nonequivalent condition.

Syntax

```
a <> b
```

Parameters

a, b   Required. Any valid numeric expression.

Returns   Object

Code Sample

```
Console.WriteLine(1 <> 2)
Console.WriteLine(1 <> 1)
```

See Also   <, <=, =, >, >=, And, Like, Not

=

Equality operator.

Description   This operator compares two values for equivalent condition.

Syntax

```
a = b
```

Parameters

a, **b**   Required. Any valid numeric expression.

Returns   Object

Code Sample

```
Console.WriteLine(1 = 1)
Console.WriteLine(2 = 1)
Console.WriteLine(True = False)
```

See Also   <, <=, <>, >, >=, And, Like, Not

> **>**

6

Greater-than operator.

Description   This operator compares two values for the greater-than condition.

Syntax

```
a > b
```

Parameters

a, **b**   Required. Any valid numeric expression.

Returns   Object

Code Sample

```
Console.WriteLine(5 > 3)
Console.WriteLine(3 > 5)
```

See Also   <, <=, <>, =, >=, And, Like, Not

> **>=**

Greater-than or equal-to operator.

Description This operator compares two values for greater-than or equivalent condition.

Syntax

```
a >= b
```

Parameters

a, b Required. Any valid numeric expression.

Returns Object type

Code Sample

```
Console.WriteLine(2 >= 1)
Console.WriteLine(2 >= 2)
Console.WriteLine(1 >= 2)
```

See Also <, <=, <>, =, >, And, Like, Not

?

Prints to the current or Immediate window.

Description For quick typing, the question mark can be used in place of the Print command.

Syntax

```
? a
```

Parameters

a Any valid expression.

Returns N/A

Code Sample

```
? "Hello"
```

See Also Print, PrintLine, Space, Tab, Write, WriteLine

\

Integer division operator.

Description   This performs like the traditional division (/) operator, except it returns the results as an integer. Before the division takes place, both numbers are converted to integers. The result is truncated rather than rounded to the nearest integer. Use the Mod operator to obtain the remainder of the division of two integers.

Syntax
```
a \ b
```

Parameters
a, b   Required. Any valid numeric expression.

Returns   Object type

Code Sample
```
Console.WriteLine(16 \ 8)
Console.WriteLine(16 \ 15)
```

See Also   *, +, -, /, ^, Mod

\=

Variable integer division assignment operator.

Description   This performs like the traditional division assignment (/=) operator, except it stores the result as an integer. Before the division takes place, both numbers are converted to integers. The result is truncated rather than rounded to the nearest integer.

Syntax
```
a \= b
```

Parameters
a   Required. A numeric variable.

b   Required. Any valid numeric expression.

Returns N/A

Code Sample

```
Dim a As Integer = 16
a \= 15
Console.WriteLine(a)
```

See Also *=, +=, −=, /=, ∧=

Exponent or caret operator.

Description This returns the number raised to the power of the provided exponent.

Syntax

```
a ^ b
```

Parameters

a, b Required. Any valid numeric expression.

Returns Object

Code Sample

```
Console.WriteLine(2 ^ 1)
Console.WriteLine(2 ^ 2)
Console.WriteLine(2 ^ 8)
Console.WriteLine(2 ^ 0)
```

See Also *, +, −, /, Mod

Variable exponent assignment operator.

Description This operator returns a number raised to the power of the exponent provided by the value in the variable and stores the result in that variable.

Syntax

```
a ^= b
```

Parameters

a   Required. A numeric variable.

b   Required. Any valid numeric expression. Provides the exponent value.

Returns   N/A

Code Sample

```
Dim a As Integer = 2
a ^= 5
Console.WriteLine(a)
```

See Also   *=, +=, −=, /=, \=

6

{ ... }

Creates an array in memory containing the values passed in the parameter list.

Description   This extremely useful function can be used to automatically create the element array and store a number of values into it. If no values are specified, an empty array with zero elements is returned. Performs the same operation that the Array() function served in previous versions of Visual Basic.

Syntax

```
Dim myArray = {arglist}
```

Parameters

myArray   Required. Any valid variable name expression.

arglist   Required. The parameters to be contained as sequential elements in the array.

Returns   Array items

Code Sample

```
Dim myArray() As String = {"McClane", "Gennero", _
  "Gruber"}
Console.WriteLine(myArray(0))
```

See Also   Dim, ReDim

Abs

Returns the absolute value of the parameter passed to it.

Description   This function returns the absolute (positive) value of a number passed to it. The same data type is returned that is passed to it (that is, pass an Integer type, and an Integer type is returned).

Syntax

```
Abs(num)
```

Parameters

num   Required. The value to convert to an absolute value.

Returns   Same type as passed

Code Sample

```
Console.WriteLine(Abs(1))
Console.WriteLine(Abs(-1))
Console.WriteLine(Abs(-45.2334))
```

See Also   Fix, Int, Log, Mod

AddHandler

Dynamically assigns a routine to handle a specified event.

Description   The AddHandler keyword will allow dynamic specification of a routine to receive a specific event type. Multiple event handlers may be specified for a single event.

Syntax

```
AddHandler eventName, handlerAddress
```

Parameters

eventName   Required. The name of the event that activates the handler.

handlerAddress   Required. Using the AddressOf routine, the name of the routine to handle the event specified.

Returns   N/A

Code Sample

```
AddHandler cmdOK.Click, AddressOf cmdOKClickHandler
```

See Also   RemoveHandler

6

AddressOf

Returns the address of a procedure.

Description   The AddressOf operator is used for Windows API calls when the API routine requires a call-back function to be passed to it. Most API functions execute and then return control to the Visual Basic application when execution is complete. When a call-back is required, this means that a function needs to be called while the API retains execution control (such as updating the current page counter while the scrollbar thumb is being dragged). This operator is used like the ByRef or ByVal command when passing a series of arguments to an API routine.

Syntax

```
AddressOf procName
```

Parameters

procName   Required. The name of the procedure to be activated by the API function.

Returns   N/A

Code Sample

```
AddHandler cmdOK.Click, AddressOf cmdOKClickHandler
```

See Also Call, Declare

And

Logical And.

Description This command can be used to compile two comparison expressions or to logically combine two numbers. The And operator returns the bitwise result of all bits that exist in both values.

Syntax

```
a And b
```

Parameters

a, b Required. Any valid numeric expression.

Returns Object

Code Sample

```
Console.WriteLine((2 > 1) And (2 > 0))
Console.WriteLine((2 > 3) And (2 > 0))
Console.WriteLine(15 And 8)
Console.WriteLine(16 And 8)
Console.WriteLine(256 And 8)
```

See Also False, Not, Or, True, XOR

AndAlso

Short-circuiting logical And.

Description The And operator returns a Boolean result based on two values. This operator works like a normal And except that short-circuiting occurs when the first expression is false, in which case the second expression is not even evaluated and the result returned is False.

Syntax

```
a And b
```

Parameters

a, b   Required. Any valid numeric expression.

Returns   Object

Code Sample

```
Console.WriteLine((2 > 1) AndAlso (2 > 0))
Console.WriteLine((2 > 1) AndAlso (2 > 3))
Console.WriteLine((2 > 3) AndAlso (2 > 4))
```

See Also   And, False, Or, True, XOR

AppActivate

6

Activates a specified application window.

Description   This command shifts the focus to any specified application currently running under the Windows system. Either the title of the window or the application ID that is returned by the Shell command may be used. Note that activating the application does not change the collapsed or expanded state of the application.

Syntax

```
AppActivate(Title[, ProcessID])
```

Parameters

Title   Required. Title of the application to be activated or the TaskID returned by the Shell function.

ProcessID   Optional. An integer holding the Win32 process ID number that represents the application.

Returns   N/A

Code Sample

```
AppActivate "Microsoft Excel"
Dim MyAppID = Shell("C:\Windows\Notepad.EXE", 1)
AppActivate MyAppID
```

See Also Environ, Shell

Asc

Returns the ASCII code of the first letter of the string.

Description This command is the exact opposite of the Chr( ) command that returns the character when given a numeric ASCII character value. When given a character, this command returns the numeric value.

Syntax
```
Asc(val)
```

Parameters

val Required. String that contains the first letter that will be converted to a numeric.

Returns Integer

Code Sample
```
Console.WriteLine(Asc("A"))
Console.WriteLine(Asc("Abbey"))
Console.WriteLine(Chr(Asc("A")))
```

See Also AscW, Chr, Mid

AscW

Returns an integer of the Unicode value of the first letter of the string.

Description This command is the exact opposite of the ChrW( ) command that returns the character when given a numeric Unicode character value. When given a character, this command returns the numeric value.

Syntax
```
AscW(val)
```

Parameters

val   Required. String that contains the first letter that will be converted to a numeric.

Returns   Integer

Code Sample

```
Console.WriteLine(AscW("A"))
Console.WriteLine(AscW("Abbey"))
Console.WriteLine(Chr(AscW("A")))
```

See Also   Asc, Chr, Mid

Atan

Returns the arctangent of a given number in radians.

Description   This function retrieves the arctangent value of a number of type Double. The Atan function is the inverse trigonometric function of the Tan function. This function is now found in the System.Math namespace.

Syntax

```
System.Math.Atan(val)
```

Parameters

val   Required. Ratio of two sides of a right triangle.

Returns   Double type

Code Sample

```
Console.WriteLine(System.Math.Atan(1.2))
```

See Also   Cos, Sign, Sin, Sqrt, Tan

Beep

Speaker beep.

Description The Beep command will simply beep the speaker. There is no other way to make sound with Visual Basic without using the Windows API routines, DirectSound, or the Multimedia control. See Chapter 4, "How-To Code Examples" for an example of playing digitized sound (a WAV file).

Syntax
```
Beep
```

Parameters N/A

Returns N/A

Code Sample
```
Beep
```

See Also ?, Declare, Print, PrintLine, Write, WriteLine

Call

Activates a procedure.

Description This executes a system or user-defined procedure. To call a subroutine, you can simply use the name of the procedure or precede the name with the Call statement to make the call more explicit in the code.

Syntax
```
Call name [(arglist)]
```

Parameters

name Required. Current procedure name.

arglist Optional. Any parameters required for the procedure.

Returns N/A

Code Sample
```
Call Beep
Call MsgBox("Hello")
```

See Also Function...End Function, Sub...End Sub

CallByName

Enables runtime binding of a method or property.

Description   This function enables a property or method to be accessed by passing a string. Use of a string allows the property or method to be chosen at runtime with a constructed string. This function can be used to get or set a property or to invoke a method.

Syntax
```
CallByName(object,procName,callType,[arglist])
```

Parameters
object   Required. Object reference for the control (such as a text box or a check box) that will be used.

procName   Required. A string of the procedure or property that will be accessed.

callType   Required. Constant of the type of call being made, including vbLet, vbGet, or vbMethod.

arglist   Optional. Arguments to pass to method if method is called.

Returns   Dependent on method/property

Code Sample
```
CallByName(Button1, "Hide", CallType.Method)
```

See Also   Call

CBool

Converts a value to the Boolean data type.

Description   A Boolean data type has a value of either True or False. Conversion can occur on any valid string or numeric expression.

Syntax
```
CBool(expression)
```

Parameters

expression Required. Valid string or numeric expression to be converted.

Returns Boolean type

Code Sample
```
Console.WriteLine(CBool(3=2))
Console.WriteLine(CBool(3>2))
```

See Also CDbl, CInt, CLng, CSng, CStr, CType

CByte

Converts to Byte data type.

Description A Byte data type takes up a single byte in the computer memory and has a value from 0 to 255. This data type is used mostly for file formats and data conversion. Converting a number greater than 255 or less than 0 results in an Overflow error.

Syntax
```
CByte(expression)
```

Parameters

expression Required. Value to be converted.

Returns Byte type

Code Sample
```
Console.WriteLine(CByte(3))
Console.WriteLine(CByte(3.2))
```

See Also CBool, CDbl, CInt, CLng, CSng, CStr, CType

CChar

Converts the variable passed to the function to a Char type variable.

Description   A Char data type holds a single character, takes up two bytes in the computer memory, and has a value from 0 to 65535. Converting a number greater than 65535 or less than 0 results in an Overflow error.

Syntax

```
CChar (expression)
```

Parameters

expression   Object, Integer, Single, Double, String

Returns   Char type

Code Sample

```
Dim myChar As Char = _
  CChar("ABC") ' Will only hold the 1st letter: A
```

See Also   CBool, CDbl, CInt, CLng, CSng, CStr, CType

6

CDate

Converts the variable passed to the function to a Date type variable.

Description   This conversion function can be used to ensure the type of a particular variable. Any valid date or time representation can be converted into a Date type. This function performs the same operation CVDate() did in previous versions of VB.

Syntax

```
CDate (expression)
```

Parameters

expression   Object, Integer, Single, Double, String

Returns   Date type

Code Sample

```
Console.WriteLine(CDate("11/2/01"))
Console.WriteLine(CDate("September 11,2001"))
```

See Also   #, CBool, CDbl, CInt, CLng, CSng, CStr, CType

CDbl

Converts to double floating-point number.

Description   The Double type can hold from
−1.79769313486232E+308 to −4.94065645841247E−324 for
negative numbers or from 4.94065645841247E−324 to
1.79769313486232E+308 for positive numbers.

Syntax
```
CDbl(expression)
```

Parameters

expression   Required. Value to be converted.

Returns   Double type

Code Sample
```
Dim myVar As Integer = 1
Dim myDVar As Double
myDVar = CDbl(myVar)
myDVar = myDVar / 3
Console.WriteLine(myDVar)
```

See Also   #, CInt, CLng, CSng, CStr, CType

CDec

Converts to variable type Decimal.

Description   The Decimal type contains numbers scaled to the
power of ten. In the background, it optimizes for numbers that do
or don't contain decimals. Without any decimals, the range is
positive and negative 79,228,162,514,264,337,593,543,950,335.
Numbers with decimal places have 28 decimal places between
positive and negative 7.9228162514264337593543950335.

Syntax
```
CDec(expression)
```

Parameters

expression   Required. Value to be converted.

Returns   Object

Code Sample
```
Console.WriteLine(CDec(100))
Console.WriteLine(CDec(-5.231))
```

See Also   CDbl, CInt, CLng, CSng, CType

ChDir

Changes the default directory.

6

Description   Use the change directory (ChDir) command to change the default directory location where Visual Basic searches for files without a fully qualified path. After you use this command, any nonqualified file reference operations will access the specified folder first.

Syntax
```
ChDir path
```

Parameters

path   Required. Any valid path.

Returns   N/A

Code Sample
```
ChDir("C:\")
```

See Also   ChDrive, CurDir, Dir, Environ, FileOpen, Kill, MkDir, RmDir

ChDrive

Changes the current default-selected drive.

Description   This command changes the current drive. This changes the default drive to the value passed in a string. If a multicharacter string is passed, only the first character is used.

Syntax
```
ChDrive Drive
```

Parameters

Drive   Required. String that contains a valid drive.

Returns   N/A

Code Sample
```
ChDrive("c:\")
ChDrive("alpha:")
```

See Also   ChDir, CurDir, Dir, Environ, FileOpen, Kill, MkDir, RmDir

Choose

Returns a specified value for a list.

Description   This function returns a value from a list of arguments based on an index number. Can be used to quickly return a selection without having to create an array.

Syntax
```
Choose(index%, expression1
   [,expression2]...[,expression13])
```

Parameters

index%   Required. Number of expression to be returned.

expression   Required. Any valid expression.

Returns   Object

Code Sample
```
Console.WriteLine(Choose(3,"Draw","Paint","Write","Build"))
```

See Also   IIf, Select Case, Switch

Chr

Returns the character string of the ASCII value passed to it.

Description This function can be used to return both normal and unprintable characters. Common characters such as a space (Chr(32)), a tab (Chr(9)), a carriage return (Chr(13)), or a linefeed (Chr(10)) can be added to a string.

Syntax
```
Chr(Charcode)
```

Parameters

Charcode Required. An Integer or Long that defines the character.

Returns String type

Code Sample
```
Console.WriteLine(Chr(86) + Chr(66) + Chr(65))
```

See Also Asc, ChrW

ChrW

Converts to character type Unicode.

Description This returns a string of the character code. This string conforms to the Unicode standard, which uses two bytes per character to handle all of the international character sets.

Syntax
```
ChrW(Charcode)
```

Parameters

Charcode An Integer or Long that defines the character.

Returns String type

Code Sample
```
Console.WriteLine(ChrW(65))
```

See Also Asc, Chr

CInt

Converts the given expression to an integer.

Description This converts the expression to an Integer data type. A fractional part rounds to the nearest even number. The number 1.5 will round to 2, but 2.5 will round to 2 also. Integers can range from −32,768 to 32,767.

Syntax
```
CInt(expression)
```

Parameters

expression Required. Value to be converted.

Returns Integer type

Code Sample
```
Console.WriteLine(CInt(1.25))
```

See Also CDbl, CLng, CSng, CStr, CType, Fix, Int

Class...End Class

Defines a new class and encapsulates the properties, methods, events, and fields that belong to that class.

Description This command allows definition of a class that may include the types of members that will be available for instances of objects created from it. A class may be defined as Public, Private, Protected (visible only to own class or derived classes), Friend (visible only to entities declared with the Friend modifier), or Protected Friend. The Shadows modifier may be used to make the class shadow an identically named class in a base class. The Implements keyword indicates the interfaces for which the class will provide implementation methods. The Inherits keyword allows the specification of a parent class from which to inherit attributes, fields, properties, methods, and events.

Syntax
```
[Public | Private | Protected | Friend | Protected Friend]
[Shadows] [MustInherit | NotInheritable]
Class className
 [Implements interfaceName]
 [Inherits parentname]
   [statements]
End Class
```

Parameters   N/A

Returns   N/A

Code Sample
```
Public Class Class1
    ' Method, property, and event definitions
End Class
```

See Also   Call, End, Exit, Function...End Function, Sub...End Sub

CLng

Converts the given expression to a Long integer.

Description   This converts the expression to a Long data type. A fractional part rounds to the nearest even number. The number 1.5 will round to 2, but 2.5 will round to 2 also.

Syntax
```
CLng(expression)
```

Parameters

expression   Required. Value to be converted.

Returns   Long type

Code Sample
```
Console.WriteLine(CLng(200000.5))
```

See Also   CDbl, CInt, CSng, CStr, CType, Fix, Int

CObj

Converts the given expression to an Object data type.

Description   This function converts a data type to the Object data type.

Syntax

```
CObj(expression)
```

Parameters

expression   Required. Value or object to be converted.

Returns   Object type

Code Sample

```
Console.WriteLine(CObj(200000.5))
```

See Also   CBool, CDbl, CInt, CSng, CStr, CType, Fix, Int

Collection

Provides a standard form of the Collection object.

Description   A Collection object holds an ordered set of items as named object references. Elements of the collection are accessed through the Items property. New items may be added to a collection with the Add() method. The Remove() method will remove individual items, while the Clear() method eliminates all items in the collection.

Syntax

```
Collection
```

Parameters   N/A

Returns   N/A

Code Sample

```
Dim myObjects As New Collection()
Dim myObj1 As New Object
myObjects.Add(myObj1)
```

See Also   CreateObject

Command

Returns the commands passed to the Visual Basic program when it is executed.

Description   This command is useful if you will have a file extension associated with your program. When the user double-clicks the document, your EXE is launched and the path and name of the document that was selected are passed in this string. The commands will also contain information passed at the command line or the filename of an icon dragged and dropped onto the program icon. If no commands were passed when the program was executed, this command will return an empty string.

Syntax

```
Command
```

Parameters   N/A

Returns   String type

Code Sample

```
Console.WriteLine(Command())
```

See Also   Environ, Shell

Const

Declares a value as a Constant.

Description   Like the Dim command, the Const command cannot be used in the Immediate window. Defining a Const creates a read-only variable, in contrast to the #Const command, which generates a temporary constant for use only in other conditional compilation statements.

Syntax

```
[Global] Const name = expression [,name = expression]
```

Parameters

name   Required. Any permitted variable name.

expression   Required. Any valid expression.

Returns   N/A

Code Sample

```
Const myName = "Dan"
```

See Also   #Const, Dim, Enum, Public, ReDim, Static

Cos

Returns the cosine of an angle specified in radians.

Description   This command requires the angle to be passed in radians. The formula *radians = (degrees * pi) / 180* can be used to determine the radians from a degree measure. This function is now found in the System.Math namespace.

Syntax

```
Cos(angle)
```

Parameters·

angle   Required. Any numeric expression holding a radian measure.

Returns   Double type

Code Sample

```
Console.WriteLine(System.Math.Cos(3.14159))
Console.WriteLine(System.Math.Cos((90*3.14159)/180))
```

See Also   Atan, Exp, Log, Sign, Sin, Sqrt, Tan

CreateObject

Creates an instance of an object.

Description   Use this function to create a new instance of any OLE or ActiveX object. Either the qualified path name (that is, "excel.application") or the entire ClassID can be used to select the class library used to create the object. Note that CreateObject is used primarily for late-binding and the New keyword should be used instead for most general operations.

Syntax
```
CreateObject(ProgId As String [,ServerName As String])
```

Parameters

ProgID   Required. Class name or GUID of the required object. Must be registered with the OLE Registry system.

ServerName   Optional. The name of the server where the object will be created.

Returns   Object reference

Code Sample
```
Dim myObject As Object
myObject = CreateObject("Excel.Application")
myObject.Visible = True
```

See Also   Dim, GetObject

CShort

Converts the given expression to a Short 16-bit integer number.

Description   This converts the given expression to a Short data type that can hold a number between −32,768 and 32,767. Fractions are automatically rounded.

Syntax
```
CShort(expression)
```

Parameters

expression   Required. Value to be converted.

Returns   Short type

Code Sample

```
Console.WriteLine(CShort(1.222))
```

See Also   CDbl, CInt, CLng, CSng, CStr, CType

CSng

Converts the given expression to a Single precision floating-point number.

Description   This converts to a Single data type that can hold negative numbers between −3.402823E38 and −1.401298E−45, or positive numbers between 1.401298E−45 and 3.402823E38.

Syntax

```
CSng(expression)
```

Parameters

expression   Required. Value to be converted.

Returns   Single type

Code Sample

```
Console.WriteLine(CSng(1.222))
```

See Also   CDbl, CInt, CLng, CStr, CType

CStr

Converts the given expression to a string.

Description   This command can be used to convert any data type to a string. Most useful are the numeric- and date-to-string conversions. Note that most objects in the .NET Framework include the ToString method to provide a custom string output tailored to the specific object. In most cases, the ToString method should be favored over the CStr function.

Syntax
```
CStr(expression)
```

Parameters
expression   Required. Value to be converted.

Returns   String type

Code Sample
```
Console.WriteLine(CStr(12))
Console.WriteLine(CStr(1+2))
```

See Also   CDbl, CInt, CLng, CSng, CType, Format

CType

Converts the given expression to a specific data type, object, structure, class, or interface.

Description   This command can be used to convert any data type to another explicit data type.

Syntax
```
CType(expression, typename)
```

Parameters
expression   Required. Value to be converted.

typename   Required. Destination type of the converted expression. Can be any keyword that is valid for the As clause of a Dim statement.

Returns   Type varies

Code Sample
```
Dim myInt As Integer = 25
Dim myDouble As Double
myDouble = CType(myInt, Double)
```

See Also CDbl, CInt, CLng, CSng, Format

CurDir

Returns the path for a specified drive.

Description This function, if passed no argument, returns the path of the selected drive. If passed a string with a drive letter, it returns the path of the requested drive.

Syntax
```
CurDir[(drive)]
```

Parameters

drive Optional. Single-letter string to indicate desired drive.

Returns Object type

Code Sample
```
Console.WriteLine(CurDir())
Console.WriteLine(CurDir("C"))
```

See Also ChDir, ChDrive, MkDir, RmDir

DateAdd

Adds a specified amount to the Date type variable passed to it.

Description The format returned by DateAdd is determined by the Windows Control Panel settings. Intervals may be year (yyyy), quarter (q), month (m), day of year (y), day (d), weekday (w), week (ww), hour (h), minute (n), or second (s).

Syntax
```
DateAdd(interval, number, dateVar)
```

Parameters

interval Required. Interval to add to the specified datetime.

number   Required. Multiplier of the interval.

dateVar   Required. The Date type to be used as the base of the addition.

Returns   Date type

Code Sample
```
Console.WriteLine(DateAdd("m", 1, Now))
Console.WriteLine(DateAdd("ww", 2, Now))
Console.WriteLine(DateAdd("h", 5, Now))
```

See Also   CDate, DateDiff, DatePart, DateSerial, DateValue, Day, Format, IsDate, Month, Now, TimeOfDay, WeekDay

DateDiff

6

Determines the difference between two dates in units of the interval passed to it.

Description   This function returns the number of intervals between the two periods. Intervals may be year (yyyy), quarter (q), month (m), day of year (y), day (d), weekday (w), week (ww), hour (h), minute (n), or second (s).

Syntax
```
DateDiff(interval, date1, date2
  [,firstdayofweek[,firstweekofyear]])
```

Parameters
interval   Required. Interval to add to the specified datetime.

date1, **date2**   Required. The Date type.

firstdayofweek   Optional. Specifies first day of week (1 = Sunday [default], 2 = Monday, and so on).

firstweekofyear   Optional. Specifies the first week of the year (1 = Jan 1 [default]).

Returns   Object type

Code Sample
```
Console.WriteLine(DateDiff("d",Now,#1/1/2000#))
```

See Also   CDate, DateAdd, DatePart, DateSerial, DateValue, Day, Format, IsDate, Month, Now, TimeOfDay, Today, WeekDay

DatePart

Returns the part of the date specified by the interval string.

Description   Intervals may be year (yyyy), quarter (q), month (m), day of year (y), day (d), weekday (w), week (ww), hour (h), minute (n), or second (s).

Syntax
```
DatePart(interval, date)
```

Parameters

interval   Required. Interval to derive from the specified datetime.

date   Required. The Date type to be used as the base of the conversion.

Returns   Object

Code Sample
```
Console.WriteLine(DatePart("m",Now))
```

See Also   CDate, DateAdd, DateDiff, DateSerial, DateValue, Day, Format, IsDate, Month, Now, TimeOfDay, Today, WeekDay

DateSerial

Returns a Date type for the specified values.

Description   This routine allows the quick creation of a date from three integer values.

Syntax
```
DateSerial(year%, month%, day%)
```

Parameters

year%, **month%**, **day%**   Required. Integers.

Returns   Object type

Code Sample
```
Console.WriteLine(DateSerial(2001,8,1))
```

See Also   CDate, DateAdd, DateDiff, DatePart, DateValue, Day,
Format, IsDate, Month, Now, TimeOfDay, Today, WeekDay

DateValue

Converts an expression to a Date type.

Description   This function works very similarly to the CDate
function.

Syntax
```
DateValue(datestring)
```

Parameters

datestring   An expression representing a date.

Returns   Object type

Code Sample
```
Console.WriteLine(DateValue("August 15, 2001"))
```

See Also   #, CDate, DateAdd, DateDiff, DatePart, DateSerial, Day,
Format, IsDate, Month, Now, TimeOfDay, Today, WeekDay

Day

Returns the day value from the passed date argument.

Description   The returned day value will be an integer between
1 and 31 representing the day of the month. This function is actually
found in the Microsoft.VisualBasic namespace. Therefore, it may be

addressed with the complete pathname reference (i.e., Microsoft.VisualBasic.Day(dateObject)).

Syntax

```
Day(dateObject)
```

Parameters

dateObject   Required. Date to be used to retrieve the requested day.

Returns   Integer type

Code Sample

```
Console.WriteLine(Day(Now))
```

See Also   CDate, DateAdd, DateDiff, DatePart, DateSerial, DateValue, Format, IsDate, Month, Now, TimeOfDay, Today, WeekDay

DDB

Returns the depreciation value of an asset.

Description   Depreciation is determined by use of a double-declining balance method, unless another factor is specified using the factor parameter. The double-declining balance uses the number 2 for the default factor parameter.

Syntax

```
DDB(cost, salvage, life, period [, factor])
```

Parameters

cost   Required. Initial cost of asset as Double type.

salvage   Required. Value at end of useful life as Double type.

life   Required. Length of useful life as Double type.

period   Required. Period for which depreciation is calculated as Double type.

factor   Optional. Rate that balance declines (default = 2) as Object type.

Returns   Double type

Code Sample

```
Console.WriteLine(DDB(10000,500,24,12))
```

See Also   FV, IPmt, IRR, MIRR, NPer, NPV, Pmt, PPmt, PV, Rate, SLN, SYD

Declare

Creates a reference to a procedure or function in an external DLL.

Description   This statement can be used to specify an external routine available in a Dynamic-Linked Library file (uses the DLL extension). The Libname is the name of the DLL to be called. The DLL extension is optional and will be added automatically if omitted. The procedure name is case sensitive, so make sure the name you use in the declaration is exact. Visual Basic includes the API Text Viewer application that contains VB declarations for all Win32 API calls.

Syntax

```
Declare Sub Procname Lib Libname
   [Alias aliasname][(argList)]
Declare Function procname [Lib Libname]
   [Alias aliasname][(arg-List)]
   [As type]
```

Parameters

Procname   Required. Case-sensitive name must match function name unless given in aliasname parameter.

Libname   Name of library containing Sub or Function.

aliasname   Name or ordinal number of the specified routine.

argList   Any parameters and their types that must be passed.

Returns   N/A

Code Sample

```
Declare Function GetVersion Lib "kernel32" () As Long
```

6

See Also   Call

Delegate...End Delegate

Defines a new delegate and encapsulates the properties, methods, events, and fields that belong to it.

Description   This command allows definition of a delegate that may include the types of members that will be available for subclasses created from it. A delegate may be defined as Public, Private, Protected (visible only to own class or derived classes), Friend (visible only to entities declared with the Friend modifier), or Protected Friend. The Shadows modifier may be used to make the delegate shadow an identically named class in a base class.

Syntax

```
[ <attrlist> ]
[Public | Private | Protected | Friend | Protected Friend]
[Shadows]
Delegate [Sub | Function] name[([arglist])] [As Type]
```

Parameters

name   Required. A valid delegate name.

Returns   N/A

Code Sample

```
Delegate Function myFunction() As Integer
```

See Also   Call, End, Exit, Function...End Function, Sub...End Sub

DeleteSetting

Deletes a setting from the application's Windows Registry entries.

Description   Eliminates an individual key or all keys contained in a section of the Windows Registry. An error will occur if you attempt to delete a key or section that doesn't exist.

Syntax

```
DeleteSetting AppName,Section[,Key]
```

Parameters

AppName   Required. The name of the application in the Registry where the key is stored.

Section   Required. Name of the section within the application area that holds the key. If key is not passed, all keys within the section are deleted.

Key   Optional. Name of the key to be deleted.

Returns   N/A

Code Sample

```
DeleteSetting("myApp","Prefs")
```

See Also   GetAllSettings, GetSetting, SaveSetting

6

Dim

Defines a variable.

Description   This statement defines a variable and can set the data type of the variable either with the As keyword or through the variable suffixes (such as $, %, and so on). This command cannot be used in the Immediate window.

Syntax

```
[<attrlist>]
[Public | Protected | Friend | Protected Friend
   | Private | Static] [Shared] [Shadows] [ReadOnly]
Dim [WithEvents] name [(boundlist)]
   [ As [ New ] type ] [= initexpr]
```

Parameters

name   Permitted names include alphanumerics and basic symbols (such as the underscore), but no spaces.

type   Required if As keyword is used. Can be set to object types as well as the data type primitives such as Boolean, Byte, Char,

Date, Decimal, Double, Integer, Long, Object, Short, Single, and String.

Returns   N/A

Code Sample

```
Dim iCounter As Integer
Dim myStr As String
Dim myShortIntArray() As Int16
```

See Also   Const, Private, Public, ReDim, Static, Structure...EndStructure, VarType

Dir

Returns the name of the file or path that matches the pattern passed in the argument.

Description   The first call to this function must contain the requested pattern. If the next call omits the pattern argument, the next file or path that matches the original pattern will be returned. An empty string will be returned if none matching the pattern is found.

Syntax

For the initial call to Dir for a pattern:

```
Dir(pattern[,attributes])
```

For each successive call for the same pattern:

```
Dir
```

Parameters

pattern   Any path or filename. May include wildcards.

attributes   Optional. Options include: vbNormal, vbReadOnly, vbHidden, vbSystem, vbVolume, vbDirectory, vbArchive, and vbAlias.

Returns   String type

Code Sample

```
Console.WriteLine(Dir("C:\Windows\Win.INI"))
Console.WriteLine(Dir("C:\Windows\*.INI"))
```

See Also   ChDir, ChDrive, CurDir

Do...Loop

Cycles through a loop until the necessary condition is met.

Description   The Do...Loop structure can continue cycling while a condition is True (While) or until it is True (Until).

Syntax

To test the condition at the top of a loop:

```
Do [While | Until condition]
   [statements] [Exit Do] [statements]
Loop
```

6

To test the condition at the bottom of the loop:

```
Do
   [statements] [Exit Do] [statements]
Loop [While | Until condition]
```

Parameters

condition   Required. Boolean condition that may be evaluated to either True or False.

Returns   N/A

Code Sample

```
Dim i As Integer = 0
Do While i < 5
  Console.WriteLine(i)
  i += 1
Loop
i = 0
Do Until i > 5
  Console.WriteLine(i)
  i = i + 1
Loop
```

See Also   Exit, For...Next, While...End While

DoEvents

Pauses to allow the system to process events.

Description A loop that is doing a great number of operations provides few processing resources for the rest of the system for tasks such as screen updates. This command pauses for the system to process other tasks. This method is now found in the System.Windows.Forms.Application namespace.

Syntax
```
DoEvents()
```

Parameters N/A

Returns N/A

Code Sample
```
DoEvents
```

See Also End, Stop

End

Stops execution or ends the definition of a Function, If structure, Select statement, Subroutine, or Structure definition.

Description The End command is used to terminate either the current execution or a definition. Only the End If statement will automatically insert the necessary space when it is typed (automatically converting "endif" to "End If").

Syntax
```
End [Function | If | Select | Sub | Type]
```

Parameters N/A

Returns N/A

Code Sample

```
If 1 > 0 Then
End If
```

See Also   Function...End Function, If...Then...Elseif...Endif, Select
Case, Stop, Structure...EndStructure, Sub...End Sub

Enum

Used to create an enumeration set of constants.

Description   Like the Structure...End Structure commands,
enumeration enables you to create a set of variables that are
referenced together. Variables and parameters can be declared
with the Enum type, although assigned values cannot be modified
at runtime.

Syntax

```
[<attrlist>]
[Public | Protected | Friend | Protected Friend | Private]
[Shadows]
Enum name [As type]
    constName1 = val1
    constName2 = val2
End Enum
```

Parameters

name   Required. Name of the enumeration set.

constName1, **constName2**   Optional. Any number of constant
names.

val1, **val2**   Optional. Values to assign to the enumerated
constants.

Returns   N/A

Code Sample

```
Enum myPrintingPrefs
    Portrait = 0
    Landscape = 1
End Enum
```

See Also   Const

Environ

Returns information on the current environment.

Description   The operating system stores a great deal of information available through this function. These variables include such information as the Path statement, the Prompt information, the Temp directory, and so on. Each returned string begins with the environmental variable, followed by an equal sign, followed by the current setting.

Syntax

```
Environ(entry-name | entry-position)
```

Parameters

entry-name   The name of the environmental variable to retrieve.

entry-position   The index of the environmental variable.

Returns   String type

Code Sample

```
Console.WriteLine(Environ("path"))
Console.WriteLine(Environ(1))
Console.WriteLine(Environ(2))
Console.WriteLine(Environ(3))
```

See Also   Command

EOF

Returns the End-of-File condition.

Description   This function may be used effectively with a Do...Loop to process a file. The code sample requires a file Test.txt located at the root of C: to function properly. Change the file and path names to use a different file.

Syntax

```
EOF(filenumber)
```

Parameters

filenumber   The current file number assigned when the file was opened.

Returns   Integer type

Code Sample

```
FileOpen(1, "C:\test.txt", OpenMode.Output)
Print(1, "File position test")
Console.WriteLine(EOF(1))
FileClose(1)
```

See Also   FileClose, FileGet, FileOpen, Input, LineInput, Loc, LOF

6

Erase

Clears the current contents of an array.

Description   This clears and releases the memory of an array. Each cleared element of the array is assigned a Nothing reference.

Syntax

```
Erase arrayname [, arrayname]
```

Parameters

arrayname   Required. The name of the array to be cleared.

Returns   N/A

Code Sample

```
Dim myArray() As Integer = {1, 5, 7, 9}
Console.WriteLine(myArray(2))
Erase myArray
Console.WriteLine(myArray(2))
```

See Also   { ... }, Dim, ReDim

Err Object

Contains complete information about an error that has occurred.

Description   The Clear method will clear the current error, while the Description and Number properties describe the error itself. The Err object is mostly used in conjunction with an On Error routine within a procedure or function.

Syntax
```
Err.Raise errornum
```

Parameters
errornum   Required. Integer with error code to be generated.

Returns   N/A

Code Sample
```
Err.Clear()
Err.Raise(6)
```

See Also   Error, On Error..., Resume

Error

Generates an error of the specified type in the system.

Description   This statement causes the Visual Basic system to receive an error of the type specified.

Syntax
```
Error errorcode
```

Parameters
errorcode   Required. Integer error code number.

Returns   N/A

Code Sample
```
Error 6
```

See Also   Err object, On Error..., Resume

ErrorToString

Returns the error message of the type specified by an error number.

Description   This statement may be passed a valid error number and will return the Description property of an error number of that type.

Syntax
```
ErrorToString(errorcode)
```

Parameters
errorcode   Required. Integer error code number.

Returns   N/A

Code Sample
```
Console.WriteLine(ErrorToString(6))
```

See Also   Err object, Error, On Error..., Resume

Event

Creates a user-defined event.

Description   Once you define an event, the RaiseEvent command may generate that event to activate the routine. This command is not available in VBA or VBScript, only in the complete Visual Basic development environment.

Syntax
```
[<attrlist>]
[Public | Private | Protected | Friend | Protected Friend]
[Shadows ]
Event eventname[(arglist)]
   [ Implements interfacename.interfaceeventname ]
```

Parameters

eventname   Required. Any permitted name for the event.

arglist   Optional. Any arguments that are to be passed to the event.

Returns   N/A

Code Sample
```
Event IDConfirmed(UserName as String)
```

See Also   Class...End Class, Function...End Function, Sub...End Sub

Exit

Terminates the current operation before the conditions are complete.

Description   You can use the Exit Do to exit a Do...Loop before the final conditions have been met. The same is possible with For...Next loops, subroutines, and functions.

Syntax
```
Exit Do
Exit For
Exit Sub
Exit Function
```

Parameters   N/A

Returns   N/A

Code Sample
```
Dim i As Integer
For i = 0 To 5
  If i = 2 Then Exit For
Next
```

See Also   Do...Loop, For...Next, Function...End Function, Sub...End Sub

Exp

Raises the base of natural logarithms (e) to a specified power.

Description   The function (known as an antilogarithm) returns a Double type based on the results of the passed exponent. The constant e is approximately 2.718282. This function is now found in the System.Math namespace.

Syntax

```
Exp(power)
```

Parameters

power   Required. Double type to be used as the exponent.

Returns   Double type

Code Sample

```
Console.WriteLine(System.Math.Exp(1))
Console.WriteLine(System.Math.Exp(20))
```

See Also   Log, Sign

False

Logical False.

Description   This constant can be used in most expressions, bitwise operations, and comparisons.

Syntax

```
False
```

Parameters   N/A

Returns   N/A

Code Sample

```
Console.WriteLine((2=2) = False)
```

See Also And, Or, True, XOR

FileAttr

Returns the mode (input, output, and so on) of the specified open file.

Description This function can be used to determine the current attributes of an open file. The OpenMode values can be Input, Output, Random, Append, or Binary.

Syntax

```
FileAttr(filenumber)
```

Parameters

filenumber Required. Any valid file number ID.

Returns OpenMode type

Code Sample

```
Dim myMode As OpenMode
FileOpen(1, "C:\test.txt", OpenAccess.Write)
Print(1, "Hello", SPC(20), "Hello2")
myMode = FileAttr(1)
Console.WriteLine("Current file mode: " & _
  myMode.ToString())
FileClose(1)
```

See Also FileClose, FileOpen, Input, Print, PrintLine

FileClose

Closes all open files or the file specified by the file number.

Description If you omit the file number and issue the Close command, all open files will be closed.

Syntax

```
FileClose ([ParamArray FileNumbers() As Integer])
```

Parameters

FileNumbers()   An integer or array of integers indicating current file numbers.

Returns   N/A

Code Sample
```
FileOpen(1, "C:\test.txt", OpenAccess.Write)
Print(1, "Hello", SPC(20), "Hello2")
FileClose(1)
```

See Also   FileOpen, Input, Print, PrintLine, Reset

FileCopy

Copies a file from the source to the destination.

Description   This routine acts as the traditional file-copy operating system call and makes a duplicate of the file (with path) described in the source to the file (with path) denoted in the destination string.

Syntax
```
FileCopy(source, destination)
```

Parameters

source, destination   Required. Strings containing paths and filenames.

Returns   N/A

Code Sample
```
FileCopy("C:\test.txt","C:\testcopy.txt")
```

See Also   ChDir, ChDrive, CurDir, FileClose, FileOpen, Kill, MkDir, RmDir

FileDateTime

Returns the date and time when a specified file was last modified.

Description   Simply passing a valid filename and path will return the last modified date of any accessible file.

Syntax

```
FileDateTime(filename)
```

Parameters

filename   Required. Any valid path and filename.

Returns   Object (Date) type

Code Sample

```
Console.WriteLine(FileDateTime("C:\test.txt"))
```

See Also   ChDir, ChDrive, CurDir, FileClose, FileLen, FileOpen, GetAttr, Kill, MkDir, RmDir

FileGet

Retrieves information from an open file and places it in a variable

Description   The FileGet command reads the data usually written into the file by a FilePut statement. All data types are supported. The code sample assumes a file named Test.txt at the C:\ root directory contains at least eight characters of data to read.

Syntax

```
FileGet(FileNumber As Integer, Value
   [,RecordNumber As Integer] )
```

Parameters

FileNumber   Required. Any valid open file number.

RecordNumber   Optional. Specifies record number in a Random file or byte number in a Binary file where reading should occur.

Value   Required. A valid variable that will have its contents read from the file. Supported data types are Object, Short, Integer, Single, Double, Decimal, Byte, Boolean, String, Data, and Array.

Returns   N/A

Code Sample

```
Dim myStr As String
FileOpen(1, "C:\test.txt", OpenMode.Input)
FileGet(1, myStr)
FileClose(1)
```

See Also   FileClose, FileOpen, FilePut, LOF, Structure

FileLen

Returns the length in bytes of a particular file.

Description   This routine can determine the length of any file available to the system. The file does not need to be opened with any of the disk access commands to get its length.

Syntax

```
FileLen(filename)
```

Parameters

filename   Required. Any valid path and filename.

Returns   Long type

Code Sample

```
Console.WriteLine(FileLen("C:\test.txt"))
```

See Also   ChDir, ChDrive, CurDir, FileClose, FileDateTime, FileOpen, GetAttr, Kill, MkDir, RmDir

FileOpen

Opens a file for reading or writing.

Description   This command is used to open a file with particular access options. Files of types Sequential, Binary, and Random may be opened. This function replaces the Open statement in previous versions of VB.

Syntax

```
FileOpen (FileNumber As Integer, FileName As String,
  Mode As OpenMode [,Access As OpenAccess [,Share
  As OpenShare [,RecordLength As Integer]]])
```

Parameters

FileNumber   Required. A valid file number (between 1 and 511) such as one returned by the FreeFile function.

FileName   Required. Any valid path and filename.

Mode   Required. May be set to Input, Output, Binary, Append, and Random.

Access   May include Read, Write, or Read Write.

Share   May include Shared, Lock Read, Lock Write, and Lock Read Write.

RecordLength   Number of characters buffered (Sequential) or record length (Random) less than or equal to 32,767.

Returns   N/A

Code Sample

```
FileOpen(1, "C:\test.txt", OpenAccess.Write)
Print(1, "Hello", SPC(20), "Hello2")
FileClose(1)
```

See Also   FileClose, FileGet, FileOpen, FilePut, FreeFile, Input, Write, WriteLine

FilePut

Writes a variable to a current file.

Description   The FilePut command works very much like the Print or PrintLine commands, except it outputs the contents of a single variable and provides no automatic formatting to the output. FilePut replaces the Put command found in previous versions of Visual Basic.

Syntax

```
FilePut(FileNumber As Integer, Value
  [,RecordNumber As Integer] )
```

Parameters

FileNumber   Required. Any valid open file number.

RecordNumber   Optional. Specifies record number in a Random file or byte number in a Binary file where writing should occur.

Value   Required. A valid variable that will have its contents written to the file. Supported data types are Object, Short, Integer, Single, Double, Decimal, Byte, Boolean, String, Data, and Array.

Returns   N/A

Code Sample

```
Dim myStr As String = "Hello World"
FileOpen(1, "C:\test.txt", OpenMode.Output)
FilePut(1, myStr)
FileClose(1)
```

See Also   FileClose, FileGet, FileOpen, LOF, Structure

6

FileWidth

Sets the line width for the output file.

Description   For formatting to a file, the FileWidth statement sets the width between 0 and 255 for text, tabs, and spaces to be formatted. If the width is set to 0 (default), there is no set line width.

Syntax

```
FileWidth(FileNumber, RecordWidth)
```

Parameters

FileNumber   Required. Any valid open file number.

RecordWidth   Required. Any width between 0 and 255.

Returns   N/A

Code Sample

```
FileOpen(1, "C:\test.txt", OpenMode.Output)
FileWidth(1, 20)
Print(1, "Hello", Spc(15), "Hello2")
FileClose(1)
```

See Also FileClose, FileGet, FileOpen, FilePut

Filter

Filters a current array and returns a new array with elements that qualify for the filter criteria.

Description This function uses criteria passed to it to filter an array. A new array is created and returned that contains only the data that qualifies under the filter specifications.

Syntax

```
Filter(Source() As Object|String, Match As String
  [,Include As Boolean [,Compare As CompareMethod]])
```

Parameters

Source Required. Array of source strings.

Match Required. String used as search string.

Include Optional. Boolean to indicate whether to return strings that contain the string. A False value (default) requires the string to match the pattern.

Compare Optional. Type of comparison to perform can be CompareMethod.Binary or CompareMethod.Text. Default is set to CompareMethod.Binary.

Returns String array type

Code Sample

```
Dim a() As String = {"Cussler", "Hill", _
  "Burgess", "Wordsworth"}
Dim b() = Filter(a,"Hill")
Console.WriteLine(b(0))
```

See Also { ... }, Join, Split

Fix

Returns an integer of the passed value.

Description   This function works almost exactly like the Int( ) function, except when handling negative numbers. Fix returns the first negative number greater than or equal to the passed value. Int() returns the first negative number that is less than or equal to the value. Fix(−1.4) would return the value −1, while Int(−1.4) would return the value −2.

Syntax
```
Fix(numericExpression)
```

Parameters
numericExpression   Required. Any valid numeric expression.

6

Returns   Integer type

Code Sample
```
Console.WriteLine(Fix(1.4))
Console.WriteLine(Fix(-1.4))
```

See Also   CInt, Int, Round

For Each...Next

Cycles through an entire collection of objects or items in an array.

Description   The For Each...Next structure will cycle through all the elements, even if they are not in numeric order. In an object collection, the element variable is set to reference the current object.

Syntax
```
For Each element In group [statements] Next [element]
```

Parameters
element   Required. A variable that will hold the current reference to the selected object or array item.

group   An array or collection reference.

Returns   N/A

Code Sample

```
Dim myArray() As Integer = {5,8,10,98}
Dim myItem As Integer
For Each myItem in myArray
  Console.WriteLine(myItem)
Next
```

See Also   CreateObject, Do...Loop, Exit, For...Next, GetObject, While...End While

For...Next

Loops until the specified value is reached.

Description   The For...Next structure will cycle through the statements in the loop until the endvalue parameter is reached.

Syntax

```
For counter = startvalue To endvalue [Step increment]
    [statements]
    [Exit For]
    [statements]
Next [counter][, counter]...
```

Parameters

counter   Required. Variable that keeps the current increment.

startvalue   Required. Begin value of loop.

endvalue   Required. End value of loop.

Step   Optional. Amount that counter is increased every time through the loop.

Returns   N/A

Code Sample

```
Dim i As Integer
For i = 1 to 10
```

```
  Console.WriteLine(i)
Next i
For i=10 to 1 step -1
  Console.WriteLine(i)
Next
```

See Also   Do...Loop, Exit, For Each...Next, While...End While

Format

Returns a string formatted in any number of ways, including styles for strings, dates, times, currency, or other types.

Description   The Format command is one of the most powerful commands for easily and quickly generating output in a desired format. Use the # within the Style argument to indicate a placeholder.

Syntax
```
Format(Expression As Object [,Style [,DayOfWeek
  [,WeekOfYear]]])
```

Parameters

Expression   Required. Valid expression including dates.

Style   Optional. String pattern required for output. Default is " ".

DayOfWeek   Constant for specifying the first day of the week in data type Microsoft.VisualBasic.FirstDayOfWeek.

WeekOfYear   Constant for specifying the first week of the year in data type Microsoft.VisualBasic.FirstWeekOfYear.

Returns   String type

Code Sample
```
Console.WriteLine(Format(Now, "hh:mm:ss AMPM"))
Console.WriteLine(Format(Now, "h:m:s"))
Console.WriteLine(Format(Now, "mmm d yyyy"))
Console.WriteLine(Format(2534.64,"##,##0"))
Console.WriteLine(Format(2534.64,"##,##0.00"))
Console.WriteLine(Format(2534.64,"##,###.##"))
```

```
Console.WriteLine(Format(-2534.64, _
  "$##,##0.00;($##,##0.00)"))
```

See Also   &, &=, CDate, CStr, DateSerial, DateValue,
FormatCurrency, FormatDateTime, FormatNumber, FormatPercent,
Now, Str, TimeSerial, Val

FormatCurrency

Returns a string formatted in a specified currency format.

Description   This command is a specialized formatting command
for easily and quickly generating output in a currency format. The
character conventions of the standard Format command also apply
to this command. The currency symbol that is specified in the
Windows Control Panel is used for formatting.

Syntax
```
FormatCurrency(Expression As Object
  [,NumDigitsAfterDecimal [,IncludeLeadingDigit
  [,UseParensForNegativeNumbers [,GroupDigits]]]])
```

Parameters

Expression   Required. Value to be formatted.

NumDigitsAfterDecimal   Optional. Number of decimal places
to appear to the right of the decimal. If left blank, −1 will be
used to indicate that the default number will be used.

IncludeLeadingDigit   Optional. Tristate value to specify whether
leading zero will be displayed for fractional values.

UseParensForNegativeNumbers   Optional. Tristate value to
specify whether to show parentheses for negative numbers.

GroupDigits   Optional. Tristate value to specify whether to group
digits using the group delimiter specified in the computer's
regional settings.

Returns   String type

Code Sample
```
Console.WriteLine(FormatCurrency(123.1232))
```

See Also   Format, FormatDateTime, FormatNumber, FormatPercent

FormatDateTime

Returns a string formatted in a specified date and time format.

Description   This command is a new specialized formatting command for easily and quickly generating output in a date and time format. The character conventions of the standard Format command also apply to this command.

Syntax
```
FormatDateTime(Expression As DateTime [,NamedFormat])
```

6

Parameters
Expression   Required.

NamedFormat   Optional. This specifies the format type based on one of five DateFormat constants: GeneralDate, LongDate, ShortDate, LongTime, and ShortTime. The default is DateFormat.GeneralDate.

Returns   String type

Code Sample
```
Console.WriteLine(FormatDateTime(Now, 0))
Console.WriteLine(FormatDateTime(Now, _
  DateFormat.LongDate))
```

See Also   Format, FormatCurrency, FormatNumber, FormatPercent

FormatNumber

Returns a string formatted in a specified numeric format.

Description   This command is a new specialized formatting command for easily and quickly generating output in a numeric format. The character conventions of the standard Format command also apply to this command.

Syntax

```
FormatNumber(Expression As Object
   [,NumDigitsAfterDecimal [,IncludeLeadingDigit
   [,UseParensForNegativeNumbers [,GroupDigits]]]])
```

Parameters

Expression   Required. Value to be formatted.

NumDigitsAfterDecimal   Optional. Number of decimal places to appear to the right of the decimal. If left blank, −1 will be used to indicate that the default number will be used.

IncludeLeadingDigit   Optional. Tristate value to specify whether leading zero will be displayed for fractional values.

UseParensForNegativeNumbers   Optional. Tristate value to specify whether to show parentheses for negative numbers.

GroupDigits   Optional. Tristate value to specify whether to group digits using the group delimiter specified in the computer's regional settings.

Returns   String type

Code Sample

```
Console.WriteLine(FormatNumber(129.222,1))
```

See Also   Format, FormatCurrency, FormatDateTime, FormatPercent

FormatPercent

Returns a string formatted in a specified percentage format.

Description   This command is a new specialized formatting command for easily and quickly generating output in a percentage format. The character conventions of the standard Format command also apply to this command. The formatted percentage is returned as the value passed multiplied by 100 (that is, 0.987 = 98.7%).

Syntax

```
FormatPercent(numericExpression
  [,numDecimalPlaces [,includeLeadDigit
  [,useParensforNegs [,groupDigits]]]])
```

Parameters

numericExpression   Required. Value to be formatted.

numDecimalPlaces   Optional. Number of decimal places to appear to the right of the decimal. If left blank, −1 will be used to indicate that the default number will be used.

includeLeadDigit   Optional. Tristate value to specify whether leading zero will be displayed for fractional values.

useParensforNegs   Optional. Tristate value to specify whether to show parentheses for negative numbers.

groupDigits   Optional. Tristate value to specify whether to group digits using the group delimiter specified in the computer's regional settings.

Returns   String type

Code Sample

```
Console.WriteLine(FormatPercent(123.456,2))
```

See Also   Format, FormatCurrency, FormatDateTime, FormatNumber

FreeFile

Returns the next valid free file number.

Description   This function returns the next available number for use as a file. Use this command if a program needs to manually specify the index number of a file to be opened. If you've been letting the system supply the file number, checking this value will reveal how many files have been opened this session.

Syntax

```
FreeFile
```

Parameters N/A

Returns Integer type

Code Sample
```
Console.WriteLine(FreeFile())
```

See Also ChDir, ChDrive, CurDir, FileClose, FileGet, FileOpen, FilePut, GetAttr, Input, MkDir, Print, PrintLine, RmDir

Friend

Like the Public keyword, but limits accessibility to within the project.

Description Using the Public keyword makes a procedure accessible throughout the project and exposes it outside the project. The Friend keyword allows the procedure to be called within the project, but hides it from the outside. For example, you may need a function in a form module or class to be available within the project, but hidden from final compilation as an ActiveX control.

Syntax
```
Friend procedureName
```

Parameters

procedureName Required. Name of procedure to make public within a project.

Returns N/A

Code Sample N/A

See Also Private, Public

Function...End Function

Creates a function in a module or form.

Description This command enables definition of a function that may include the types of arguments that will be received by the function as well as the arguments that will be returned.

Syntax

```
[Static] [Private]
Function function-name [(arguments)] [As type]
  [Static var[,var]...] [Dim var[,var]...]
    [statements]
    [function-name = expression]
    [Exit Function]
    [statements]
    [function-name = expression]
End Function
```

Parameters

arguments   Required. Any arguments to be received by the function.

Returns   Any defined type

Code Sample

```
Function myFunc() As Int64
' Enter code
End Function
```

See Also   End, Exit, Sub...End Sub

FV

Returns the future value of an annuity.

Description   The value that is returned is calculated from the period, the fixed payments, and the fixed interest rate.

Syntax

```
FV(Rate, NPer, Pmt As Double [,PV [,Due]])
```

Parameters

Rate   Required. Double type of interest rate per period.

NPer   Required. Integer of total number of payments.

Pmt   Required. Double type of the amount of each payment.

PV   Optional. Object of the present value.

Due   Optional. Payments due at end of period or the beginning of the period. Default is DueDate.EndOfPeriod.

Returns   Double type

Code Sample
```
Console.WriteLine(FV(.0081,48,-1500.75))
```

See Also   DDB, IPmt, IRR, MIRR, NPer, NPV, Pmt, PPmt, PV, Rate, SLN, SYD

GetAllSettings

Retrieves all of the settings from a section of the Windows Registry.

Description   This command will return a list of key settings within a section of the application's Registry area. The settings are returned in a two-dimensional array where the first column contains the key name and the second contains the value of the related key.

Syntax
```
GetAllSettings(appName, section)
```

Parameters

appName   Required. Application area within the Windows Registry to access.

Section   Required. Section of the Registry to be retrieved.

Returns   Array type

Code Sample
```
SaveSetting("myApp", "Prefs", "Velo", 500)
Dim a = GetAllSettings("myapp","Prefs")
```

See Also   DeleteSetting, GetSetting, SaveSetting

GetAttr

Returns the attributes of a given file.

Description   As opposed to FileAttr, which returns information about open files, GetAttr returns such information as VbNormal(0), VbReadOnly(1), VbHidden(2), VbSystem(4), VbDirectory(16), VbArchive(32), or VbAlias designations about a file or directory on the disk.

Syntax
```
GetAttr(PathName)
```

Parameters
PathName   Required. A valid path and filename.

Returns   Integer type

Code Sample
```
Console.WriteLine(GetAttr("c:\test.txt"))
```

See Also   EOF, FileAttr, FileClose, FileDateTime, FileLen, FileOpen, Loc, LOF

6

GetChar

Obtains a single Char value from a string given an index position.

Description   This function retrieves a single character from a string at the specified index position.

Syntax
```
GetChar(Str As String, Index As Integer)
```

Parameters
Str   Required. String to parse.

Index   Required. Index value that is greater than or equal to 1 and less than the length of the string.

Returns   Char

Code Sample
```
Dim myStr As String = "Hello World"
Console.WriteLine("5th char: " & GetChar(myStr,5))
```

See Also   Asc, Chr, ChrW

GetException

Returns the exception type that caused an error.

Description   This method is available through the Err object as a method to return the exception type.

Syntax
```
myException = Err.GetException()
```

Parameters

myException   Exception returned as a System.Exception type.

Returns   Exception

Code Sample
```
Dim myException As System.Exception
Error 6
myException = Err.GetException
Console.WriteLine(myException.Message)
```

See Also   Err object, Error, RaiseEvent

GetObject

Returns a reference to a current object or creates the object if unavailable.

Description   This function checks whether an instance of the object exists and uses the current one. If no object is available in memory, it attempts to instantiate it. GetObject can also be used to open a file that has an ActiveX/OLE Automation server.

In the Immediate window example, the GetObject statement expects the Excel application to already be launched and open. A reference is then created to the Application object.

Syntax
```
GetObject([pathName] [,className])
```

Parameters

pathName   Optional. Path to the file that will be opened with the GetObject.

className   Optional. Class of OLE Automation Server to be used.

Returns   N/A

Code Sample

```
Dim myObject1 = GetObject(,"Excel.Application")
Dim myObject2 = GetObject("test.xls", _
  "Excel.Application")
```

See Also   CreateObject

GetSetting

6

Reads a key setting from the application's area of the Windows Registry.

Description   This function will return the key value given the application, section, and key name from the Windows Registry. If no value is included as the default and the key is not found, a zero-length string ("") is returned.

Syntax

```
GetSetting(AppName, Section, Key [,default])
```

Parameters

AppName   Required. Name of the application for the proper area of the Windows registry.

Section   Required. Name of the section where the key will be retrieved.

Key   Required. Name of the key.

default   Optional. Value to return if no key is found.

Returns   Object

Code Sample

```
SaveSetting("myApp", "Prefs", "Velo", 500)
Console.WriteLine(GetSetting("myApp", "Prefs", _
    "Left"))
```

See Also   DeleteSetting, GetAllSettings, SaveSetting

GetType

Retrieves an object of the type specified.

Description   This function returns the type object specified for access to properties, methods, and events of the type.

Syntax

```
GetType(TypeName)
```

Parameters

TypeName   Required. Type of object to be returned.

Returns   Varies by specified object type

Code Sample

```
Dim miscObject As Object
miscObject = GetType(Integer)
miscObject = GetType(Form1)
miscObject = GetType(String())
Console.WriteLine(miscObject.Name)
```

See Also   CType, Structure...End Structure

GoTo

This command will jump execution within a procedure or function.

Description   Use the GoTo command to jump to an out-of-sequence set of code. VB prohibits using a Goto statement to jump from outside into a code block sequence (For...Next, For

Each...Next, SyncLock...End SyncLock, Try...Catch...Finally, or With...End With).

Syntax

```
GoTo [linenumber | linelabel]
```

Parameters

linenumber | linelabel   Required. Numeric or alphanumeric anchor that a GoTo command can jump to.

Returns   N/A

Code Sample

```
If 1 = 1 Then Goto Branch1
Beep()
Branch1:
Console.WriteLine("Jump!")
```

See Also   Call

Hex

Converts a number to its hexadecimal equivalent.

Description   This function will create a string containing the hexadecimal (base 16 number) from the passed value. Each value may contain the numbers 0–9 and the letters A–F.

Syntax

```
Hex(Number)
```

Parameters

Number   Required. Any numeric expression.

Returns   String type

Code Sample

```
Console.WriteLine(Hex(9))
Console.WriteLine(Hex(10))
Console.WriteLine(Hex(255))
Console.WriteLine(Hex(256))
```

See Also Oct

Hour

Returns the hour portion of a date and time value.

Description   The returned hour value will be an integer between 0 and 23 representing the hour of the day.

Syntax

```
Hour(TimeValue)
```

Parameters

TimeValue   The date that the hour is to be extracted from.

Returns   Integer type

Code Sample

```
Console.WriteLine(Hour(Now))
```

See Also   Minute, Now, Second, TimeOfDay, TimeSerial, TimeValue

If...Then...ElseIf...End If

Conditional execution of statements.

Description   The If...Then structure enables evaluation of conditions for a change in the program execution flow. If the statements to be executed are placed on a single line (without using the colon (:) command to simulate multiple lines), the End If statements may be omitted. However, for code clarity, it is often a good idea to include them. The TypeOf keyword may also be used within the If...Then structure to determine whether a object matches a specific object type. For example, the statement "If TypeOf myControl Is TextBox Then" will evaluate to True if the myControl variable holds a reference to a textbox control.

Syntax

```
If condition-1 Then
    [actions-1]
[ElseIf condition-2 Then]
    [actions-2]
[ElseIf condition-n Then]
    [actions-n]
[Else]
    [else-actions]
End If
```

Parameters

conditions Required. Boolean expressions.

Returns N/A

Code Sample

```
Dim a = 1
If a = 1 Then Console.WriteLine("Equal") Else _
    Console.WriteLine("Not equal")
a = 2
If a = 1 Then Console.WriteLine("Equal") Else _
    Console.WriteLine("Not equal")
```

See Also Choose, If...Then...Elseif...Endif, IIf, Select Case, Switch

IIf

Returns one of two values depending on the evaluation of an expression.

Description This function, like Switch, compactly and quickly returns a value based on the evaluation of an expression. The IIf works very well to substitute Null values.

Syntax

```
IIf(expression, valueIfTrue, valueIfFalse)
```

Parameters

expression Required. Any expression that can be resolved to a Boolean condition.

valueIfTrue, valueIfFalse   Required. Values to be returned from the function depending on the expression.

Returns   Object

Code Sample

```
Dim i=1
Console.WriteLine(IIf(i=1,"It's true","It's not true"))
i=2
Console.WriteLine(IIf(i=1,"It's true","It's not true"))
```

See Also   Choose, If...Then...Elseif...Endif, Select Case, Switch

Implements

Indicates one or more interfaces that will be implemented by a class definition.

Description   Using the Implements statement, a class definition can indicate an interface that it will comply with and include implementation for members such as properties, methods, and events.

Syntax

```
Implements interfacename
```

Parameters

interfacename   Required. Either the name of the interface or the class to be implemented.

Returns   N/A

Code Sample

```
Interface myInterface
    Property ContactName As String
End Interface
Public Class PIMinfo Implements myInterface
   Public ContactName As String
End Class
```

See Also   Class...End Class, Environ, Shell

Imports

Imports the names of members (methods, properties, enumerations, etc.) of the specified assembly or project.

Description   Using the Imports keyword allows names (for classes, object types, etc.) to be used without full namespace references (i.e., System.Xml). The Imports statements must appear in a form, module, or class before any other code or definition. The aliasname parameter may be used to allow two namespaces that have identical member names to be differentiated.

Syntax
```
Imports [aliasname=] namespace.element
```

Parameters

aliasname   Optional. Dereferencing name to be used to refer to the namespace elements.

namespace   Required. The name of the namespace to be imported.

element   Optional. Specific class, property, or method to be imported.

Returns   N/A

Code Sample
```
Imports System
Imports System.Xml
```

See Also   With...End With

Input

Returns a string from the open stream of an Input or Binary file.

Description   By using the FileOpen command, once a file is open, the input stream can be read. The Input command can read information directly into the specified variable.

Syntax

```
Input(FileNumber, Value)
```

Parameters

FileNumber   Required. Integer filenumber value of file for input stream.

value   Required. Variable name to read input.

Returns   N/A

Code Sample

```
Dim myStr As String
FileOpen(1, "C:\test.txt", OpenMode.Input)
Input(1, myStr)
FileClose(1)
Console.WriteLine(myStr)
```

See Also   FileOpen, FilePut, Write, WriteLine

InputBox

Presents an input dialog box that allows the user to enter text information.

Description   InputBox functions in much the same way as MsgBox(), except it accepts user-entered information. If the user clicks the Cancel button, the returned string will be empty.

Syntax

```
InputBox(Prompt [,Title [,DefaultResponse
   [,XPos [,YPos]]]])
```

Parameters

Prompt   Required. String that contains the message to display in the input box.

Title   Optional. Title of the dialog box that will be shown.

DefaultResponse   Optional. Default string to place in the input box.

XPos, **YPos**   Optional. The x and y position (in twips) where the input box should be displayed.

Returns   String type

Code Sample
```
Dim uName = InputBox("Please enter your name:", _
  "Name Entry")
Console.WriteLine(uName)
```

See Also   MsgBox, Show

InputString

Reads a string from an Input or Binary file.

Description   In contrast to the Input statement, the InputString function reads and returns all nonalpha characters such as commas, carriage returns, linefeeds, quotation marks, and leading spaces.

6

Syntax
```
InputString(FileNumber As Integer, CharCount As Integer)
```

Parameters

FileNumber   Required. Current file number to read from.

CharCount   Required. Number of bytes to read.

Returns   String type

Code Sample
```
Dim myStr As String
FileOpen(1, "C:\test.txt", OpenMode.Input)
myStr = InputString(1, 5)
FileClose(1)
Console.WriteLine(myStr)
```

See Also   FileClose, FileOpen, Input, Write, WriteLine

InStr

Returns the first place within a string that another string occurs.

Description   This function can be used to search for the occurrence of a string and its location within a larger string. The Start parameter begins the search at a particular position with the string. The returned value will be either 0 (string1 is empty), start value (string2 is empty), 0 (search string not found), position value (where pattern is located), or 0 (if Start parameter is greater than string2 length).

Syntax
```
InStr( [Start], String1, String2, Compare )
```

Parameters

Start   Optional. The position within the string to begin search. Index values begin at 1.

String1   Required. String that is to be searched.

String2   Required. The pattern string that the function attempts to locate.

Compare   Required. The compare type is of type Microsoft.VisualBasic.CompareMethod and may be either BinaryCompare(0) or TextCompare(1).

Returns   Integer type

Code Sample
```
Console.WriteLine(InStr("Hello World from Dan","Dan"))
Console.WriteLine(InStr(3,"Hello World from Dan","World"))
```

See Also   InStr, InStrRev, LBound, Left, Option Compare, Right, Split, UBound

InStrRev

Returns the postion of the first occurence from the end of the string that a target string appears.

Description   This function can be used to search for the occurrence of a string and returns its location within a larger string. The reverse InStr works like the InStr function, but it starts at the end of the string.

Syntax

```
InStrRev(StringCheck, StringMatch [,Start [,Compare]])
```

Parameters

StringCheck Required. String that is to be searched.

StringMatch Required. The pattern string that the function will attempt to locate.

Start Optional. The position within the string to begin search.

Compare Optional. Type of comparison to perform as either BinaryCompare or TextCompare.

Returns Integer type

Code Sample

```
Console.WriteLine(InStrRev("Hello World","Dan"))
Console.WriteLine(InStrRev("Hello World","World",6))
```

See Also InStr, LBound, Left, Option Compare, Right, Split, UBound

Int

Converts a number to an Integer data type.

Description This function works almost exactly like the Fix() function, except when concerning negative numbers. Int returns the first negative number less than or equal to the passed value. Int( ) returns the first negative number less than or equal to the value. Fix(−1.4) would return the value −1, while Int(−1.4) would return the value −2.

Syntax

```
Int(Number)
```

Parameters

Number Required. Any valid numeric expression.

Returns Integer type

Code Sample

```
Console.WriteLine(Int(1.4))
Console.WriteLine(Int(-1.4))
```

See Also CDbl, CInt, CStr, Fix, Round

Interface...End Interface

Defines a new interface and encapsulates the properties, methods, events, and fields that belong to it.

Description This command allows the definition of an Interface. An Interface may include the prototypes of members that will be available for instances of child objects created from it. An interface may be defined as Public, Private, Protected (visible only to its own class or derived classes), Friend (visible only to entities declared with the Friend modifier), or Protected Friend. The Shadows modifier may be used to make the class shadow an identically named class in a base class.

Syntax

```
[<attrlist>]
[Public | Private | Protected | Friend | Protected Friend]
[Shadows ]
Interface name [ Inherits interfacename[, interfacename ]]
   [statements]
End Interface
```

Parameters

name Required. A valid interface name.

Returns N/A

Code Sample

```
Interface mySortRoutines
   Sub BubbleSort(ByVal ValueArray() As String)
   Sub QuickSort(ByVal ValueArray() As String)
End Interface
```

See Also Call, End, Exit, Function...End Function, Sub...End Sub

IPmt

Returns the interest rate per period calculated from an annuity.

Description   The payment is calculated from the values of periodic fixed payments and a fixed interest rate. This function returns the interest rate per period that is calculated from the supplied arguments.

Syntax
```
IPmt(Rate, Per, NPer, PV [,FV, Due])
```

Parameters

Rate   Required. Interest rate for the calculations.

Per   Required. Current period must be greater than 1 and less than the total periods (NPer).

NPer   Required. The total periods for the calculation.

PV   Required. Present value of payments.

FV   Optional. Future value (final cash value) desired.

Due   Optional. When payments are due. Either end or beginning of payment period, with the default of DueDate.EndOfPeriod.

Returns   Double type

Code Sample
```
Console.WriteLine(IPmt(.0081,2,48,20000))
```

See Also   DDB, FV, IRR, MIRR, NPer, NPV, Pmt, PPmt, PV, Rate, SLN, SYD

IRR

Returns the internal return rate of a series of payments or receipts.

Description   This financial function will use an array that must contain at least one negative (payment) and one positive (receipt)

value to estimate the internal return rate value. You may include a guess as to the final value, which, if omitted, is set to 0.1 (10 percent).

Syntax

```
IRR(ValueArray() [,Guess])
```

Parameters

ValueArray   Required. An Array containing positive (receipt) and negative (payment) information.

Guess   Optional. Your estimate of the return rate final value. A default value of 0.1 (10%) is used if none is supplied.

Returns   Double type

Code Sample

```
Dim myArray() As Double = {-50000#, 12000#, 15000#, 10000#}
Console.WriteLine(IRR(myArray))
```

See Also   DDB, FV, IPmt, MIRR, NPer, NPV, Pmt, PPmt, PV, Rate, SLN, SYD

Is

Compares two objects.

Description   This determines whether both object references point to the same object.

Syntax

```
a Is b
```

Parameters

a, b   Required. Any valid object references.

Returns   Boolean

Code Sample

```
Dim A As Object = CreateObject("Excel.Application")
Dim B As Object
Console.WriteLine(A Is B)
Set A = B
Console.WriteLine(A Is B)
```

See Also   CreateObject, GetObject

IsArray

Determines whether a variable holds a reference to an array.

Description   This command indicates if an array is stored within the given variable.

Syntax
```
IsArray(VarName)
```

Parameters
VarName   Required. Name of the variable to be evaluated.

Returns   Boolean type

Code Sample
```
Dim myArray() As String
Console.WriteLine(IsArray(myArray))
myArray = New String() {"Michelangelo", "Da Vinci"}
Console.WriteLine(IsArray(myArray))
```

See Also   { ... }, Dim, LBound, UBound

IsDate

Returns whether the value contains a valid date.

Description   This function checks the value passed to it (string, Object, and so on) and determines whether there is either a valid date or a valid time contained in it.

Syntax
```
IsDate(Object)
```

Parameters
Object   Required. Object or variable data type.

Returns Boolean type

Code Sample

```
Console.WriteLine(IsDate(#1/2/01#))
Console.WriteLine(IsDate("1/2/01"))
Console.WriteLine(IsDate(""))
```

See Also CDate, DateAdd, DateDiff, DatePart, DateSerial, DateValue, Format, IsDbNull, IsNumeric, Now, Month, TimeOfDay, WeekDay

IsDbNull

Returns whether the value represents a null value.

Description This function checks the value passed to it (string, Object, and so on) and determines whether it evaluates to a System.DBNull value. The DBNull value is not the same as the object condition of Nothing, which indicates that an object has not been initialized. Instead, it indicates missing or nonexistent data such as a database column that holds no information. Nulls in a database field cannot be detected with traditional comparison operators such as "If a = Null Then beep()." This function can be used in the same manner as the IsNull() function could be used in previous versions of VB.

Syntax

```
IsDbNull(Object)
```

Parameters

Object Required. Object or variable data type.

Returns Boolean type

Code Sample

```
Console.WriteLine(IsDBNull(""))
Console.WriteLine(IsDBNull(System.DBNull.Value))
```

See Also IIf, IsDate, IsNumeric

IsError

Determines whether the passed variable is a valid error object.

Description   This command will check the passed variable and determine if the object is a valid instance of an Exception class in the System namespace.

Syntax
```
IsError(Expression)
```

Parameters
Expression   Required. Variable of error object to be evaluated.

Returns   Boolean type

Code Sample
```
Dim myError = New System.Exception()
Console.WriteLine(IsError(myError))
```

See Also   Error

IsNothing

Determines if variable is empty and has no object assigned to it.

Description   The IsNothing function returns True if the variable passed to it has no assigned object. This function can be used in the same manner as the IsEmpty() function could be used in previous versions of VB.

Syntax
```
IsNothing(Object)
```

Parameters
Object   Required. Object or variable data type.

Returns   Boolean type

Code Sample

```
Dim myObj As New Object
Dim myNothingObj As Object
Console.WriteLine(IsNothing(myObj))
Console.WriteLine(IsNothing(myNothingObj))
```

See Also   IsDate, IsDbNull, IsNumeric, VarType

IsNumeric

Determines if a variable contains a numeric value.

Description   The IsNumeric function is most often used for user field entry confirmation.

Syntax

```
IsNumeric(Object)
```

Parameters

Object   Required. Object or variable data type.

Returns   Boolean type

Code Sample

```
Console.WriteLine(IsNumeric("123"))
Console.WriteLine(IsNumeric("abc"))
```

See Also   IsDate, IsDbNull

IsReference

Determines whether a variable is a valid object variable.

Description   This command determines whether the variable holds a reference to an Object, but it does not determine whether the object itself is valid.

Syntax

```
IsReference(Expression As Object)
```

Parameters

Expression   Required. Name of variable to be evaluated.

Returns   Boolean

Code Sample

```
Dim myObject As Object
Dim myInt As Integer
Console.WriteLine(IsReference(myInt))
' There is no difference if a valid object
' is held or not
Console.WriteLine(IsReference(myObject))
myObject = GetObject("Excel.Application")
Console.WriteLine(IsReference(myObject))
```

See Also   CreateObject, GetObject

Join

Concatenates strings contained in an array into a single string.

Description   This command is the opposite of the Split command in that it reforms all the individual strings from an array into a single string.

Syntax

```
Join(SourceArray() [,Delimiter])
```

Parameters

SourceArray()   Required. One-dimensional array containing strings or objects.

Delimiter   Optional. The string to be placed between each of the entries. If not specified, a single space is used.

Returns   String type

Code Sample

```
Dim myItem() As String = {"Osborne", "books", _
   "are", "great!"}
Console.WriteLine(Join(myItem))
```

See Also   { ... }, Split

Kill

Deletes the file specified.

Description   The Kill command supports the wildcard characters * (multiple character) and ? (single character) to delete one or more filenames. If an attempt to delete an open file occurs, an error will be generated.

Syntax

```
Kill(pathname)
```

Parameters

pathname   Required. Any valid path and filename may be used.

Returns   N/A

Code Sample

```
Kill("c:\test.txt")
```

See Also   ChDir, ChDrive, Dir, EOF, FileLen, FileOpen, MkDir, RmDir

LBound

Returns the lowest subscript available in the array.

Description   This function can be used to determine the lower bound of an array. If the array is multidimensional, use the rank argument to specify the lower bounds to be returned.

Syntax

```
LBound(arrayname [,rank])
```

Parameters

arrayname   Required. The name of the array required to determine the limit.

rank   Optional. The subscript dimension of a multidimensional array.

Returns   Integer type

Code Sample

```
Dim boundArray(6,4,2,5,2,4,6)
Console.WriteLine(LBound(boundArray))
```

See Also   { ... }, Dim, UBound

LCase

Returns an all-lowercase string

Description   This function converts all of the characters in the passed string to lowercase. This function is effective when you're comparing two strings to make sure they match apart from case.

Syntax

```
LCase(value)
```

Parameters

value   Required. Any valid string.

Returns   String type

Code Sample

```
Console.WriteLine(LCase("hElLo"))
```

See Also   UCase

Left

Returns a string containing the specified amount of the left portion of the passed string.

Description   This function can be used to take any specified substring from the left to the right and to return it as a separate string. This function is found in the Microsoft.VisualBasic namespace.

Syntax

```
Left(Str, Length)
```

Parameters

Str   Required. Any string expression.

Length   Required. Number of characters to return in the substring.

Returns   String

Code Sample

```
Console.WriteLine( _
  Microsoft.VisualBasic.Left("Hello World", 4))
```

See Also   Format, InStr, Len, LTrim, Mid, Right, RTrim, Str

Len

Returns the length of a specified string.

Description   This function is used to determine the length in characters of a string. Either a string itself or a variable containing the string may be passed to this routine.

Syntax

```
Len(expression)
```

Parameters

expression   Required. Any valid string.

Returns   Integer type

Code Sample

```
Dim myGreeting As String = "Hello World"
Console.WriteLine(Len(myGreeting))
```

See Also   Format, InStr, Left, LTrim, Mid, Right, RTrim, Str

Like

Compares a string with a pattern.

Description   The Like command supports a number of wildcard characters to create the pattern string for searching the primary string. These characters include ?= single character, * = zero or more characters, # = any single digit, [charlist] = any char in charlist, and [!charlist] = any single character not in charlist.

Syntax
```
a Like b
```

Parameters

a   Required. String to search.

b   Required. Pattern to search for.

Returns   String type

Code Sample
```
Console.WriteLine("c:\test.txt" Like "*.txt")
```

See Also   <, <>, =, >, And, Is, Not, Split

LineInput

Reads a single line from a Sequential file.

Description   This command will read directly into a variable a single line delimited by a Chr(13) carriage return or Chr(13) + Chr(10) carriage return and linefeed. The carriage return + linefeed combination is not included with the returned string.

Syntax
```
LineInput(FileNumber)
```

Parameters

FileNumber   Required. Any valid open file number.

Returns   String type

Code Sample
```
Dim myStr As String
FileOpen(1, "C:\test.txt", OpenMode.Input)
myStr = LineInput(1)
FileClose(1)
Console.WriteLine(myStr)
```

See Also   Input, Print, PrintLine

Loc

Gets or sets the current read or write position with the open file.

Description   This function positions the current read or write access to an exact record (Random), current byte position divided by 128 (Sequential), or exact byte location (Binary).

Syntax
```
Loc(FileNumber)
```

Parameters
FileNumber   Any valid open file number.

Returns   Long type

Code Sample
```
Console.WriteLine(Loc(1))
```

See Also   EOF, FileGet, FileLen, FileOpen, FilePut, LOF, Print, PrintLine, Write, WriteLine

Lock...Unlock

Locks or unlocks access to parts of the current file for other processes.

Description   These commands may be used to control access to a single file to ensure no data is corrupted or destroyed by concurrent reads or writes.

Syntax
```
Lock(FileNumber [,FromRecord] [,ToRecord] )
[statements]
Unlock(FileNumber [,FromRecord] [,ToRecord] )
```

Parameters

FileNumber   Required. Any valid open file number.

FromRecord   Number of first byte or record.

ToRecord   Number of last byte or record.

Returns   N/A

Code Sample
```
FileOpen(1, "C:\test.txt", OpenMode.Input)
Lock(1)
Unlock(1)
FileClose(1)
```

See Also   FileClose, FileGet, FileOpen, FilePut, Loc

LOF

Returns the length of a currently open file.

Description   This function, when passed a file number, returns the size, in bytes, of the open file.

Syntax
```
LOF(FileNumber)
```

Parameters

FileNumber   Required. Any valid file number.

Returns   Long type

Code Sample
```
Console.WriteLine(LOF(1))
```

See Also EOF, FileAttr, FileLen, Loc

Log

Returns the logarithmic expression for the given expression.

Description This function returns the natural log of the passed expression. This function is now found in the System.Math namespace.

Syntax
```
Log(numericExpression)
```

Parameters
numericExpression Required. Any valid numeric expression.

Returns Double type

Code Sample
```
Console.WriteLine(System.Math.Log(1.3))
```

See Also Exp, Sign

LSet

Left-justifies a string within the destination string and fills the remainder with spaces.

Description This command essentially copies the Source argument into a new string of the size of Length with spaces if the Length is longer than the current string. For example, if the length of Length is ten characters, a five-character Source would be copied to it and padded with five space characters. This command can also be used to copy from one user-defined variable to another of the same length.

Syntax
```
LSet(Source,Length)
```

Parameters

Source   Required. Left-justified string to copy.

Length   Required. Destination for the new string.

Returns   String type

Code Sample

```
Dim a As String = "Hello"
a = LSet(a, 10)
Console.WriteLine(a + "<--end")
```

See Also   Input, Let, LTrim, RSet

LTrim

Returns a substring with the leading spaces from left to right removed from the passed string.

Description   The LTrim function is the complement of the RTrim function, but it returns a string taken from left to right. Any spaces on the left side of the string are removed.

Syntax

```
LTrim(Expression)
```

Parameters

Expression   Required. Any valid string.

Returns   String type

Code Sample

```
Console.WriteLine(LTrim("     Hello"))
```

See Also   Left, Mid, Right, RTrim, Trim

Me Property

This command returns to the currently active form.

Description   Use the Me command to write code that will work independently of the form on which it is executed. The code sample needs to be executed when a form is displayed on the screen.

Syntax

```
Me
```

Parameters   N/A

Returns   N/A

Code Sample

```
Me.Hide
```

See Also   Show

Mid

Returns a substring of the passed string of a specified length and start position.

Description   This function allows access to an exact substring within a string. The start argument determines where the desired string should begin. The lowest character position is 1. The length, if omitted, will be automatically set to the remaining length of the string.

Syntax

```
Mid(Str, Start [,Length])
```

Parameters

Str   Required. Any valid string.

Start   Required. Start position within the string. Must be greater than or equal to 1.

Length   Optional. Length of substring to return.

Returns   String type

Code Sample

```
Console.WriteLine(Mid("Hello",2))
Console.WriteLine(Mid("Hello",2,3))
```

See Also   Left, Len, Right

Mid

Replaces a substring of the passed string of a specified length and start position.

Description   This function allows replacement of a substring within a string. The start argument determines where the desired string should begin. The lowest character position is 1. The length, if omitted, will be automatically set to the remaining length of the string.

Syntax

```
Mid(Target, Start [,Length]) = Str
```

Parameters

Target   Required. Any valid string.

Start   Required. Start position within string must be greater than or equal to 1.

Length   Optional. Length of substring to return.

Str   Required. Any valid string.

Returns   N/A

Code Sample

```
Dim myStr As String = "My new world"
Mid(myStr,4,3) = "big"
Console.WriteLine(myStr)
```

See Also   Left, Mid (previous definition), Right

Minute

Returns the minute portion of the date and time passed to it.

Description The Minute function will return the minute portion of a DateTime type. An integer between 0 and 59 is returned.

Syntax

```
Minute(dateObject)
```

Parameters

dateObject Required. The date from which the minute value will be extracted.

Returns Integer type

Code Sample

```
Console.WriteLine(Minute(Now))
```

See Also Hour, Now, Second, TimeSerial, TimeValue

MIRR

Returns the modified internal rate of return.

Description This function works similarly to the IRR() function. The finance and reinvestment rates are supplied to complete the calculations.

Syntax

```
MIRR(ValueArray(), FinanceRate, ReinvestRate)
```

Parameters

ValueArray Required. An Array containing at least one positive (receipt) and one negative (payment) item.

FinanceRate Required. The cost of accounting interest rate.

ReinvestRate Required. The capital gains interest received from cash reinvestment.

Returns Double type

Code Sample

```
Dim myArray() As Double = {-50000,12000,15000,10000}
Console.WriteLine(MIRR(myArray, .1, .12))
```

See Also   DDB, FV, IPmt, IRR, NPer, NPV, Pmt, PPmt, PV, Rate, SLN, SYD

MkDir

Creates a new directory at a specified path.

Description   This command will create a single directory. The command requires all directories leading up to where the new one is going to be created to already exist. If current path information is omitted, the directory will be created in the default path.

Syntax

```
MkDir(Path)
```

Parameters

Path   Any valid path string.

Returns   N/A

Code Sample

```
MkDir("C:\vbtemp")
```

See Also   ChDrive, ChDir, CurDir, Environ, FileCopy, FileOpen, Kill, RmDir

Mod

Modulo arithmetic operator.

Description   The Mod operator allows you to obtain the remainder. If the divisor divides evenly, the value of zero will be returned.

Syntax

```
B Mod C
```

Parameters

B, C   Any numeric expressions.

6

Returns   Integer type

Code Sample
```
Console.WriteLine(9 Mod 5)
Console.WriteLine(9 Mod 2)
Console.WriteLine(9 Mod 3)
```

See Also   /, CInt, Int

Month

Returns the Month portion of the passed Date type.

Description   This function will return an integer value between 1 and 12 that represents the month of the date passed to it.

Syntax
```
Month(DateValue)
```

Parameters

DateValue   A valid DateTime object from which the Month will be extracted.

Returns   Integer type

Code Sample
```
Console.WriteLine(Month(Now))
```

See Also   CDate, DateAdd, DateDiff, DateSerial, DateValue, Day, IsDate, Now, WeekDay, Year

MonthName

Provides a string of the specified month.

Description   This command will return the name of the month specified by its numeric equivalent (1 = January, 2 = February, and so on). It can provide either the full month name or the abbreviation.

Syntax
```
MonthName(Month [, abbreviate])
```

Parameters
Month   Required. Number of the month.

abbreviate   Optional. Boolean to determine if the returned string is a month abbreviation. Default is False.

Returns   String type

Code Sample
```
Console.WriteLine(MonthName(3))
Console.WriteLine(MonthName(12,True))
```

See Also   CDate, Format, FormatDateTime

6

MsgBox

Displays a dialog box presenting information and possibly retrieving a user selection.

Description   The message box is one of the most useful functions in the Visual Basic language because it can quickly present information to the user or retrieve simple information without requiring the construction of a complete form. Since the MsgBox command can be used as either a function or a statement, the Immediate window example shows many of the ways it can be called. Note that the preferred method of displaying this dialog in VB.NET is through the MessageBox.Show() command.

Box types are numbers that represent the types of buttons shown, the icons displayed, and the modal setting. The buttons can include the OK button (0); the OK and Cancel buttons (1); the Abort, Retry, and Ignore buttons (2); the YesNoCancel buttons (3); the Yes and No buttons (4); or the Retry and Cancel buttons (5).

Icons include the Critical (16), the Question (32), the Exclamation (48), and the Information (64) icons. Including a SystemModel setting (4096) suspends all applications until the user dismisses the message box. Returned values include OK (1), Cancel (2), Abort (3), Retry (4), Ignore (5), Yes (6), and No (7).

Syntax

```
MsgBox(message [,boxtype] [,windowtitle])
```

Parameters

message   Required. A String containing the message to be displayed.

boxtype   Optional. The compilation of all the box type numbers to display the desired buttons, icons, and dialog type.

windowtitle   Optional. Title of the message box.

Returns   Integer type

Code Sample

```
MsgBox("Hello World")
Dim result = MsgBox("Hello World")
result = MsgBox("What should I do?",2+16+4096,"Proceed?")
```

See Also   InputBox, Show

Namespace...End Namespace

Declares the name of a namespace.

Description   This command organizes classes within the namespace hierarchy.

Syntax

```
Namespace name[.name]
   componenttypes
End Namespace
```

Parameters

name[.name]   Required. Unique name of the namespace.

componenttypes   Required. Elements such as Classes, Delegates, Enums, Interfaces, Structures, etc., that make up the namespace.

Returns   N/A

Code Sample

```
Namespace myNS1
  Namespace myNS2
    Class myClass
      ' Method, properties, events
    End Class
  End Namespace
End Namespace
```

See Also   Class...End Class, Delegate...End Delegate, Interface...End Interface

---

Not

6

Logical negation.

Description   Using the Not operator on a number will actually create its bitwise negative, but this is not the same as a true negative. Try using the Not in the Immediate window to demonstrate this yourself.

Syntax

```
Not expression
```

Parameters

expression   A valid mathematical expression.

Returns   Object

Code Sample

```
Console.WriteLine(Not True)
Console.WriteLine(Not 2=2)
Console.WriteLine(Not 10)
```

See Also   And, Exp, Or, XOR

Now

Returns the current system date and time.

Description   This function will return a DateTime type value containing the current date and time of the system.

Syntax

Now

Parameters   N/A

Returns   Object type

Code Sample

Console.WriteLine(Now)

See Also   DateAdd, DateDiff, DateSerial, DateValue, Day, Hour, IsDate, Minute, Month, Second, TimeOfDay, Timer, TimeSerial, TimeValue, Today, WeekDay, Year

NPer

Returns the number of periods in an annuity.

Description   The returned value is based on periodic fixed payments and a fixed interest rate. The interest rate must specify the rate per period, such as 0.0821 per month. The periodic payment specifies the size of payment made each period. The present value determines the value of a series of future receipts and payments.

The future value is the desired cash value you wish to have once all of the payments are complete. The Due parameter instructs the function to calculate whether the payments are due at the end of the period (0), the default, or at the beginning of the period (1).

Syntax

NPer(Rate, Pmt, PV [, FV, Due])

Parameters

Rate   Required. Interest rate for the calculations.

Pmt   Required. Size of each periodic payment.

PV   Required. Present value of payments.

FV   Optional. Future value or final cash value desired.

Due   Optional. Whether the payment is due at the end or beginning of payment period. Default is DueDate.EndOfPeriod.

Returns   Double type

Code Sample
```
Console.WriteLine(NPer(.0821,400,2000))
```

See Also   DDB, FV, IPmt, IRR, MIRR, NPV, Pmt, PPmt, PV, Rate, SLN, SYD

NPV

6

Returns the net present value based on payments, receipts, and discount rate.

Description   This function determines the current value of the future series of investments. These include the cash flow values of payments (negatives) and receipts (positives). The discount rate is stated as a percentage over the life of the investment.

Syntax
```
NPV(Rate, ValueArray())
```

Parameters

Rate   The discount rate of interest expressed as a decimal (that is, 5 percent = 0.05).

ValueArray   Required. Array that must contain at least one payment and one receipt.

Returns   Double type

Code Sample
```
Dim myArray() As Double = {-50000,12000,15000,10000}
Console.WriteLine(NPV(.05, myArray))
```

See Also   DDB, FV, IPmt, IRR, MIRR, NPer, Pmt, PPmt, PV, Rate, SLN, SYD

Oct

Converts a number to its octal equivalent.

Description This function will create a string containing the octal (base 8 number) equivalent of the passed value.

Syntax
```
Oct(Expression)
```

Parameters
Expression Required. Any numeric expression.

Returns String type

Code Sample
```
Console.WriteLine(Oct(7))
Console.WriteLine(Oct(8))
Console.WriteLine(Oct(63))
Console.WriteLine(Oct(64))
```

See Also Hex, Val

On Error...

Creates an error-trapping routine and jumps to prespecified areas of code when an error occurs.

Description The On Error routine will seize control when an error occurs. If the On Error routine instructs, the GoTo command will jump to a specified error handler or line number. The On Error Resume Next command will simply ignore the error and execute the instruction that follows it. The On Error GoTo 0 command will disable the current error handler in the procedure or function.

Syntax
```
On Error GoTo error-handler
error-handler:
    [statements]
Resume [[0] | Next | line-number | line-label ]
```

To cause the Err flag to be set:

```
On Error Resume Next
```

or

```
On Error GoTo 0
```

Parameters
error-handler   Label to indicate location of the error handler.

Returns   N/A

Code Sample
```
Sub mysub()
   On Error Resume Next
   Error 6
   Beep()
End Sub
```

See Also   Err object, Error, Resume

Option Compare

Sets the default comparison method for strings.

Description   When strings are being compared, they can be compared by use of the Binary method, which differentiates between case, foreign alphabets, and so on, and the Text method, which does not. The default is set to Binary mode.

Syntax
```
Option Compare (Binary | Text)
```

Parameters
Binary | Text   Required. Specifies the comparison method.

Returns   N/A

Code Sample
```
Option Compare Text
```

See Also   Option Explicit, StrComp

Option Explicit

Requires that all variables be explicitly defined.

Description   The Option Explicit command makes any execution generate an error if a variable is not explicitly defined with a Dim command.

Syntax
```
Option Explicit On | Off
```

Parameters   N/A

Returns   N/A

Code Sample
```
Option Explicit On
```

See Also   Dim

Option Strict

Prevents any implicit data type conversion that results in loss of data by requiring the destination type to be as wide or wider than the source.

Description   Using the Option Strict command requires that in any implicit data conversions, the destination type be the same or longer than the source. This statement must appear before any program code. Option Strict also prevents any late binding.

Syntax
```
Option Strict On | Off
```

Parameters   N/A

Returns   N/A

Code Sample
```
Option Strict On
```

Or

Logical Or.

Description   The Or operator will perform a logical Or on two numbers, or it will do a logical truth on two Boolean values.

Syntax

```
a Or b
```

Parameters

a, b   Required. Any valid numeric expressions.

Returns   Object

Code Sample

```
Console.WriteLine(True Or False)
Console.WriteLine(True Or True)
Console.WriteLine(False Or False)
Console.WriteLine(1=2 Or 1=1)
```

See Also   And, False, Not, True, XOR

OrElse

Short-circuiting logical Or.

Description   The Or operator returns a Boolean result based on two values. This operator works like a normal Or except that short-circuiting occurs when both expressions are false, in which case the result returned is False.

Syntax

```
a OrElse b
```

Parameters

a, b   Required. Any valid numeric expressions.

Returns Object

Code Sample
```
Console.WriteLine(True OrElse False)
Console.WriteLine(True OrElse True)
Console.WriteLine(False OrElse False)
Console.WriteLine(1=2 OrElse 1=1)
```

See Also And, AndAlso, False, Not, True, XOR

Partition

Returns a string denoting where the passed number occurs within specified numeric ranges.

Description This function calculates ranges and the particular range in which the specified number falls. The returned string describes the range in the format *start*:*end*.

Syntax
```
Partition(Number, Start, Stop, Interval)
```

Parameters

Number Required. Number that will be evaluated against the ranges.

Start Required. Number. The number 0 is used as the beginning of the overall range.

Stop Required. Number. The endRange is used as the end of the overall range.

Interval Required. Number. The number 1 is used as the interval spanned by each range.

Returns String type

Code Sample
```
Console.WriteLine(Partition(20,0,400,30))
```

See Also InStr

Pmt

Returns a payment value for an annuity.

Description The payment is calculated from the values of periodic fixed payments and fixed interest rate. The interest rate is specified in a decimal percentage for each period.

Syntax

```
Pmt(Rate, NPer, PV [,FV ,Due])
```

Parameters

Rate Required. Interest rate for the calculations.

NPer Required. Total number of payments or periods.

PV Required. Present value of payments.

FV Optional. Future value or final cash value desired.

Due Optional. Indicates whether the payment is due at the end or the beginning of payment period. The default is set to DueDate.EndOfPeriod.

Returns Double type

Code Sample

```
Console.WriteLine(Pmt(.0081,48,10000))
```

See Also DDB, FV, IPmt, IRR, MIRR, NPer, NPV, PPmt, PV, Rate, SLN, SYD

PPmt

Returns the principal payment value for an annuity.

Description This function calculates the principal payment based on periodic payments and a fixed interest rate.

Syntax

```
PPmt(Rate, Per, NPer, PV [, FV, Due])
```

Parameters

Rate   Required. Interest rate for the calculations.

Per   Required. The specified period.

NPer   Required. Total number of payments or periods.

PV   Required. Present value of payments.

FV   Optional. Future value or final cash value desired.

Due   Optional. Indicates whether the payment is due at the end or the beginning of payment period. The default is set to DueDate.EndOfPeriod.

Returns   Double type

Code Sample

```
Console.WriteLine(PPmt(.0081,12,48,10000))
```

See Also   DDB, FV, IPmt, IRR, MIRR, NPer, NPV, Pmt, PV, Rate, SLN, SYD

Print, PrintLine

Writes text data to a specified Sequential file.

Description   The Print and PrintLine statements output variables or formatted text to the file denoted by the file number. Print and PrintLine function identically except that PrintLine adds a linefeed at the end of each line.

Syntax

```
Print(FileNumber As Integer, ParamArray Output()
  As Object)
PrintLine(FileNumber As Integer, ParamArray Output()
  As Object)
```

Parameters

FileNumber   Required. Any valid open file number.

Output   Required. Any number of items may be included in the output list, such as strings, spaces, tabs, or expressions.

Returns   N/A

Code Sample
```
FileOpen(1, "c:\test.txt", OpenMode.Output)
Print(1, "1... ")
Print(1, "2... ")
Print(1, "3... ")
Print(1, "Bang!")
PrintLine(1) ' Blank line
PrintLine(1, "Hello ", "World")
PrintLine(1, "Col 1", TAB(), "Col 2", SPC(5), _
   "Col 3")
FileClose(1)
```

See Also   FileClose, FileOpen, FilePut

Private

6

Makes the variable scope private to a particular class, form, module, or routine.

Description   Use of the Private statement will limit the scope of the form, module, procedure, or function.

Syntax
```
Private [Function|Sub|Class|methodname|variablename]
```

Parameters   N/A

Returns   N/A

Code Sample
```
Private a As Integer
```

See Also   Dim, Friend, Function...End Function, Public, Sub... End Sub

Property...End Property

Declares a property management routine.

Description   Use of the Property statements allows the program to minimize the direct access to internally used (often Private) properties. In object-oriented programming, using these statements is known as "information hiding." By creation of an indirect method to access properties, internal changes do not affect programs that access properties. Also, bounds checking can be performed before changes are made to the properties.

Syntax

```
[Public|Private] [Static]
Property name [(arglist)] [As type]
   Get [statements] End Get
   Set [statements] End Set
End Property
```

Parameters

name   Required. Any valid name expression.

arglist   Required. List of variables to be passed when the property is called.

Returns   N/A

Code Sample

```
Private NumBeersInPack As Integer = 1
Property Beer() As Integer
   Get
      Beer = NumBeersInPack
   End Get
   Set(ByVal Value As Integer)
      If Value < 1 Or Value > 6 Then
         '   Not allowed
      Else
         Beer = Value
      End If
   End Set
End Property
```

See Also   Function...End Function, Sub...End Sub

Public

Makes the variable scope Public for access outside a form, class, or module.

Description   Using the Public statement will increase the scope of the class, form, module, procedure, or function so that it may be accessed from another object. References to a Public member from an external object require the hosting object name to be referenced (that is, "myPublicForm.myPublicSub").

Syntax
```
Public [Function|Sub|Class|variablename]
```

Parameters   N/A

Returns   N/A

Code Sample
```
Public a As Integer
```

See Also   Dim, Friend, Function...End Function, Private, Property...End Property, Sub...End Sub

PV

Returns the present value of an annuity.

Description   This function calculates the present value based on periodic payments and a fixed interest rate.

Syntax
```
PV(Rate, NPer, Pmt [, FV, Due])
```

Parameters

Rate   Required. Interest rate for the calculations.

NPer   Required. Total number of payments or periods.

Pmt   The payment amount to be made each period.

FV Optional. Future value or final cash value desired.

Due Optional. Indicates whether the payment is due at the end or the beginning of payment period. The default is set to DueDate.EndOfPeriod.

Returns Double type

Code Sample
```
Console.WriteLine(PV(.0081,48,2000))
```

See Also DDB, FV, IPmt, IRR, MIRR, NPer, NPV, Pmt, PPmt, Rate, SLN, SYD

QBColor

Returns a standard Long color value from a QuickBasic color.

Description This command provides quick access to simple colors that are supported in the QuickBasic system included with most older versions of Windows. QuickBasic color values include black (0), blue (1), green (2), cyan (3), red (4), magenta (5), yellow (6), white (7), gray (8), light blue (9), light green (10), light cyan (11), light red (12), light magenta (13), light yellow (14), and bright white (15).

Syntax
```
QBColor(color)
```

Parameters
color Required. A number between 0 and 15.

Returns Integer value

Code Sample
```
Console.WriteLine(QBColor(7))
```

See Also RGB

RaiseEvent

Simulates an event occurrence for user-created events.

Description   This command will create an event for a form, class, or document. The event must be a user-defined event that is explicitly declared within the module.

Syntax
```
RaiseEvent eventName [(argumentList)]
```

Parameters

eventName   Required. Name of the event to be activated.

argumentList   Optional. List of any arguments to be passed to the event.

Returns   N/A

Code Sample
```
' Module level with a class module.
Event IDConfirmed(UserName as String)

Sub
    RaiseEvent IDConfirmed("Osborne")
End Sub
```

See Also   Call

Randomize

Initializes the seed of the random generator.

Description   This statement sets the random seed to a new number. Call this function before the first call to the Rnd() function to have a custom-seeded random outcome.

Syntax
```
Randomize [Number]
```

Parameters

Number Optional. Any valid numeric expression. If seed is omitted, the system timer is used for the seed.

Returns N/A

Code Sample

```
Randomize
Console.WriteLine(Rnd)
```

See Also Rnd, Timer

Rate

Returns the interest rate per period calculated from an annuity.

Description The payment is calculated from the values of periodic fixed payments and a fixed interest rate. The Rate function returns the interest rate per period given the other factors.

Syntax

```
Rate(NPer, Pmt, PV [,FV, Due, Guess])
```

Parameters

NPer Required. Total number of payments or periods.

Pmt The payment amount to be made each period.

PV Required. Present value of payments.

FV Optional. Future value or final cash value desired.

Due Optional. Indicates whether the payment is due at the end or the beginning of payment period. The default is set to DueDate.EndOfPeriod.

Guess Optional. Your estimate of the rate. If omitted, guess is set to 0.1 (10 percent).

Returns Double type

Code Sample

```
Console.WriteLine(Rate(24,-2000,12000))
```

See Also   DDB, FV, IPmt, IRR, MIRR, NPer, NPV, Pmt, PPmt, PV, SLN, SYD

ReDim

Redimensions an array size and can leave the data within the array intact

Description   This command can be used to resize an array. If the array is made bigger, the new array items are left blank. If smaller, the array is truncated and values outside the new array size are lost. Note that in VB.NET, the Redim statement cannot be used to create an array as could be done in previous versions of VB. An array must be first created with a Dim command before Redim may be used.

Syntax

```
ReDim [Preserve] name[subscript-range][As type]
[, namesubscript-range)As type]]...
```

Parameters

Preserve   Optional. Preserve the data that exists with the array.

Returns   N/A

Code Sample

```
Dim myPainters() As String =
  {"Da Vinci", "Michelangelo", "Raphael"}
Redim myPainters(10)
```

See Also   Dim, Erase

Rem

Makes any text following it on the current line invisible to the compiler.

Description   The remark command can be used anywhere on a code line. Any text that follows it until the end of the line will be ignored.

Syntax

```
Rem comment
' comment
```

Parameters

comment   Optional. Any text.

Returns   N/A

Code Sample

```
Rem This does nothing
Dim a As Integer
```

See Also   ' (apostrophe)

RemoveHandler

Removes the association between a handler and a specified event added with the AddHandler statement.

Description   The RemoveHandler keyword removes the link between a handler routine and a specific event.

Syntax

```
RemoveHandler(eventName,handlerAddress)
```

Parameters

eventName   Required. The name of the event that activates the handler.

handlerAddress   Required. The name of the routine set to handle the event.

Returns   N/A

Code Sample

```
RemoveHandler cmdOK.Click,AddressOf cmdOKClickHandler
```

See Also   AddHandler

Rename

Renames a file, directory, or folder.

Description   The new pathname and old pathname must match except for the final change value. You cannot change the name of an open file. This statement is used in the same way that the Name statement was used in previous versions of VB.

Syntax
```
Rename(OldPath As String, NewPath As String)
```

Parameters

OldPath, NewPath   Required. OldPath must be a valid path or file. NewPath can't already exist or an error will be generated.

Returns   N/A

Code Sample
```
Rename("test.txt","test2.txt")
```

See Also   ChDir, ChDrive, CurDir, Environ, Kill, Open

Replace

Returns a string with the replacement substring the specified number of times.

Description   This command begins at the position specified by the Start parameter and replaces a substring a number of times optionally set by the Count parameter.

Syntax
```
Replace(Expression, Find, Replacement
    [,Start [,Count [,Compare]]])
```

Parameters

Expression   Required. Initial string to search for replacements.

Find   Required. The string to search for within the string.

Replacement   Required. The string to replace the found strings.

Start   Optional. Character position where the searching is to begin that is greater than or equal to 1.

Count   Optional. Number of substitutions to perform. If omitted, all found replacements are made.

Compare   Optional. Type of comparison used for replacement specified by one of the constants: vbBinaryCompare (0) or vbTextCompare (1). Binary compare is the default.

Returns   String

Code Sample
```
Console.WriteLine(Replace( _
   "Hello ab this ab is ab a ab test ab.", _
   "ab", "**"))
```

See Also   InStr

Reset

Closes all open files.

Description   Any files that were opened using the FileOpen command will be closed, and their file buffers will be written to disk. This works in the same manner as the FileClose command when FileClose is not passed any parameters.

Syntax
```
Reset()
```

Parameters   N/A

Returns   N/A

Code Sample
```
Reset()
```

See Also   ChDir, ChDrive, End, FileClose, FileOpen, FreeFile

Resume

Resumes execution after an error-handling routine has completed processing.

Description   The Resume command can resume to the beginning of the procedure (Resume 0), with the next available statement (Resume Next), or with a particular anchor line or label.

Syntax
```
Resume [[0] | Next | line-number | line-label ]
```

Parameters
line-number | line-label   An anchor where execution is to resume.

Returns   N/A

Code Sample
```
Resume Next
```

See Also   On Error...

Return

Returns from a subroutine call.

Description   The Return command moves execution back to the original caller of the subroutine.

Syntax
```
Return [expr]
```

Parameters   N/A

Returns   expr

Code Sample
```
Function myRoutine() As Integer
  Return 1
End Function
```

See Also Call

RGB

Returns an Integer value representing the three RGB values passed to it.

Description This function converts a Red value, a Green value, and a Blue value into the Integer format typically used by the Windows system for everything from drawing to window background colors.

Syntax
```
RGB(red, green, blue)
```

Parameters

red Integer value between 0 and 255.

green Integer value between 0 and 255.

blue Integer value between 0 and 255.

Returns Integer type

Code Sample
```
Console.WriteLine(RGB(0,255,0))
```

See Also QBColor

Right

Returns a string containing the specified amount of the right portion of the passed string.

Description This function can be used to take any specified substring from the right to the left and to return it as a separate string.

Syntax
```
Right(Expression, Length)
```

Parameters

Expression   Any string expression.

Length   Number of characters to return in the substring.

Returns   String type

Code Sample

```
Console.WriteLine( _
  Microsoft.VisualBasic.Right("Hello World",4))
```

See Also   Left, Mid

RmDir

Removes the specified empty directory.

Description   The directory to be removed must not contain any files or an exception will be thrown. You can use the Kill command to delete the files before removing the directory.

Syntax

```
RmDir Path
```

Parameters

Path   String must be in the format of [drive:][dir[subdir][subdir]...

Returns   N/A

Code Sample

```
RmDir "c:\tempdir"
```

See Also   CurDir, Kill, MkDir

Rnd

Returns a random number.

Description   This function returns a Single number between 0 and 1 that contains a seeded random number. You may include a specific seed for the random number. For random numbers within a range, use *Int((ub – lb + 1) * Rnd + lb)*, where lb = lower bound and ub = upper bound.

Syntax
```
Rnd[(number)]
```

Parameters
number   Any valid numeric expression.

Returns   Single type

Code Sample
```
Console.WriteLine(Rnd)
Console.WriteLine(Int((25-5+1)*Rnd+5))
```

See Also   Randomize

Round

Rounds the passed number to the specified decimal places.

Description   This function will round a numeric expression (including Int, Double, Single, and Object types) to a specified number of decimal places. If the number of decimal places is not specified, a rounded integer will be returned.

Syntax
```
Round(num [,numDecimalPlaces])
```

Parameters
num   Required. Number to round.

numDecimalPlaces   Optional. Number of places to the right of the decimal to include in the answer.

Returns   Double

Code Sample
```
Console.WriteLine(System.Math.Round(1.2268))
Console.WriteLine(System.Math.Round(1.2268, 2))
```

See Also   Fix, Format, Int

RSet

Right-justifies a string within the destination and fills the remainder with spaces.

Description   This command essentially copies the source string into the new string, padded with spaces if the specified length is longer. For example, if the length is ten characters, a five-character source would be copied to it and padded with five space characters. This command can also be used to copy from one user-defined variable to another of the same length.

Syntax
```
RSet(Source, Length)
```

Parameters
Source   Right-justified string to copy.

Length   Required. Length of string to be returned.

Returns   String type

Code Sample
```
Dim a As String = RSet("Hello", 10)
Console.WriteLine(a + "<--end")
```

See Also   LSet

RTrim

Returns a substring with the trailing spaces from the right removed from the passed string.

Description   The RTrim function is the complement of the LTrim function, but it returns a string taken from right to left. Any spaces on the right side of the string are removed.

Syntax
```
RTrim(Expression)
```

Parameters
Expression   Required. Any valid string.

Returns   String type

Code Sample
```
Console.WriteLine(Rtrim("Hello      ") + "<-end")
```

See Also   LTrim

SaveSetting

Writes an entry into the Windows Registry.

Description   This writes an entry into the Windows Registry in the specified application section.

Syntax
```
SaveSetting(AppName, Section, Key, Setting)
```

Parameters
AppName   Required. Name of the application section in the Registry.

Section   Required. Section in which the setting is to be stored.

Key   Required. Name of the key to be saved.

Setting   Required. The value to be stored in the key.

Returns   N/A

Code Sample
```
SaveSetting("myApp", "Prefs", "Indy", 500)
```

See Also   DeleteSetting, GetAllSettings, GetSetting

Second

Returns the seconds portion of the date and time passed to it.

Description   The Second function will return the seconds portion of a Date type. An integer between 0 and 59 is returned.

Syntax

```
Second(DateValue)
```

Parameters

DateValue   Required. The DateTime from which the second value will be extracted.

Returns   Integer type

Code Sample

```
Console.WriteLine(Second(Now))
```

See Also   Hour, Minute, Now, Time, TimeSerial, TimeValue

Seek

6

Returns the current read/write position of an open file.

Description   When passed a file number, this function will return a Long value that varies depending on the type of file accessed. If the file is a Random file, the number of the next record is returned. If a Binary, Output, Append, or Input file is used, the byte position (beginning at byte 1) will be returned.

Syntax

```
Seek(FileNumber [,Position])
```

Parameters

FileNumber   Required. Number of a currently open file.

Position   Optional. Position to move the read/write pointer as a record number (Random files) or byte offset number.

Returns   Long type

Code Sample

```
Console.WriteLine(Seek(1))
```

See Also   FileGet, FileLen, FileOpen, FilePut, Loc

Select Case

Executes a group of statements when an expression equals the test expression.

Description   The Select Case statement is an advanced form of an If...Then...Else structure, where one expression is entered and compared against multiple values. The Case Else statement allows statements to be executed if none of the values matches the expression.

Syntax

```
Select Case testexpression
   Case expression1
      [statements]
   [Case expression2]
      [statements]
   [Case Else]
      [statements]
End Select
```

Parameters

testexpression   Main value used for all comparisons.

expression   Value to be compared with testexpression.

Returns   N/A

Code Sample

```
Dim myNum = 3
Select Case myNum
  Case 1 : Console.WriteLine("1")
  Case 2 : Console.WriteLine("2")
  Case Else : Console.WriteLine("Other")
End Select
```

See Also   Choose, If...Then...Elseif...End If, IIf, Switch

SendKeys

Class used for sending keystrokes to the active window.

Description   This can be used to simulate keyboard entry and to access system functions, such as Cut, Copy, and Paste, not normally available to a Visual Basic program.

Syntax
```
SendKeys.Send(keys)
```

Parameters

keys   Required. String containing the keystrokes to be sent to the window.

Returns   N/A

Code Sample
```
Dim myKeys As SendKeys()
SendKeys.SendWait("ENTER")
SendKeys.Send("F1")
SendKeys.Send("PrtSc")
```

See Also   DoEvents

SetAttr

Sets the attributes of a file given a proper filename and path.

Description   SetAttr designates the information of files as VbNormal (0), VbReadOnly (1), VbHidden (2), VbSystem (4), VbVolume (8), VbDirectory (16), VbArchive (32), or VbAlias. These attributes can be set for any file on the disk. The Code Sample makes the Test.txt file read-only.

Syntax
```
SetAttr PathName, Attributes
```

Parameters

PathName   Required. A valid path and filename.

Attributes   Required. New attribute settings.

Returns   N/A

Code Sample
```
SetAttr("c:\test.txt", vbReadOnly)
```

See Also   GetAttr

Shell

Executes a command at the command prompt.

Description   Use of the Shell command gives complete access to all command-prompt (MS-DOS) or console functions. This command is most often used to launch another program. Using traditional command-line parameters, information can be passed to the launching application including toggle commands or parameters.

A taskID is returned if the command is successful. The mode enables you to control the execution window so that it's hidden (0), normal with focus (1), minimized with focus (2), maximized with focus (3), normal without focus (4), or minimized without focus (6).

Syntax
```
Shell(Pathname As String [,Style [,Wait [,Timeout]]] )
```

Parameters

Pathname   Required. Fully qualified path and filename of program.

Style   Optional. Specifies the mode to execute the command with the default as AppWinStyle.MinimizedFocus.

Wait   Optional. Determines whether VB execution will halt until shell program is finished executing. Default is False.

Timeout   Optional. Number of milliseconds to wait with execution if Wait argument is true. The default of −1 will make VB wait indefinitely until completion if Wait is True.

Returns   Integer type

Code Sample

```
Shell "c:\windows\calc.exe"
```

See Also   AppActivate

Show

Makes the current window visible.

Description   This method can be used on a unloaded form to load and display it. If the form window was previously hidden, the Show method will make it visible.

Syntax

```
window.Show
```

Parameters

window   Required. The Name property of a window within the project.

Returns   N/A

Code Sample

```
MessageBox.Show("Hello World")
```

See Also   AppActivate

Sign

Returns the sign (+/–) of the number passed to it.

Description   The Sign function can be used to determine the sign of a number. A positive number returns a 1; a negative number returns a –1. If the passed value is 0, a 0 is returned. This function is now found in the System.Math namespace.

Syntax

```
Sign(Expression)
```

Parameters

Expression   Required. Any valid numeric expression.

Returns   Integer type

Code Sample

```
Console.WriteLine(System.Math.Sign(5))
Console.WriteLine(System.Math.Sign(-5))
Console.WriteLine(System.Math.Sign(0))
```

See Also   Abs, Atan, Cos, Exp, Log, Sin, Tan

Sin

Returns the sine of an angle specified in radians.

Description   This command requires the angle to be passed in radians. The formula *radians = (degrees * pi) / 180* can be used to determine the radians from a degree measure. This function is now found in the System.Math namespace.

Syntax

```
Sin(angle)
```

Parameters

angle   Required. Any numeric expression holding a radian measure.

Returns   Double type

Code Sample

```
Console.WriteLine(System.Math.Sin(System.Math.PI))
Console.WriteLine(System.Math.Sin((90 * 3.14159) / 180))
```

See Also   Abs, Atan, Cos, Exp, Log, Sign, Sqrt, Tan

SLN

Returns the value for a single period of straight-line depreciation.

Description   Depreciation is determined by use of a straight-line method for a single period where the period should be specified in the same units as the Life argument. All arguments must be expressed as positive numbers.

Syntax

```
SLN(Cost, Salvage, Life)
```

Parameters

Cost   Required. Initial cost of asset as Double type.

Salvage   Required. Salvage value at end of useful life as Double type.

Life   Required. Lifespan or length of useful life as Double type.

Returns   Double

Code Sample

```
Console.WriteLine(SLN(10000,500,24))
```

See Also   DDB, FV, IPmt, IRR, MIRR, NPer, NPV, Pmt, PPmt, PV, Rate, SYD

Space

Returns a string containing the number of spaces specified.

Description   This function can be used for formatting to pad any number of spaces required.

Syntax

```
Space(number)
```

Parameters

number   Required. Numeric expression containing the number of spaces to create.

Returns   String type

Code Sample

```
Console.WriteLine(Space(10) + "Hello")
```

See Also   ?, Print, PrintLine, Spc, StrDup

Spc

Adds spaces for formatting specifically for Print and PrintLine commands.

Description   The Spc function adds spaces to the current print position. If the number of spaces exceeds the line width, the spaces will be placed on the next line in the next print position.

Syntax

```
Spc(Count)
```

Parameters

Count   Required. Numeric expression containing the number of spaces to create.

Returns   N/A

Code Sample

```
FileOpen(1, "C:\test.txt", OpenAccess.Write)
Print(1, SPC(5), "Hello", SPC(5), "Hello2")
FileClose(1)
```

See Also   Space, Tab

Split

Splits a string into a number of smaller strings based on the specified delimiter.

Description   This function will take a string and break it into an array of substrings. If the delimiter is set to an empty string (" "), the entire string will be returned in the first index position of the array.

Syntax

```
Split(Expression [,delimiter [,limit [,compare]]])
```

Parameters

Expression   Required. String to be processed.

delimiter   Optional. Delimiting string; if it is not specified, a space is used.

limit   Optional. Number of strings to be returned.

compare   Optional. Type of comparison specified by a constant: vbBinaryCompare (0), vbTextCompare (1).

Returns   Array

Code Sample

```
Dim myArray = Split("This is a test")
Console.WriteLine(myArray(0))
Console.WriteLine(myArray(1))
```

See Also   { ... }, Dim, Input, Join

6

Sqrt

Returns the square root of a given number.

Description   The square root function will return the square root of any number greater than or equal to zero. This function is now found in the System.Math namespace.

Syntax

```
Sqrt(numericExpression)
```

Parameters

numericExpression   Required. Any valid numeric expression.

Returns   Double type

Code Sample

```
Console.WriteLine(System.Math.Sqrt(9))
Console.WriteLine(System.Math.Sqrt(2))
```

See Also   Abs, Atan, Cos, Exp, Log, Sign, Sin, Tan

Static

Makes a variable persistent even after the procedure has completed executing.

Description The Static command will make a variable that is local to a particular routine keep its value. The next execution of the routine can access the remaining value.

Syntax

For declaring the data type of a simple variable:

```
Static name [As type][, name [As type]]...
```

For declaring an array:

```
Static name[(subscript-range)][As type]
[, name [(subscript-range)][As type] syntax as type]
```

Parameters Standard variable definitions.

Returns N/A

Code Sample

```
Static Dim a As Int32
```

See Also Dim, Private, Public, ReDim, Structure

Stop

Halts execution of the program.

Description Including a Stop statement in your program places a semipermanent breakpoint at the location of the command. The debugger will be activated when execution reaches the line that contains the Stop. Since breakpoints don't save with a file, the Stop command allows the creation of a breakpoint that will be stored in the program.

Syntax

```
Stop
```

Parameters   N/A

Returns   N/A

Code Sample
```
Beep()
Stop
Beep()
```

See Also   End

Str

Converts an expression to a string.

Description   The Str function will return a string representation of a numeric value; it recognizes only the period (.) as a decimal separator.

Syntax
```
Str(Expression)
```

Parameters

Expression   Required. Any valid numeric expression.

Returns   String type

Code Sample
```
Console.WriteLine(Str(5))
Console.WriteLine(Str(5+10))
```

See Also   CStr, Format, InStr, Val

StrComp

Compares two strings.

Description   This function will compare two strings using a specified method and return a result of the comparison. The compare type can be a binary comparison (0, default), a textual comparison (1), or, for Microsoft Access, a comparison based on information in a database. The results returned by the comparison can indicate that string1 < string2 (–1), string1 = string2 (0), string1 > string2 (1), or either string1 or string2 = Null (Null).

Syntax

```
StrComp(string1, string2 [, compare])
```

Parameters

string1, **string2**   Required. Any valid strings.

compare   Optional. Specifies comparison method.

Returns   Integer

Code Sample

```
Console.WriteLine(StrComp("Hello","hello"))
Console.WriteLine(StrComp("Hello","hello",1))
Console.WriteLine(StrComp("Hello","jello",1))
```

See Also   =, InStr, Like, Option Compare

StrConv

Converts the passed string in a number of ways, such as uppercase, lowercase, international, and so on.

Description   This command is powerful in its ability to make conversions of the entire string for common needs. Passing a conversion type constant determines how the string will be converted: vbUppercase (1); vbLowercase (2); vbPropercase (3)—first letter of every word is capitalized; vbWide (4)—changes byte character string to two-byte character string; vbNarrow (8)—converts two-byte character string to byte character string; vbKatakana (16)—converts Hirigana to Katakana; vbHirigana (32)—converts Katakana to Hirigana; vbUnicode (64); or vbFromUnicode (128).

Syntax

```
StrConv(Str, Conversion[, LocaleID])
```

Parameters

Str Required. String to be converted.

Conversion Required. Value indicating the type of conversion.

LocaleID Optional. Locale ID if different conversion is desired from the one set in the System Locale ID. The default is 0.

Returns String

Code Sample
```
Console.WriteLine(StrConv("Demon Baby",1))
Console.WriteLine(StrConv("Demon Baby",vbLowercase))
```

See Also Len

StrDup

Returns a string made of a character repeated one or more times.

Description This command duplicates the first character in a String, Char, or Object the number of times specified in a passed argument. Therefore, passing the string "Hello World" and the number of repetitions as 5 will return the string "HHHHH."

Syntax
```
StrDup(Number As Integer, Character As Object)
```

Parameters

Number Required. Number of times to repeat passed character. Determines the length of the returned string.

Character Required. The Char, String, or Object data type that holds the character for duplication.

Returns String

Code Sample
```
Console.WriteLine(StrDup(10, "D"))
Console.WriteLine(StrDup(5, "Demon Baby"))
```

See Also StrReverse

StrReverse

Reverses the string that is passed to it.

Description   Reverses the string character by character and returns the reversed string. If the string passed to this function is a Null, an error will occur.

Syntax
```
StrReverse(str)
```

Parameters
str   Required.

Returns   String

Code Sample
```
Console.WriteLine(StrReverse("Reef Brazil"))
```

See Also   StrConv

Structure...EndStructure

Creates a user-defined variable type.

Description   User-defined types are ideal when you need to format a set of information into a single structure such as rectangle data, data records, and so on.

Syntax
```
[<attrlist>]
[Public | Protected | Friend | Protected Friend | Private]
Structure name
    [variabledeclarations]
    [statements]
End Structure
```

Parameters
name   Required. Any valid name.

Returns   N/A

Code Sample
```
Structure Contact
   Public ContactName As String
   Dim Address As String
   Public ZipCode As Long
   Private creditRating As Integer
End Structure
```

See Also   CType, Dim, Private, Public, ReDim

Sub...End Sub

Creates a subroutine in a module or form.

Description   This command allows definition of a subroutine that may include the types of arguments that will be received when the routine is called.

Syntax
```
[<attrlist>]
[Overloads | Overrides | Overridable | NotOverridable
  | MustOverride | Shadows | Shared]
[Public | Protected | Friend | Protected Friend | Private]
Sub sub-name[(arguments)]
   [Static var[,var]...] [Dim var[,var]...]
   [ReDim var[,var]...] [statements] [Exit Static]
    [statements]
End Sub
```

Parameters

arguments   Required. Any arguments to be received by the function.

Returns   N/A

Code Sample
```
Sub mysub()
   Console.WriteLine("Sub_Root_Ine")
End Sub
```

See Also   Call, Class...End Class, End, Exit, Function...End Function

Switch

Evaluates a passed value against a series of values and returns the expression associated with the first matching value.

Description   The Switch function can be used to perform a quick series of related comparisons. The code sample demonstrates converting an abbreviation to a complete string. This function is now found in the Microsoft.VisualBasic namespace. Therefore, it may be addressed with the complete pathname reference (i.e., Microsoft.VisualBasic.Switch).

Syntax
```
Switch(expression1, value [, expression2, value2
   [,. . . expression7, value7]])
```

Parameters

expression   Boolean. Can be an evaluative expression.

value   Any valid Object type variable.

Returns   Object type

Code Sample
```
Dim a$ = "CA"
Console.WriteLine(Switch( _
   a$="WI","Wisconsin",a$="OR","Oregon", _
   a$="CA","California"))
```

See Also   Choose, IIf, Select Case

SYD

Returns the sum depreciation of the years digits of an asset.

Description   Depreciation is determined for the sum-of-years digits of an asset for the specified period.

Syntax
```
SYD(Cost, Salvage, Life, Period)
```

Parameters

Cost   Required. Initial cost of asset as Double type.

Salvage   Required. Salvage value at end of useful life as Double type.

Life   Required. Lifespan or length of useful life as Double type.

Period   Required. Period for which depreciation is calculated as Double type.

Returns   Double type

Code Sample

```
Console.WriteLine(SYD(10000,500,24,12))
```

See Also   DDB, FV, IPmt, IRR, MIRR, NPer, NPV, Pmt, PPmt, PV, Rate, SLN

6

SyncLock...End SyncLock

Synchronizes enclosed statements to execute as a single expression.

Description   This statement is used to create indivisible execution units that prevent the individual operations (lines of code) of the unit from being distributed over multiple threads and possibly being executed simultaneously.

Syntax

```
SyncLock expression
   statementlines
End SyncLock
```

Parameters

expression   Required. A number of expressions that provide a single result. The expression must be a class, module, interface, array, or delegate.

Returns   N/A

Code Sample

```
Public Class Class1
    Public Shared Sub Add(ByVal myObj As Object)
```

```
      SyncLock GetType(Class1)
      End SyncLock
   End Sub
   Public Shared Sub Remove(ByVal myObj As Object)
      SyncLock GetType(Class1)
      End SyncLock
   End Sub
End Class
```

See Also Lock...Unlock

Tab

Adds a tab to the formatting for a Print or PrintLine statement.

Description The Tab statement can be used to properly format columns for output to files. If the position specified in the column has already passed, the characters will automatically be aligned with the next column position.

Syntax

```
Tab([column])
```

Parameters

column Optional. Integer that specifies the column to tab into.

Returns N/A

Code Sample

```
FileOpen(1, "C:\test.txt", OpenAccess.Write)
Print(1, TAB(), "Hello", TAB(5), "Hello2")
FileClose(1)
```

See Also ?, Print, PrintLine, Spc

Tan

Returns the tangent of an angle specified in radians.

Description   This command requires the angle to be passed in radians. The formula *radians = (degrees * pi) / 180* can be used to determine the radians from a degree measure. This function is now found in the System.Math namespace.

Syntax

```
Tan(angle)
```

Parameters

angle   Required. Any numeric expression holding a radian measure.

Returns   Double type

Code Sample

```
Console.WriteLine(System.Math.Tan(3.14159))
Console.WriteLine(System.Math.Tan((90*3.14159)/180))
```

See Also   Atan, Cos, Sin, Sqrt

Throw

Generates an exception that can be captured by a Try...Catch structure.

Description   This function generates an error by throwing an instance of a class derived from the System.Exception class at runtime.

Syntax

```
Throw [ Expression ]
```

Parameters

Expression   Required. Valid Exception object or derived class.

Returns   N/A

Code Sample

```
Throw New Exception("6")
```

See Also   Error, RaiseEvent

TimeOfDay

Gets or sets the current system time.

Description   This property sets the actual system time, so be careful with its use.

Syntax
```
TimeOfDay = timesetting
```

Parameters

timesetting   Required. DateTime containing a valid time setting. Date portion is ignored.

Returns   N/A

Code Sample
```
TimeOfDay = "2:40"
Console.WriteLine(TimeOfDay)
```

See Also   Now, TimeValue, Today

Timer

Returns the number of seconds that have elapsed since midnight.

Description   This function, available in both VBA and VBScript, where there are no Timer controls available, can be used to track time values. This function is actually found in the Microsoft.VisualBasic namespace. Therefore, it may be addressed with the complete pathname reference (i.e., Microsoft.VisualBasic.Timer()).

Syntax
```
Timer
```

Parameters   N/A

Returns   Single type

Code Sample

```
Console.WriteLine(Timer)
Dim curTimer = Timer
Console.WriteLine(Timer - CurTimer)
```

See Also   Randomize

TimeSerial

Returns a time based on serial parameters passed to it.

Description   This routine allows the quick creation of a DateTime value from three integer values.

Syntax

```
TimeSerial(hour, minute, second)
```

Parameters

hour, minute, second   Required. Integers representing the hour, minute, and second of the desired time.

Returns   DateTime type

Code Sample

```
Console.WriteLine(TimeSerial(14,34,15))
```

See Also   CDate, DateSerial, DateValue, Day, Format, Month, Now, TimeOfDay, TimeValue, Today, Year

TimeValue

Creates a DateTime value holding the specified time.

Description   This function can be used to create a date and time value from a string containing a time string.

Syntax

```
TimeValue(StringTime)
```

Parameters
StringTime Required. Any valid string holding a time value.

Returns DateTime type

Code Sample
```
Console.WriteLine(TimeValue("2:15:23 PM"))
```

See Also Now, TimeSerial

Today

Sets or returns the current date as a DateTime type.

Description This routine can return the current date of the system or set a new date. The format of the date will be set to the format specified in the Windows Control Panel. Standard format will show the date in a format such as "6/28/01." This function can be used to set the actual system date, so be careful with its use.

Syntax
```
Today
```

Parameters N/A

Returns DateTime type

Code Sample
```
Console.WriteLine(Today)
```

See Also CDate, DateAdd, DateDiff, DatePart, DateSerial, DateValue, Day, Format, IsDate, Month, Now, TimeOfDay, WeekDay

Trim

Returns a string with both leading and trailing spaces removed.

Description Just as the LTrim command removes leading spaces and the RTrim removes trailing spaces, Trim removes both.

Syntax

```
Trim(Expression)
```

Parameters

Expression   Required. Any valid string.

Returns   String type

Code Sample

```
Console.WriteLine(Trim(" Hello "))
```

See Also   LTrim, RTrim

True

Logical True.

Description   This constant can be used in most expressions, bitwise operations, and comparisons.

Syntax

```
True
```

Parameters   N/A

Returns   N/A

Code Sample

```
Console.WriteLine((2=2) = True)
```

See Also   And, False, Or, XOR

Try...Catch...Finally

Conditional execution for structured exception handling.

Description   The Try structure enables evaluation of error events for a change in the program flow. Blocks of code can be encapsulated within the structure, and conditional error-handling routines can be activated based on exceptions that occur within the code. The code block in the Finally clause of the structure will execute regardless of whether an error occurs or not. This clause is often used for cleanup such as closing files or flushing buffers.

Syntax

```
Try
    [actions-1]
Catch [filter]
    [errorHandler]
Finally
    [finallyActions]
End Try
```

Parameters

filter   Optional. An instance of a child of an exception class may specify the type of error to be filtered and receive the appropriate information.

Returns   N/A

Code Sample

```
  Dim myStr As String = "Hello World"
Try
  FileOpen(1, "C:\test.txt", OpenMode.Output)
  FilePut(1, myStr)
Catch fileException as Exception
   MsgBox("File cannot be opened.")
Finally
  FileClose(1)
End Try
```

See Also   Throw

TypeName

Returns a string of the variable type passed to the function.

Description   This function receives a variable name and returns the data type specified by the variable name. Data types such as Double, Date, Null, and others are returned as a string.

Syntax

```
TypeName(varName)
```

Parameters

varName   Required. The variable to be typed.

Returns   String

Code Sample

```
Dim a = CStr("Hello"), b = CInt(53)
Console.WriteLine(TypeName(a))
Console.WriteLine(TypeName(b))
```

See Also   #, %, Dim

UBound

6

Returns the highest subscript available in the array.

Description   This function can be used to determine the upper bound of an array. If the array is multidimensional, use the rank argument to specify the upper bound to be returned.

Syntax

```
UBound(Array [,Rank])
```

Parameters

Array   Required. The name of the array required to determine the limit.

Rank   Optional. The subscript dimension of a multidimensional array.

Returns   Long type

Code Sample

```
Dim myArray() As Integer = {6, 4, 2, 5, 2, 4, 6}
Console.WriteLine(UBound(myArray))
```

See Also   { ... }, Dim, LBound

UCase

Returns a completely uppercase string.

Description   This function converts all the characters in the passed string to uppercase.

Syntax

```
UCase(expression)
```

Parameters

expression   Required. Any valid string.

Returns   String type

Code Sample

```
Console.WriteLine(UCase("hElLo"))
```

See Also   LCase

Val

Returns the value contained in a string.

Description   This function will convert the value contained within a string to a numeric value. If there is no numeric value contained in the string, a zero will be returned.

Syntax

```
Val(Expression)
```

Parameters

Expression   Required. Any string containing a numeric value.

Returns   Object

Code Sample

```
Console.WriteLine(Val("100"))
Console.WriteLine(Val("54.55"))
```

See Also   &, &=, Format, Str

Value Property

Holds the value for a specific control property.

Description   The Value property is the most common property available for objects. It typically holds the central data for the control. For example, in a scroll bar control, the Value property holds the current thumb position.

Syntax
```
object.Value [= value]
```

Parameters
value   Dependent on the object type.

Returns   N/A

Code Sample
```
Console.WriteLine(myScroll1.Value)
```

See Also   Collection, With...End With

VarType

Returns the type of variable stored in the passed reference.

Description   This function can be used to determine the type of variable being used. The returned type number may indicate Empty (0), Null (1), Integer (2), Long (3), Single (4), Double (5), Currency (6), Date (7), String (8), Object (9), Error (10), Boolean (11), Object (12), Data Object (13), Decimal (14), Byte (17), or Array (8192).

Syntax
```
VarType(Object)
```

Parameters
Object   Required. A value to be evaluated.

Returns   Integer type

Code Sample
```
Dim a As String = "Hello"
Console.WriteLine(VarType(a))
Dim b As Long = 15
Console.WriteLine(VarType(b))
```

See Also   CByte, CDbl, CInt, CStr, Dim

WeekDay

Returns the weekday portion of the passed Date type.

Description   This function will return an Integer value between 1 (Sunday) and 7 (Saturday) that represents the weekday of the date passed to it.

Syntax
```
WeekDay(DateValue)
```

Parameters

DateValue   A valid date from which the weekday will be extracted.

Returns   Integer type

Code Sample
```
Console.WriteLine(WeekDay(Now))
```

See Also   DateSerial, DateValue, Day, Format, Month, Now, WeekdayName, Year

WeekdayName

Returns a string with the name of the weekday.

Description   This command will return a string with the specified day of the week in the format specified. The WeekDay

and FirstDayOfWeekValue parameters are specified using one of
the following constants: vbUseSystem (0), vbSunday (1), vbMonday
(2), vbTuesday (3), vbWednesday (4), vbThursday (5), vbFriday (6),
or vbSaturday (7).

Syntax

```
WeekdayName(WeekDay [,Abbreviate [,FirstDayOfWeekValue]])
```

Parameters

WeekDay   Required. Numeric constant of the day of the week that
should be returned in the string.

Abbreviate   Optional. Boolean to indicate whether the returned
string should be abbreviated.

FirstDayOfWeekValue   Optional. Numeric constant indicating the
first day of the week.

Returns   String

Code Sample

```
Console.WriteLine(WeekdayName(1))
Console.WriteLine(WeekdayName(1, True))
```

See Also   Day, Format, WeekDay

While...End While

Cycles through a loop until the necessary condition is met.

Description   The While...End While structure will continue
cycling while a condition is True. Note that in VB.NET, the Wend
keyword no longer exists, so End While should be used in its place.

Syntax

```
While condition : [statements] : End While
```

Parameters

condition   Required. Boolean value.

Returns   N/A

Code Sample

```
Dim i As Integer = 0
While i < 5 : Console.Write(i) : i += 1 : End While
```

See Also   Do...Loop, For Each...Next, For...Next

With...End With

Used for a series of object references.

Description   The With...End With structure enables any statement contained within it to reference the current object with a simple dot (.) command. For example, number held in the Value property of an Excel cell may be changed inside the proper With operator using the simple ".Value = 3" command.

Syntax

```
With object [statements] End With
```

Parameters

object   Required. Any valid object reference.

Returns   N/A

Code Sample

```
Dim myWithStr As String = "Hello World"
With myWithStr
  Console.WriteLine(.Length())
  Console.WriteLine(.ToString())
End With
```

See Also   CreateObject, GetObject

Write, WriteLine

Writes data to a specified open sequential file.

Description   Unlike the Print and PrintLine commands, Write and WriteLine can write formatted data to a file. These commands use commas to separate data fields and enclose string values within quotes. WriteLine operates exactly like Write except it also adds a newline (Chr(13)+Chr(10)) at the end of each line.

Syntax

```
Write(FileNumber As Integer,
  ParamArray Output() As Object)
WriteLine(FileNumber As Integer,
  ParamArray Output() As Object)
```

Parameters

FileNumber   Required. Any valid open file number.

Output   Required. Any number of items may be included in the output list, such as strings, spaces, tabs, or expressions.

Returns   N/A

Code Sample

```
Dim a As String = "Hello"
Dim b As Single = 20.5
FileOpen(1, "c:\test.txt", OpenMode.Output)
Write(1, a,a,a,a)
WriteLine(1)
WriteLine(a,b)
FileClose(1)
```

See Also   FileClose, FileOpen, FilePut, Print, PrintLine

XOR

Exclusive Or.

Description   This operator can be used to logically combine two numbers using logical exclusion. Within the bits of the numbers, if a 1 value exists in one of the bit positions but not the other, a 1 is returned in that bit position. If both bits are set to zero or 1, a zero is returned in that bit position.

Syntax

```
a Xor b
```

Parameters

a, b   Required. Any valid numeric expression.

Returns   Object type

Code Sample
```
Console.WriteLine(255 Xor 8)
```

See Also   And, False, Not, Or, True

Year

Returns the Year portion of the passed Date type.

Description   This function will return a Object value between 0 and 9999 that represents the year of the date passed to it.

Syntax
```
Year(DateValue)
```

Parameters

DateValue   A valid DateTime object from which the year will be extracted.

Returns   Integer type

Code Sample
```
Console.WriteLine(Year(Now))
```

See Also   #, CDate, DateSerial, DateValue, Day, Format, Month, Now, WeekDay

Chapter 7
Object Model Diagrams

Microsoft's Component Object Model (COM) has been the cornerstone of object integration on the Windows platform for years. The .NET Framework now supplants the COM technology in many areas such as reusable components. Because .NET uses namespaces and strong names for hierarchical identification, components and programs don't need to be registered with a central catalog (such as the COM Registry) to be used. Many .NET components and programs can be activated simply by copying them to a client hard drive without any registration process required.

Despite the advantages of .NET components, COM will remain important in many areas, such as network distributed components, for years to come. Microsoft has created the necessary infrastructure to enable objects in both COM and .NET to communicate and interact almost seamlessly.

7

COM Access from Visual Basic.NET

In either direction—COM to .NET or .NET to COM—object wrappers are necessary to present a recognizable interface to the destination infrastructure. COM objects are handled in .NET as unmanaged entities. This means that although the instance of the component itself is managed by the memory and garbage collection functionality of the .NET Framework, memory operations that occur on the inside of the COM component are not part of the unified management system of .NET.

In COM, each class uses a Globally Unique Identifier (GUID) for independent unique identification. The .NET Framework has supplanted this type of identity with the use of strong names. A strong name provides context for the assembly within the namespace hierarchy under which the assembly can be located. One clear advantage of the strong name system over the GUID system: Changes to the object interface can be accommodated after the initial strong name is generated. Any changes to a COM interface requires the generation of a new GUID.

To enable the two different systems to interact, therefore, requires automation included with .NET. A COM component needs to be placed in a namespace, so a wrapper for an existing COM component is generated to allow .NET access to the control. The placement in the namespace occurs through a strong name based on the component name and other information supplied by the COM registration information included in the OCX (OLE custom control) header, TLB file, or OLB file. Likewise, a .NET component is given a GUID to be published into the COM system.

Accessing COM Objects from .NET

With the significant investment in COM technology that has been made by organizations over the years, it is critical that .NET be able to effectively address the objects created in COM. The wrapper for a COM object is a set of metadata elements that are held in the assembly file. This metadata describes the component and enables .NET to understand its members (that is, methods, properties, events, and so on).

There are four ways to create this metadata:

- **Visual Studio**   Through the Add Reference dialog box, all of the COM objects on the current system may be accessed.

- **Type Library Importer**   An import utility included with the .NET SDK (software development kit) that can read a specified type library and generate the necessary metadata for .NET access.

- **TypeLibConverter class**   All of the functionality of the Type Library Importer utility, but available as an accessible class. By programming the TypeLibConverter class, .NET access to a COM type library may be automated.

- **Custom wrapper**   A manually created custom wrapper that provides the bridge between a COM object and the .NET system. This option is complicated and rarely chosen.

Visual Studio

Visual Studio will transparently create the necessary metadata required for access to any COM component file. Figure 7-1 shows the new Add Reference dialog box, available through the Project | Add Reference menu item. The COM tab displays all of the COM components currently registered on the system and enables you to browse for components stored in unregistered files.

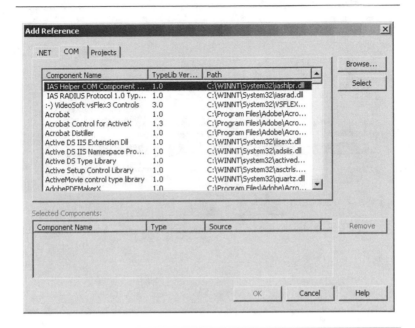

Figure 7-1.   The Add Reference dialog box allows COM objects to be added to a .NET project.

If you select a COM component that hasn't had an interoperability metadata file already created for it, the dialog box shown in Figure 7-2 will be displayed. If the Yes button is clicked, the component is queried for the necessary information and the file is created.

NOTE: If you make changes to the COM component (adding methods, deleting properties, and the like) you will have to rebuild the class library yourself by using a tool such as the Type Library Importer to provide access to the changes.

Type Library Importer

To create your own metadata wrapper file for a COM object, the Type Library Importer utility has been included with the .NET SDK. The application, named TLBIMP.EXE, is executed from the command line. The default directory of the application is usually:

```
c:\Program Files\Microsoft.NET\FrameworkSDK\Bin\TLBIMP.EXE
```

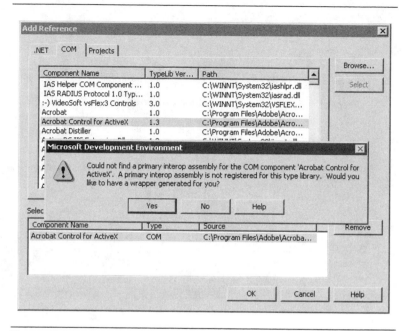

Figure 7-2. When no metadata exists, .NET prompts for the creation of a type library metadata file.

To generate the metadata file, simply execute the utility with the name of the source COM component:

```
tlbimp myComponent.DLL
```

The metadata file will be generated for all of the classes and interfaces in the dynamic link library (DLL) component file. Table 7-1 lists the switches that are available to control the process of compiling the metadata.

When importing a module containing multiple type libraries, a resource ID can be appended to the library name to specify the desired library. For example:

```
TlbImp MyModule.dll\1
```

If an assembly has multiple type libraries, more than one can be specified for import by using the /reference option several times.

Option	Description
/? or /help	Display the help information.
/asmversion:Version	Set the version number for the generated assembly. Version number should be specified in the format: Major.Minor.Build.Revision
/delaysign	Delay signing strong name.
/keycontainer:FileName	Specify container file that contains strong name key pair.
/keyfile:FileName	Specify file that contains strong name key pair.
/namespace:Namespace	Set the namespace of the assembly to be created.
/nologo	Suppress the display of the of importer logo.
/out:FileName	Name of the output file that will contain the metadata.
/primary	Generate a primary interop assembly.
/publickey:FileName	Create with strong name public key held in specified file.
/reference:FileName	Resolve references with specified file.
/silent	Disable display of all information except error messages.
/strictref	Use only those assemblies found in the /reference switch.
/sysarray	Import the SAFEARRAY as the type System.Array.
/unsafe	Disable the .Net Framework security checks and produce the file.
/verbose	Display the extra information generated during compilation.

Table 7-1.   Type Library Importer Switches

7

TypeLibConverter Class and Custom Wrappers

Through the TypeLibConverter class, it is also possible to automate
the creation of COM wrappers for the .NET system. This class
creates the same metadata information as the TlbTmp.EXE utility.
The library converter can be found under the System.Runtime
.InteropServices.TypeLibConverter namespace. The conversion
process can convert any in-memory type library for availability to
programs within the .NET runtime. The class can also be used to
create a COM type library wrapper for a .NET assembly.

Providing COM Access to a .NET Class

A public class can be called by other programs within the .NET
system without any additional work. If the class is properly
constructed, publishing it into the COM system is a fairly simple
process. To access any class or library created with .NET by using
COM technology, an assembly must be created.

An assembly can be created as either an EXE or DLL file. After the
assembly has been compiled, it can be automatically registered in
the COM catalog on the current machine. Alternately, there are two
utilities included with the .NET Framework SDK that will take the
metadata of the assembly (called the assembly manifest) and create
an entry for the assembly in the COM registry. Once registered, the
published assembly can be addressed like any other COM component.
The example in the next section creates a public class that is stored
in an assembly, registered with the COM system, and instantiated
from Microsoft Excel.

Creating a VB.NET Public Class

A simple component provides a useful reference for how construction
and registration within the COM system works. In this example, a
component that has a couple of properties and a single method is
created and stored within an assembly. After the proper settings
are made, this assembly will be automatically registered with the
COM system.

NOTE: In many examples in this book, the names of elements
have included the prefix "my" (for example, myVar or myString.) to
indicate that they are being newly defined and are not system data
types or keywords. In VB.NET, however, the name myClass is a
keyword that is used like the "this" keyword in C# or the "Me"
keyword on a VB form. For this reason, the following example uses
the name myNewClass for the class it creates.

To create the sample COM component, follow these steps:

1. Begin a new Visual Basic project and set the name to myAssembly and the template to Class Library.

2. In the Solution Explorer, right-click on the default class file that's named Class1.vb and select the Properties option.

3. Change the Filename property to myNewClass.vb.

4. In the code window for the class, place the following code:

```
Public Class myNewClass
    ' Read/write accessible to all
    Public myCounter As Integer
    ' Read only
    Public ReadOnly myGreeting As String
    ' Only available to methods within the class
    Private myPrivate As Long _ 0

    Public Sub New()
        ' A read-only variable can only be set
        ' within the constructor of the class.
        myGreeting = "Hello World"
        myCounter = 0
    End Sub

    Public Function AddCounter() As String
        myCounter += 1
        AddCounter = myCounter.ToString()
    End Function
End Class
```

5. Right-click on the myAssembly item in the Solution Explorer and select the Properties option.

6. Under the Common Properties folder, select the Strong Name item in the option list.

7. Click the Generate Strong Name Using checkbox to activate the key generation system.

8. Click the Generate Key button. After the key is created, the text box will display the name of the key file (KeyFile.snk) as shown in Figure 7-3. A key is required to place an assembly in the Global Assembly Cache so that any program on the system can address it.

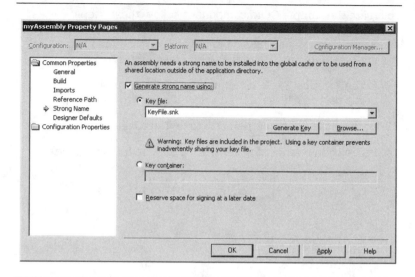

Figure 7-3. Clicking the Generate Key button creates a key file.

9. Under the Configuration Properties folder, select the Build item.

10. Check the Register for the COM Interop check box (as shown in Figure 7-4).

11. Click the OK button.

12. Select the Build | Build menu option

If you look at the output window of Visual Studio, the last line of the build process should read "Registering project output for COM Interop..." to indicate proper registration has taken place.

Calling the Class from Excel

Now that the simple component has been created and published, it can be accessed from any COM-compatible environment. Available in all of the Microsoft Office applications, the VBA programming environment provides the perfect place to test the execution of the component you just created.

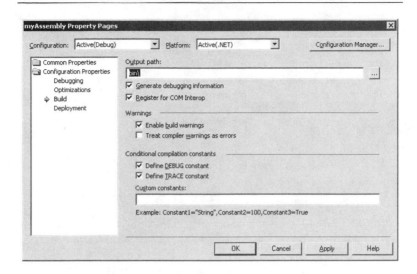

Figure 7-4. The COM Interop check box will register the component in the COM system.

Follow these steps to create and use an instance of the new class:

1. @ =

2. Open the Visual Basic environment under the Tools | Macro | Visual Basic Editor menu option or press ALT-F11.

3. Select the References option under the Tools menu to display the alphabetical list of available COM libraries.

4. Scroll down until you reach the myAssembly entry, check the box to the left of it, and click the OK button.

5. Display the Object Browser by pressing the F2 key.

6. In the top left-hand corner of the browser, use the ComboBox to select the myAssembly library.

7. Click the myNewClass entry in the left pane and all of the available methods and properties will display as shown in Figure 7-5. Most of the displayed methods are those inherited by myNewClass from its parent.

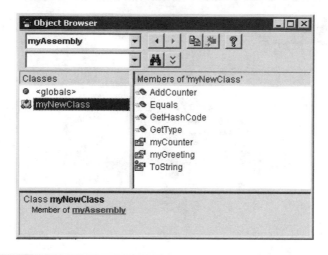

Figure 7-5. Displaying myNewClass in the Object Browser

8. Select the View | Immediate Window menu option or press CTRL-G to show the Immediate window.

9. To demonstrate the different aspects of the class component, enter the following commands in the Immediate window one line at a time:

```
Set myInst1 = New myNewClass
? myInst1.myGreeting
? myInst1.myCounter
myInst1.AddCounter
? myInst1.myCounter
Set myInst2 = New myNewClass
? myInst2.myCounter
myInst1.AddCounter
myInst2.AddCounter
? myInst1.myCounter
? myInst2.myCounter
```

From the VBA environment, there are two ways of creating an instance of the class. The first way is to use the keyword New shown in the example above. However, if the class isn't activated in the Reference dialog, you can still create an instance of the object by using the second way:

```
Set myobj = CreateObject("myAssembly.myNewClass")
```

Manual Component Registration

The VB.NET component example shows how to make a few setting changes so Visual Studio automatically handles all of the processing and registration. By using utilities that are included with the .NET SDK, you can handle this registration process manually if necessary. Before the component can be added to the Global Assembly Cache, a key pair must be created for it.

Generating a Key Pair Manually

While the Project Properties dialog in VB.NET will generate a public/private key pair, you can also create one manually and simply use the Browse button in that dialog to select it. To manually create a key pair, use the SN utility by entering the following at the command prompt:

```
sn -k myNewClass.key
```

After you create the key pair and point to it in the Project Properties dialog box, the component must be compiled. After it is compiled, it can be added to the Global assembly.

Manual Registration in the Global Assembly Cache

To make the assembly available to every application on the current machine, it can be installed to the *global assembly cache*. There are five primary reasons to install an assembly into the global assembly:

- **Shared access**   After an assembly is placed in the global cache, any application on the machine can address it, eliminating the need for a separate copy with each program.
- **COM access**   To be available as a COM component for the entire system, it should be registered to the global assembly.
- **File security**   Following initial installation, only an administrator can delete an assembly from the global cache.
- **Multiple versions**   Multiple versions of an assembly that have the same name but a different version can be kept in the global cache.

- **Search predominance** In the search tree for external assemblies, .NET searches global assemblies first. If no reference is found there, the local codebase is used.

To register an assembly to the global assembly cache, the Global Assembly Cache (gacutil) tool is most commonly used from the command line like this:

```
gacutil /i myNewClass.dll
```

This execution places the assembly in the global assembly cache.

➤ Programming Tip

From the command prompt, you may have to switch to the Bin directory of the project to execute the registration. Typing the extensive pathname to reach this directory can be tedious. If you have the folder currently open on the Windows desktop, right-click on it and select Properties. In the Properties window, the Location entry will display the complete path. Select the path and use CTRL-C to copy it to the clipboard. Now you can right-click in the command prompt window to paste the path at the present cursor location. You have to delete the drive reference at the beginning of the path string for the cd\ command to work properly.

Manual Registration for COM Interop

The only remaining step to make the assembly available to the COM system is placing the appropriate entry in the Registry. The regasm utility can be used at the command line like this:

```
regasm /install myNewClass.dll
```

Regasm will confirm success by returning the message "Types registered successfully." After the object is registered, an instance of the component can be created from a COM-compliant development system.

Chapter 8
ActiveX Data Objects.NET

To reflect the changes to the database world, ActiveX Data Objects
.NET (ADO.NET) has evolved dramatically from ADO (ActiveX Data
Objects). Widespread access to the Internet has made inexpensive
WAN connectivity available to nearly anyone. To leverage the new
opportunities created by the growth of the Internet and maximize
Web-related database interaction, Microsoft adapted ADO to play
to the strengths of the Web infrastructure.

The restructuring of ADO occurs both on the surface as well as
underneath in the plumbing. Under ADO.NET, XML has become
the standard format for data exchange. Almost all underlying
exchange of data between clients and servers takes place through
XML-compatible files and streams. This enables more efficient
interaction in a sessionless environment such as the Internet. By
adopting discontinuous database access as the standard, it also
makes a system more scalable.

ADO.NEXT Overview

8

On the surface of ADO.NET, most of the older ADO objects to
which you're accustomed (Command, Connection, Parameter, and
so on) have been reconstituted. The new DataSet object replaces
the Recordset, which was the key data management object in the
old system. Even more fundamentally, there has been a new object
added called the DataAdapter object that provides the foundation
level of communication between a data source and the objects that
handle the data processing.

DataAdapter Object

The DataAdapter object provides the bedrock method of communication
between a DataSet and a data source. Calls to the adapter enable
data to be loaded from a database into the memory-resident DataSet,
and provide the capability to write modified data back to the source.
Data adapters may exist to populate a DataSet from nearly any type
of data source, from SQL Server databases to Microsoft Exchange stores.

A data adapter can retrieve rows from a data source and store them in either a DataSet or DataReader object. It also handles writing any changes made in rows of a DataSet back into the data store.

ADO.NET provides two different types of data adapters:

- **SqlDataAdapter** Created specifically to integrate with Microsoft SQL Server 7 or later; it provides the fastest throughput.

- **OleDbDataAdapter** Made to provide connectivity with all supported OLE DB data sources.

Figure 8-1 shows that the object layouts of the SQL and OLE DB adapters are nearly identical. While the objects have been named to reflect their data source type (SQL or OLE DB), they have nearly identical methods, properties, and events. Converting code between one and the other typically involves more tedium from renaming objects than it involves actual code rewrite.

NOTE: For read-only data, a data adapter can be used to read data quickly into an array-like memory structure without loading it into a DataSet at all. This feature is particularly useful when you need the fastest access to reference or lookup data. This functionality is provided through the data reader objects (OleDbDataReader and SqlDataReader). These objects are used for forward-only, read-only queries. An example of using a data reader can be found under the CommandText property entry.

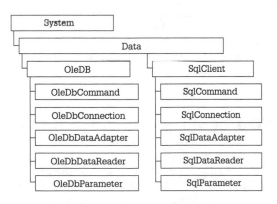

Figure 8-1. The object layouts of SqlDataAdapter and OleDbDataAdapter are nearly the same.

For a standard multitable database operation, Microsoft recommends that you set up a separate data adapter for each table (see Figure 8-2). In ADO.NET, this is a much more efficient method than creating a single data adapter with a multiple join. In the figure, a generalized setup is shown with a SQL Server data source and three data adapters. Each adapter connects to a DataTable object contained in the DataSet, while the Relation object provides the join between two of these tables.

The Fill method of the data adapter is the routine that is actually used to read data from a source and place it into the DataSet. The Update method writes DataSet changes to the source. A data adapter maps each item in a data source to its equivalent item in a DataSet by using a collection called TableMappings.

Connection Objects

ADO.NET uses Connection objects to provide the actual link between the data adapter and the data source. The Connection object, however, is much different in the new ADO.NET than it has been in previous versions of ADO. Each Connection has four references that relate directly to SQL functions of Select, Update, Insert, and Delete.

8

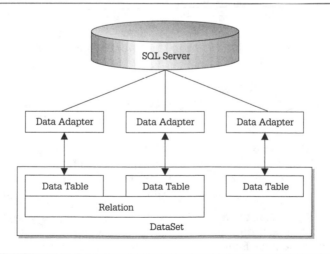

Figure 8-2.   Use a separate DataAdapter for each DataTable.

A Connection object represents a session connection to the database. The login information (server name, password, user ID, and so on) is stored in each Connection object along with the transaction functionality for that data adapter.

DataSet Object

The DataSet object provides a memory-resident image of data and data connections for both continuous (session based) and discontinuous data scenarios. Each DataSet object contains references for the Relations, Tables, and ExtendedProperties to replicate the schema of a database (see Figure 8-3). A DataSet often contains data that is retrieved from more than one data adapter.

A DataSet object can be populated manually, from a data source, or from an XML file (with the ReadXML method). No matter which option is used, the DataSet uses the XML format for internal structuring. This allows any data stored in any DataSet to be written into an XML file by using the WriteXML method.

NOTE: If the ReadXML method is used to load data into a DataSet and that data is subsequently written back to the file with the WriteXML() method, there could be a substantial difference between the original file and the updated one. When a DataSet is created with ReadXML, a great deal of formatting is lost, including text comments, element order, white space, and any data not specified to be read by the schema. If you wish to keep an existing XML data file intact, use the XMLDataDocument object. This object creates a memory-resident link to the XML file and can read and write to it much like a database, yet it leaves all existing formatting and data intact.

Information contained in a DataSet object can be written to disk for export, backup, or serialization. An example of writing XML data can be found under the WriteXML method entry. Any DataSet can be written as an XML file (which contains the DataSet data) or an XSD file (which contains the DataSet structure or schema). Additionally, a single XML file may be created that contains the schema (in XSD form) followed by the DataSet data.

A DataSet can be set to synchronize with an XMLDataDocument for real-time updating. Any changes to the data in one source (the DataSet or the XML file) will cause an immediate update to the other. If you have an existing DataSet, you can synchronize this data with a

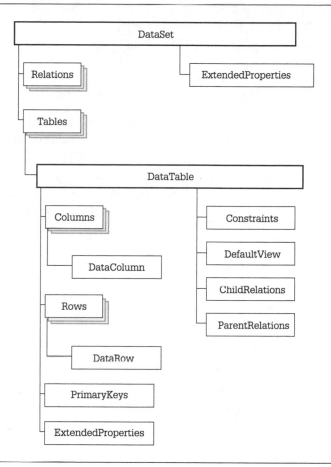

Figure 8-3. The DataSet object contains all of the structures necessary to represent the schema of a database.

new XMLDataDocument. The synchronization will create the proper XML data file and schema to mirror the existing data.

Within the DataSet object, tables are presented as a collection of one or more DataTable objects. Each DataTable holds the rows and columns (in DataRow and DataColumn objects, respectively) of the table as well as the items of the schema such as the primary keys of the table. For ADO.NET, all of the primary objects of a schema may be created separately and located in the .NET framework hierarchy at the same level (see Figure 8-4).

For connections between tables, the DataRelation object codifies what is traditionally considered a join relationship. Each DataRelation object holds the connecting columns (primary and foreign key columns) and the definition of the type of relation between two or more tables in the DataSet. In the DataRelation, the ForeignKeyConstraints may put limits on the connected tables to ensure that any changes to data rows in either table do not invalidate the current relation.

The DataSet also includes a collection of ExtendedProperties that are used to configure how the data will be treated. This collection is also present for each DataRow and DataColumn object, although the properties held in each collection are different from those used by the DataSet. For DataRow and DataColumn objects, the ExtendedProperties allow the developer to store custom information with each object.

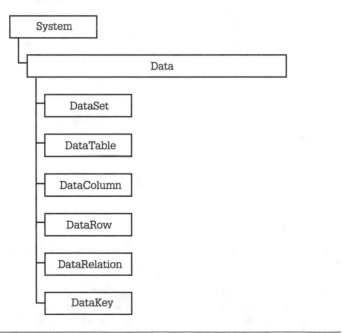

Figure 8-4.   The data objects of ADO.NET may be created separately.

BeginEdit Method

This method activates the editing mode for a record/row.

Description   This method is used to begin editing a row in a DataTable. Validation events are suspended until the EndEdit() or the CancelEdit() method is called. EndEdit() is called implicitly when the AcceptChanges() or the RejectChanges() methods are called for the DataTable itself.

Class Occurrence
System.Data.DataRow.BeginEdit

System.Data.DataRowView.BeginEdit

Syntax
```
myTable.BeginEdit()
```

Parameters   N/A

Returns   N/A

Code Sample
```
' Edit the uniqueid column
myTable.Rows(0).BeginEdit()
myTable.Rows(0)("uniqueid") = 100
myTable.Rows(0).EndEdit()
```

See Also   RowState

Clone Method

Creates a clone of the specified DataSet or DataTable object.

Description   This method duplicates the current DataSet or DataTable including all DataTable schema, relations, and constraints. On a DataTable, it can save a great deal of processing time if a duplicate recordset is needed, because a clone does not execute an entirely new query.

Class Occurrence

System.Data.DataSet.Clone

System.Data.DataTable.Clone

Syntax

```
myDS = datasetObject.Clone()
myDT = datatableObject.Clone()
```

Parameters   N/A

Returns   DataSet or DataTable object

Code Sample

```
Dim oldDS As DataSet
Dim newDS As DataSet

newDS = oldDS.Clone
```

See Also   Open, Parameters

CommandText Property

Holds the string that specifies the action to be taken by the Command object.

Description   This property contains the text of the command to be sent when the ExecuteNonQuery(), the ExecuteReader(), the ExecuteScalar(), or the ExecuteXMLReader() method is activated. This property is usually set to equal a SQL command. If the data provider can support multiple statements or stored procedures in a single command, use the semicolon (;) character to delimit between them.

Class Occurrence

System.Data.OleDb.OleDbCommand.CommandText

System.Data.SqlClient.SqlCommand.CommandText

System.Data.IDbCommand.CommandText

Syntax

```
commandObject.CommandText = myStr
```

Parameters

myStr   String type containing the text to send the Data Provider,
most often in the form of a SQL command.

Returns   N/A

Code Sample

```
Imports System.Data.OLEDB
Private Sub Button1_Click(ByVal sender As System.Object, _
  ByVal e As System.EventArgs)  Handles Button1.Click
    Dim myConn As OleDbConnection, myCmd As OleDbCommand
    Dim myReader As OleDbDataReader, myConnStr As String

    ' Create a connection string to the FrontPage edition
    ' of the Northwind database that installs with Office
    myConnStr = "Provider=Microsoft.Jet.OLEDB.4.0;" & _
      "Password=;User ID=Admin;" & _
      "Data Source=C:\myData\FPNWIND.MDB;" & _
      "Mode=Share Deny None;"
    myConn = New OleDbConnection(myConnStr)
    myCmd = New OleDbCommand()
    myCmd.CommandType = CommandType.Text
    myCmd.CommandText = "Select * from Employees"
    myCmd.Connection = myConn
    myConn.Open()
    ' Execute a forward-only read version of the command
    myReader = myCmd.ExecuteReader()
    ' Step through the data, displaying it to the console
    Do While myReader.Read()
        Console.WriteLine(myReader.GetInt32(0) & "," & _
          myReader.GetString(1))
    Loop
    myConn.Close()
End Sub
```

See Also   CommandType, ConnectionString, Provider

CommandType Property

Specifies the type of Command object.

Description This property indicates the type of execution expected of the Command object and how the text in the CommandText property will be interpreted. Constant values contained in this property include Text (1), StoredProcedure (4), and TableDirect (512). The default is Text.

Class Occurrence

System.Data.OleDb.OleDbCommand.CommandType

System.Data.SqlClient.SqlCommand.CommandType

System.Data.IDbCommand.CommandType

Syntax

```
commandObject.CommandType = myCommandType
```

Parameters

myCommandType Integer value of one of the constants of the command type.

Returns   N/A

Code Sample

```
Imports System.Data.SqlClient
Private Sub Button1_Click(ByVal sender As System.Object, _
  ByVal e As System.EventArgs) Handles Button1.Click
    Dim myConn As SqlConnection, myCmd As SqlCommand
    Dim myReader As SqlDataReader, myConnStr As String
    myConnStr = "user id=sa;password=;" & _
        "initial catalog=northwind;" & _
        "data source=mySQLServer;Connect Timeout=30"
    myConn = New SqlConnection(myConnStr)
    myCmd = New SqlCommand()
    myCmd.CommandType = CommandType.Text
    myCmd.CommandText = "Select * from Employees"
    myCmd.Connection = myConn
```

```
    myConn.Open()
    myReader = myCmd.ExecuteReader()
    Do While myReader.Read()
        Console.WriteLine(myReader.GetInt32(0) & "," & _
            myReader.GetString(1))
    Loop
    myConn.Close()
End Sub
```

See Also   CommandText

Commit Method

Commits any records held in the current transaction.

Description   A transaction can contain one or more changes to one or more records. When the Commit method is called, either all of the current operations stored in the transaction are written successfully, or a single failure will abort the update. A transaction begins with calling the Begin method call; a transaction can complete with either the Commit or RollBack methods.

8

Class Occurrence

System.Data.IDbTransaction.Commit

System.Data.SqlClient.SqlTransaction.Commit

System.Data.OleDb.OleDbTransaction.Commit

Syntax

```
transaction.Commit
```

Parameters   N/A

Returns   N/A

Code Sample

```
Private Sub cmdTransCommit_Click( _
  ByVal sender As System.Object, _
  ByVal e As System.EventArgs) Handles cmdTransCommit.Click
    Dim myCommand As New OleDbCommand()
    Dim myConnStr As String
```

```
myConnStr = "Provider=Microsoft.Jet.OLEDB.4.0;" & _
    "Password=;User ID=Admin;" & _
    "Data Source=C:\myData\FPNWIND.MDB;" & _
    "Mode=Share Deny None;"

Dim myConnection As New OleDbConnection(myConnStr)
myConnection.Open()
myCommand.Transaction = myConnection.BeginTransaction()

myCommand.CommandText = "Insert into Customers " & _
    "(CustomerID, CompanyName) VALUES (100, 'Pecos Bill')"
' Execute the Insert statement to add a record
myCommand.ExecuteNonQuery()
myCommand.Transaction.Commit()
myConnection.Close()
End Sub
```

See Also   CommandText, ConnectionString, Provider

ConnectionString Property

Holds the string that indicates the data provider.

Description   The text of the ConnectionString can also contain the data provider, the filename of the connection data, as well as the user name and password for transmission when the Connection is opened. If the user name and password are not supplied to the source through the ConnectionString, they are passed through the UserID and Password parameters to identify the user for login.

The following parameters are valid for use in the string: Application Name, AttachDBFilename/Initial File Name, Connection Timeout/Connect Timeout, Connection Lifetime, Connection Reset, Current Language, Data Source/Server /Address/Addr/Network Address, Enlist, Initial Catalog/Database, Integrated Security/Trusted_Connection, Max Pool Size, Min Pool Size, Network Library/Net, Packet Size, Password/Pwd, Persist Security Info, Pooling, User ID/UID, and Workstation ID.

Class Occurrence

System.Data.OleDb.OleDbConnection.ConnectionString

System.Data.SqlClient.SqlConnection.ConnectionString

System.Data.IDbCommand.ConnectionString

Syntax
`connectionObject.ConnectionString = myStr`

Parameters
myStr   String that holds the connection parameters.

Returns   N/A

Code Sample
```
' OLEDB connection to MS Access
myConnStr = "Provider=Microsoft.Jet.OLEDB.4.0;" & _
   "Password=;User ID=Admin;Data Source=" & _
"C:\myData\FPNWIND.MDB;Mode=Share Deny None;"
' OLEDB connection to SQL Server
myConnect.ConnectionString = "Provider=SQLOLEDB;Data Source=localhost;" & _
   "Initial Catalog=Northwind;Integrated Security=SSPI;"
' SQLClient connection to SQL Server
myConnect.ConnectionString = "driver=SQL Server;" & _
   "server=MarinerServ;uid=sa;pwd=;database=pubs"
' Another SQLClient connection to SQL Server
myConnect.ConnectionString = "user id=sa;password=;initial " & _
   "catalog=northwind;data source=mySQLServer;Connect Timeout=30"
```

See Also   CommandText, CommandType, Provider

DataType Property

Specifies the data type of a column in a DataTable.

Description   Holds the schema type of the data that will be stored in a particular column. The data types specified by this property may include the base .NET Framework types: Boolean, Byte, Char, DateTime, Decimal, Double, Int16, Int32, Int64, SByte, Single, String, TimeSpan, UInt16, UInt32, and UInt64. However, Visual Basic does not support four of these base types: UInt16, UInt32, UInt64, and TimeSpan.

Class Occurrence   System.Data.DataColumn.DataType

Syntax

```
myDataColumn.DataType = myDataType
```

Parameters

myDataType   Holds a reference to a System.Type object.

Returns   N/A

Code Sample

```
Private Sub MakeTable()
    Dim myDataTable As DataTable = New DataTable()
    Dim myColumn As DataColumn, myRow As DataRow

    myColumn = New DataColumn()
    myColumn.DataType = System.Type.GetType("System.Int16")
    myColumn.ColumnName = "uniqueid"
    myDataTable.Columns.Add(myColumn)

    myRow = myDataTable.NewRow()
    myRow("uniqueid") = 1
    myDataTable.Rows.Add(myRow)
End Sub
```

See Also   RowState

Delete Method

Deletes a row from the DataRows collection.

Description   The Delete method allows you to remove a row from the DataRows collection. The code example removes the first record from myDataTable. The deletion isn't processed until either the AcceptChanges() or RejectChanges() method is called for the table.

Class Occurrence

System.Data.DataRow

System.Data.DataRowView

Syntax
```
myDataRow.Delete()
```

Parameters   N/A

Returns   N/A

Immediate Window Sample
```
' Delete the first row in DataTable
myDataTable.Rows(0).Delete()
myDataTable.AcceptChanges()
```

See Also   BeginEdit, RowState

ExecuteNonQuery Method

This method executes nonquery SQL code against a Connection.

Description   This method is used to send SQL code to the data source to execute a stored procedure, create a database object, and so on. After the execution has occurred, it will return the number of records affected by the command. If the operation doesn't affect records (for example, code that creates a stored procedure), the number returned is zero.

Class Occurrence
System.Data.IDbCommand.ExecuteNonQuery

System.Data.SqlClient.SqlCommand.ExecuteNonQuery

System.Data.OleDb.OleDbCommand.ExecuteNonQuery

Syntax
```
recordsAffected = commandObject.ExecuteNonQuery()
```

Parameters
recordsAffected   The records that will be affected by the operation.

8

Returns Integer

Code Sample
```
myCommand.Connection.Open()
myCommand.ExecuteNonQuery()
```

See Also ConnectionString, Open

Fill Method

Fills a DataSet or DataTable with information retrieved from the specified DataAdapter.

Description This method adapts the Select command found in the DataAdapter to fill or refresh a DataSet or a DataTable with new records. When used on a DataSet, any DataTable objects that do not yet exist in the set but are specified in the DataAdapter are created and automatically populated.

Class Occurrence

System.Data.IDataAdapter.Fill

System.Data.Common.DataAdapter.Fill

System.Data.Common.DbDataAdapter.Fill

System.Data.OleDb.OleDbDataAdapter.Fill

Syntax
```
numRows = dataAdapter.Fill(myDataSet)
numRows = dataAdapter.Fill(myDataSet, sourceTable)
numRows = dataAdapter.Fill(myDataSet, _
  ADOrecordset, sourceTable)
numRows = dataAdapter.Fill(myDataTable, myIDataReader)
numRows = dataAdapter.Fill(myDataSet, startRecord, _
  maxRecords, sourceTable)
numRows = dataAdapter.Fill(myDataTable, myIDBCommand, _
```

```
    myCommandBehavior)
numRows = dataAdapter.Fill(myDataTable, startRecord, _
    maxRecords, sourceTable, myIDBCommand, _
    myCommandBehavior)
```

Parameters

numRows Integer of the number of rows added or refreshed in the DataSet or DataTable.

myDataSet DataSet object that is to be filled.

myDataTable DataTable object that is to be filled.

myIDbCommand A SQL Select statement used to retrieve rows for the source.

myCommandBehavior Integer specifying the update behavior as one of the following six enumerated values: SingleRequest (1), SchemaOnly (2), KeyInfo (4), SingleRow (8), SequentialAccess (16), or CloseConnection (32).

myIDataReader Used to match names in the data source to the updating DataTable.

sourceTable The table that will be read from on the data source.

startRecord Starting record number for update with the very first record numbered zero (0).

maxRecords Maximum number of records to retrieve. Passing a value of zero will retrieve all records. Note that if the Select statement was created to retrieve multiple result sets, this parameter is only applied to the first returned set.

ADOrecordset Enables copying an ADO recordset into an ADO .NET DataSet. Provides a bridge from the old technology to the new.

Returns Integer

Code Sample

```
numrecords = myDataAdapter.Fill(myDataSet, "Categories")
```

See Also BeginEdit, CommandText, DataType

GetXml Method

Returns a string of the specified DataSet in XML format.

Description   This method, when executed on a DataSet object, returns a string containing the XML definitions and data for all of the rows in the set. It performs essentially the same function as the WriteXML method, except the XML data is stored to a memory-resident string rather than being written to a specified storage location.

Class Occurrence   System.Data.DataSet.GetXml

Syntax

```
myXML = myDataSet.GetXml()
```

Parameters

myXML   A string containing the XML code of the data contained in the DataSet.

Returns   String type

Code Sample

```
Private Sub cmdGetXML_Click(ByVal sender As _
   System.Object, ByVal e As System.EventArgs) _
   Handles cmdWriteXML.Click
      Dim myDS As DataSet
      Dim myConn As OleDbConnection, myCmd As OleDbCommand
      Dim myConnStr As String
      Dim myDataAdapter As OleDbDataAdapter

      myConnStr = "Provider=Microsoft.Jet.OLEDB.4.0;" & _
        "Password=;User ID=Admin;Data Source=" & _
        "C:\myData\FPNWIND.MDB;Mode=Share Deny None;"
      myDataAdapter = New OleDbDataAdapter()
      myConn = New OleDbConnection(myConnStr)
      myCmd = New OleDbCommand()

      myCmd.CommandType = CommandType.Text
      myCmd.CommandText = "Select * from Employees"
      myCmd.Connection = myConn
      myDataAdapter.TableMappings.Add("Table", "Employees")
      myConn.Open()
```

```
myDataAdapter.SelectCommand = myCmd
myDS = New DataSet("myEmployees")
myDataAdapter.Fill(myDS)
myConn.Close()

Console.Write(myDS.GetXml())
End Sub
```

See Also   WriteXml

NewRow Method

Creates a new record/row in the DataSet.

Description   This method, when used with a DataTable, creates a new record in the current DataSet. Once the NewRow method has been used, the cursor points to this new record. Therefore, any modification to the current columns/fields will be saved in the new record.

To create a new record, the NewRow method will append a record to the end of the DataRows collection in the DataTable. The code example shows a record being added to a table named myDataTable that contains two columns. The second column is set to the name "Joe," and the row is then added to the existing rows.

Class Occurrence   System.Data.DataTable

Syntax

```
myDataTable.NewRow()
```

Parameters   N/A

Returns   DataRow

Code Sample

```
myRow = myDataTable.NewRow()
myRow("id") = 4
myRow("name") = "Joe"
myDataTable.Rows.Add(myRow)
```

See Also   Commit, RowState

Open Method

Opens the specified connection.

Description A Connection object may open a session with the Open method. This method uses the ConnectionString property to provide the access details of the data source that will be used.

Class Occurrence

System.Data.IDbConnection.Open

System.Data.SqlClient.SqlConnection.Open

System.Data.OleDb.OleDbConnection.Open

Syntax
`connectionObject.Open()`

Parameters N/A

Returns N/A

Code Sample
`myConnection.Open()`

See Also ConnectionString, Provider

Parameters Property

The Parameters property holds the reference to the Parameters collection.

Description This property holds the object reference to the SqlParameterCollection that provides the variables of a Command object. Parameters are typically variables passed to SQL queries such as substitution variables for a SQL Where clause.

Class Occurrence

System.Data.IDbCommand.Parameters

System.Data.SqlClient.SqlCommand.Parameters

System.Data.OleDb.OleDbCommand.Parameters

Syntax

```
myParameter = commandObject.Parameters(myIndex)
```

Parameters

myParameter   Object to receive the specified Parameter object.

myIndex   Numeric or string that selects desired Parameter element.

Returns   N/A

Code Sample

```
queryParm = "%Dan%"
' Using a parameter index value on the DataAdapter
myOleDbDA.SelectCommand.Parameters(1).Value _
    = queryParm
' Using a named parameter
myOleDbDA.SelectCommand.Parameters("FirstName").Value _
    = queryParm
```

See Also   CommandText, CommandType

ParentTable Property

The ParentTable property holds a reference to the parent table of a DataRelation.

Description   This property holds the object reference to the parent DataTable of the specified DataRelation. A DataRelation object forms a database join relationship between two tables. The

8

join occurs between a column in one table that specifies a primary key and a column in the other table that holds the matching foreign key. The table with the primary key is considered the parent table and this property in the DataRelation object holds the reference to it.

Class Occurrence   System.Data.DataRelation.ParentTable

Syntax

```
myParentTable = dataRelationObject.ParentTable
```

Parameters

DataRelationObject   Object that holds the join relation that connects two tables.

myParentTable   Variable to hold parent DataTable reference.

Returns   N/A

Code Sample

```
Private Sub cmdGetParent_Click(ByVal sender As _
    System.Object, ByVal e As System.EventArgs) _
    Handles cmdGetParent.Click
    Dim myTable As DataTable, myRelation As DataRelation
    Dim myDS As DataSet, myConn As OleDbConnection
    Dim cmdSuppliers As OleDbCommand
    Dim cmdProducts As OleDbCommand
    Dim myConnStr As String
    Dim suppliersDA As OleDbDataAdapter
    Dim productsDA As OleDbDataAdapter
    Dim relCustOrder As DataRelation
    Dim parentCol As DataColumn, childCol As DataColumn

    myConnStr = "Provider=Microsoft.Jet.OLEDB.4.0;" & _
        "Password=;User ID=Admin;Data Source=" & _
        "C:\myData\FPNWIND.MDB;Mode=Share Deny None;"
    suppliersDA = New OleDbDataAdapter()
    productsDA = New OleDbDataAdapter()
    myConn = New OleDbConnection(myConnStr)
    cmdProducts = New OleDbCommand()
    cmdSuppliers = New OleDbCommand()
    suppliersDA.TableMappings.Add("Table", "Suppliers")
    cmdSuppliers.CommandType = CommandType.Text
    cmdSuppliers.CommandText = "Select * from Suppliers"
    cmdSuppliers.Connection = myConn
    suppliersDA.SelectCommand = cmdSuppliers
```

```
myConn.Open()
myDS = New DataSet("myEmployees")
suppliersDA.Fill(myDS)

productsDA.TableMappings.Add("Table", "Products")
cmdProducts.CommandType = CommandType.Text
cmdProducts.CommandText = "Select * from Products"
cmdProducts.Connection = myConn
productsDA.SelectCommand = cmdProducts

productsDA.Fill(myDS)
myConn.Close()

parentCol = _
  myDS.Tables("Suppliers").Columns("SupplierID")
childCol = _
  myDS.Tables("Products").Columns("SupplierID")
relCustOrder = _
  New DataRelation("SPJoin", parentCol, childCol)
myDS.Relations.Add(relCustOrder)

myRelation = myDS.Relations("SPJoin")
myTable = myRelation.ParentTable
Console.WriteLine("ParentTable=" & myTable.TableName)
End Sub
```

See Also   DataType

Provider Property

In the Connection object, the Provider property holds the name of
the OLE DB Data Provider.

Description   The Provider property holds the name of the provider
for the particular data source. If the Provider will be an ODBC
driver, or if there is no Provider set, the MSDASQL provider will be
used as the default. This variable holds the same value that can be
established with the Provider= parameter in the ConnectionString
property. Two common providers are Microsoft.Jet.OLEDB.4.0 and
SQLOLEDB.

Class Occurrence

System.Data.OleDb.OleDbConnection.Provider

System.Data.OleDb.OleDbPermission.Provider

System.Data.OleDb.OleDbPermissionAttribute.Provider

Syntax
```
connectionObject.Provider
```

Parameters N/A

Returns N/A

Code Sample
```
MsgBox myConnectObj.Provider
```

See Also ConnectionString

RowState Property

Indicates the current state of a record/row.

Description This property indicates the status of the current row within a DataSet. The property contains a value that signals whether the row has been Detached (1), Unchanged (2), Added (4), Deleted (8), or Modified (16).

Class Occurrence System.Data.DataRow.RowState

Syntax
```
currentState = myRow.RowState
```

Parameters

currentState Integer type enumerating the current row condition.

Returns N/A

Code Sample
```
MsgBox myRow.RowState
```

See Also BeginEdit, Commit

Table Property

Holds a reference to the table that matches the object schema.

Description When an object such as a row or column is created, it is not automatically added to the table from which its schema is derived. Therefore, the Table property holds a reference to the table of the object's owner unless the RowState property indicates that the row is Detached.

Class Occurrence

System.Data.DataColumn.Table

System.Data.DataRow.Table

System.Data.DataView.Table

System.Data.DataViewSetting.Table

Syntax

```
currentTable = myRow.Table
```

Parameters

currentTable DataTable reference to table with matching schema.

Returns N/A

Code Sample

```
currentTable = myRow.Table
```

See Also DataType

8

WriteXml Method

Writes the specified DataSet into an XML-format file.

Description   When this method is executed, the schema and all rows and columns of the specified DataSet are written to a XML file. The XML file can be written using either the TextWriter or the XmlWriter.

Class Occurrence

System.Data.DataSet.WriteXml

System.XML.Serialization.IXmlSerializable.WriteXml

Syntax

```
myDataSet.WriteXml(fileName)
myDataSet.WriteXml(fileName, mode)
myDataSet.WriteXml(stream)
myDataSet.WriteXml(textWriter)
myDataSet.WriteXml(textWriter, mode)
myDataSet.WriteXml(xmlWriter)
myDataSet.WriteXml(xmlWriter, mode)
```

Parameters

fileName   The filename and path to which the XML file is written.

stream   A Stream object that will accept the XML output from this method.

mode   XmlWriteMode is an integer that specifies one of three modes: WriteSchema, IgnoreSchema, and DiffGram. WriteSchema (0) is the default setting that stores the XSD data in the file, in addition to the data. The IgnoreSchema (1) option instructs the method not to write the XSD data schema into the file, but only the data itself. DiffGram (2) writes the DataSet, including both the original values and any value changes that haven't yet been updated to the data source.

textWriter   A textWriter object that will accept the XML output from this method.

xmlWriter   An xmlWriter object that will accept the XML output from this method.

Returns   N/A

Code Sample

```
Private Sub cmdWriteXML_Click(ByVal sender As _
  System.Object, ByVal e As System.EventArgs) _
  Handles cmdWriteXML.Click
    Dim myDS As DataSet
    Dim myConn As OleDbConnection, myCmd As OleDbCommand
    Dim myConnStr As String
    Dim myDataAdapter As OleDbDataAdapter

    ' Open the Northwind database
    myConnStr = "Provider=Microsoft.Jet.OLEDB.4.0;" & _
      "Password=;User ID=Admin;Data Source=" & _
      "C:\myData\FPNWIND.MDB;Mode=Share Deny None;"
    myDataAdapter = New OleDbDataAdapter()
    myConn = New OleDbConnection(myConnStr)
    myCmd = New OleDbCommand()

    myCmd.CommandType = CommandType.Text
    myCmd.CommandText = "Select * from Employees"
    myCmd.Connection = myConn
    myDataAdapter.TableMappings.Add("Table", "Employees")
    myConn.Open()
    myDataAdapter.SelectCommand = myCmd
    myDS = New DataSet("myEmployees")
    ' Grab all of the data for the employees
    myDataAdapter.Fill(myDS)
    myConn.Close()

    ' Create a file stream
    Dim myFileStream As New _
      System.IO.FileStream("c:\Employees.xml", _
      System.IO.FileMode.Create)
    ' Create an XML writer to send XML to the file stream
    Dim myXmlWriter As New System.Xml.XmlTextWriter( _
      myFileStream, System.Text.Encoding.Unicode)
    ' Write the DataSet myDS into the XML file
    myDS.WriteXml(myXmlWriter)
    myXmlWriter.Close()
End Sub
```

See Also   GetXml

8

Chapter 9
Excel XP Object Model Diagrams

Excel was the first application to incorporate VBA and provides a robust object implementation. Spreadsheets break down in a very hierarchical manner, so the Excel XP object model will appear in a way that is logical and consistent. By browsing through the object model diagram to understand the basic organization, you will be able to quickly locate the object that you need.

All open files are stored as Workbook objects in the Workbooks collection. In turn, each Worksheet in a Workbook is stored within the Worksheets collection. Cells can be accessed individually or selected as a set. All cells are accessible from the Range object. Note that there is only a single Range object, not a collection of Range objects. Therefore, if you need to access several different ranges simultaneously, each has to be individually stored.

Although all of the objects in the model are shown in this chapter's object diagram, only the most useful properties and objects are detailed in the following section. For complete object and member declarations, examine the model itself in the Object Browser.

9

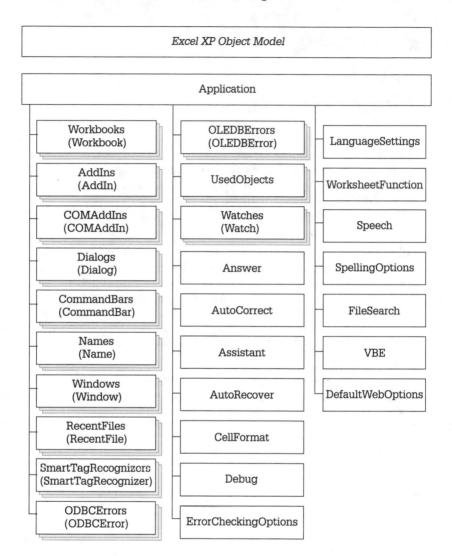

Excel XP Object Model

Application

Workbooks (Workbook)	OLEDBErrors (OLEDBError)	LanguageSettings
AddIns (AddIn)	UsedObjects	WorksheetFunction
COMAddIns (COMAddIn)	Watches (Watch)	Speech
Dialogs (Dialog)	Answer	SpellingOptions
CommandBars (CommandBar)	AutoCorrect	FileSearch
Names (Name)	Assistant	VBE
Windows (Window)	AutoRecover	DefaultWebOptions
RecentFiles (RecentFile)	CellFormat	
SmartTagRecognizers (SmartTagRecognizer)	Debug	
ODBCErrors (ODBCError)	ErrorCheckingOptions	

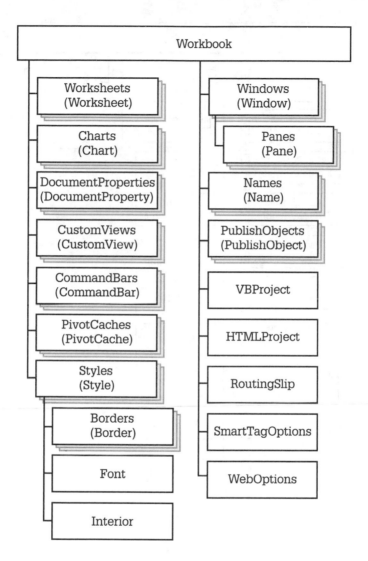

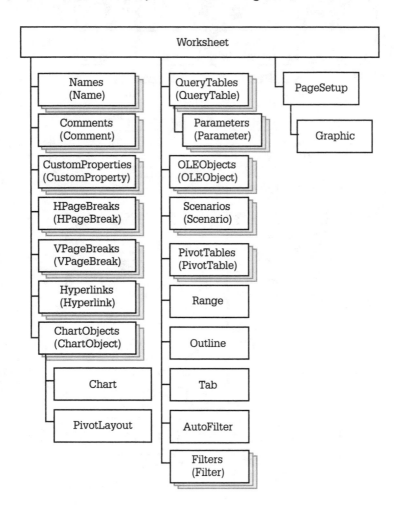

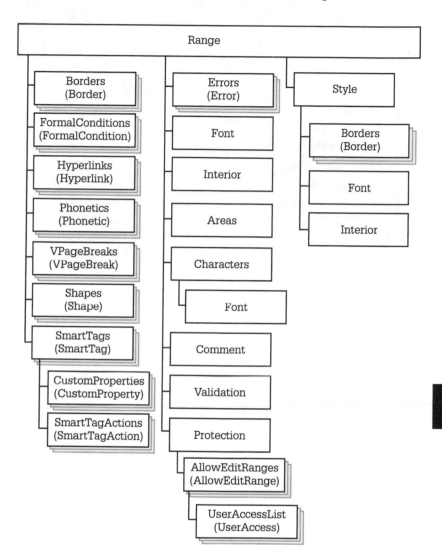

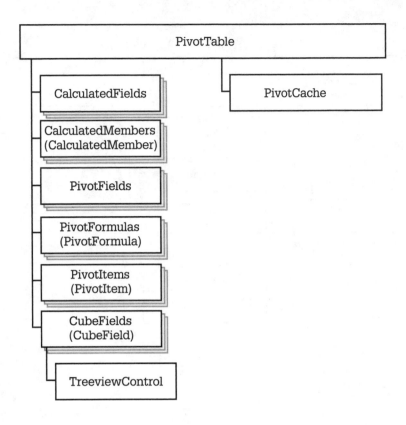

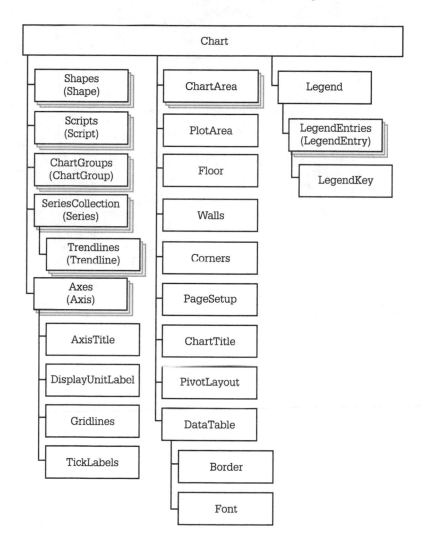

9

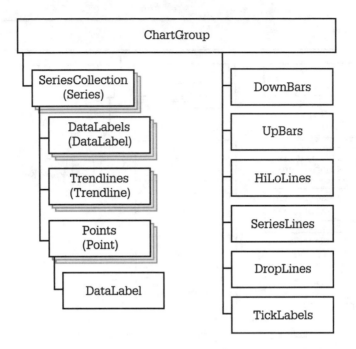

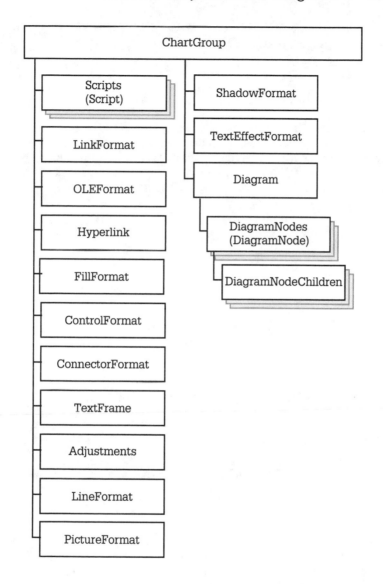

Activate Method

Activates the current specified object.

Description   The Activate method can be used to activate a
Workbook, Worksheet, Chart, Window, Pane, Range, or OLE object.
It functions essentially like the Select method for Workbook,
Worksheet, Chart, Range, and OLE objects. To activate a single
cell (with the Range object), it is recommended you use this
method instead of Select.

Syntax
```
[object.] Activate
```

Parameters   N/A

Returns   N/A

Immediate Window Sample
```
WorkSheets("Sheet2").Activate
' A shorthand version of the same command
Sheets("Sheet2").Activate
```

See Also   ActiveSheet, ActiveWorkbook, Select

ActiveCell Property

Returns an object reference to the currently active cell of the active
sheet of the active workbook.

Description   The ActiveCell property can be used to quickly
set or determine information about the current cell. The value
contained within a cell, the formula, and the formatting are all
obtainable through this property.

Syntax
```
[Application.] ActiveCell
```

Parameters   N/A

Returns   Variant type

Immediate Window Sample
```
? ActiveCell.Value
```

See Also   ActiveSheet, ActiveWorkbook

ActiveSheet Property

Returns an object reference to the current active sheet of the active workbook.

Description   This property gives instant access to the currently selected sheet. It is especially useful when a button or macro is used to modify a worksheet the user has selected. If no sheet is selected, access through the ActiveSheet object generates an error.

Syntax
```
[Application.] ActiveSheet
```

Parameters   N/A

Returns   N/A

Immediate Window Sample
```
? ActiveSheet.Name
```

See Also   ActiveCell, ActiveWorkbook

9

ActiveWorkbook Property

Returns an object reference to the currently active workbook.

Description   This read-only property gives access to the current workbook displayed in the active window. If no window is open or only the clipboard window or info window is displayed, this property contains the value of Nothing.

Syntax

```
[Application.] ActiveWorkbook
```

Parameters   N/A

Returns   N/A

Immediate Window Sample

```
? ActiveWorkbook.Name
```

See Also   ActiveCell, ActiveSheet

Add Method

Used to add worksheets, workbooks, and so on.

Description   Use this method to add an object to the current object collection. The Immediate window example demonstrates how a Workbook object can be added to the current Excel workspace and a worksheet can be added to the current Workbook. The Add method creates instances of these objects in memory, but doesn't automatically save them. When creating an automated solution that will be transparent to the user, make sure to save or close the documents that you've added or modified. Otherwise, the program will stop execution and wait for the user to supply information to the Save File dialog box.

Syntax

```
Set myObject = object.Add
```

Parameters   N/A

Returns   Object type

Immediate Window Sample

```
Application.Workbooks.Add
Set a = ActiveWorkbook.Sheets.Add
```

See Also   ActiveSheet, ActiveWorkbook, DisplayAlerts

AutoFilter Method

Toggles the AutoFilter setting to place the current sheet or selection in Filter mode.

Description   Using the AutoFilter from a VBA program can be the quickest way to do multivariable queries. The AutoFilter may be used to select columns of information that match specific criteria. The rows that match these criteria can be copied to the Clipboard and pasted into another sheet. Use the Macro Recorder to understand how this works.

An idiosyncrasy of the AutoFilter is the first row inclusion. If the first physical row in the sheet matches the criteria, it becomes the first logical row in the AutoFilter. However, if the first physical row does not match the criteria, the second logical row on the sheet begins the set that matches the criteria. If your program uses the AutoFilter, be sure to manually check the first row to determine where to begin copying.

Syntax

```
range.AutoFilter([Field], [Criteria1], [Operator],
   [Criteria2], [VisibleDropDown])
```

9

Parameters

range   Range object to begin AutoFilter.

Field   Field # to conduct filter.

Criteria1, Criteria2   Values to match for the filter.

Operator   Optional. Can be set to determine how filtered results are displayed. Also allows Criteria1 and Criteria2 to have And or Or logical operators. Values may include xlAnd, xlBottom10Items, xlBottom10Percent, xlOr, xlTop10Items, or xlTop10Percent.

VisibleDropDown   Boolean value to determine whether to display the dropdown combobox.

Returns   N/A

Immediate Window Sample
```
Selection.AutoFilter Field:=1, Criteria1:="1/1/97"
Selection.AutoFilter ' Toggles autofilter off
```

See Also   ActiveSheet, ActiveWorkbook

Calculation Property

Holds the mode of calculation for open spreadsheets.

Description   This property determines when changes to a sheet will activate recalculation. Three modes are available: xlCalculationAutomatic, xlCalculationManual, and xlCalculationSemiautomatic. Setting the mode to manual can speed value insertion.

Syntax
```
[Application.] Calculation
```

Parameters   N/A

Returns   N/A

Immediate Window Sample
```
Application.Calculation = xlCalculationManual
```

See Also   Formula

Cells Property

Enables row and column number access to information stored in a particular cell.

Description   This property provides a quick way to access information stored in a cell by its ordinal index values. When creating a program to access individual cells, using this method is often much faster than selecting a range of cells and then retrieving or setting values. The Immediate window example will print the value stored in the cell in row 10, column 8.

Syntax

```
sheetname.Cells(row,col)
```

Parameters

row   Long value containing the row number to access.

col   Long value containing the column number to access.

Returns   Object type

Immediate Window Sample

```
? ActiveSheet.Cells(10,8).Value
```

See Also   Value

Close Method

Closes a window or a workbook.

Description   The Close method is used to close a window (which requires no parameters) or to close a workbook (which can specify saving and routing information). This method can be used to close all current workbooks by issuing the command to the Workbooks collection without any parameters.

Syntax

```
[object.] Close([savechanges,filename,routeworkbook])
```

Parameters

savechanges   Boolean. Specifies whether changes should be saved to current filename or the one specified in the filename parameter. If parameter is omitted, user is prompted to save changes.

9

filename   Filename to save changes into.

routeworkbook   Boolean. Specifies whether changes should be routed. If parameter is omitted, user is prompted for routing instructions.

Returns   N/A

Immediate Window Sample

```
ActiveWorkbook.Close True,"C:\Changes.xls"
Workbooks.Close
ActiveWindow.Close
```

See Also   ActiveSheet, ActiveWorkbook

ColorIndex Property

Holds the color of a border, font, or interior for a cell or group of cells.

Description   The ColorIndex specifies a color based on its position within the Excel palette. For a font, the constant xlColorIndexAutomatic can be used to have the font filled in the default color. An interior can use either the constant xlColorIndexAutomatic or xlColorIndexNone to specify the types of fill.

For the numbers of the other color indexes, see the Excel VBA help file under the ColorIndex entry. Several primary colors in the default Excel color palette are black = 1, white = 2, red = 3, light green = 4, blue = 5, yellow = 6, purple = 7, light blue = 8, dark red = 9, and green = 10.

Syntax

```
[object.] ColorIndex = indexnum
```

Parameters

indexnum   Palette index value.

Returns   N/A

Immediate Window Sample

```
Selection.Interior.ColorIndex = 6
```

See Also   ActiveCell, Cells, Select, Value

Copy Method

Copies the contents of the current object to the Clipboard or to a different part of the worksheet or workbook.

Description   This method can be used to copy a selection or object to the Clipboard, to a range within a workbook, or to a worksheet within a workbook.

Syntax

```
object.Copy
object.Copy(destination)
object.Copy(before,after)
```

Parameters

destination   Range object to which selection will be copied.

before   Worksheet that the sheet will be copied before. If before is specified, after should remain blank.

after   Worksheet that the sheet will be copied after. If after is specified, the before parameter should remain blank.

Returns   N/A

Immediate Window Sample

```
Selection.Copy
Selection.Copy(Cells(5,5))
```

See Also   ActiveSheet, ActiveWorkbook, AutoFilter

9

Delete Method

Deletes an object or range.

Description   Delete can be used to eliminate a specified object or information in a range of cells. When specifying a range to delete, the type of shift (up or left) to the surrounding cells may be passed.

Syntax

```
[object.] Delete
[object.] Delete(shift)
```

Parameters

shift   Direction to shift remaining cells after range is deleted. May be the constants xlShiftToLeft or xlShiftUp.

Returns   N/A

Immediate Window Sample

```
Cells(1,1).Delete
Cells(1,1).EntireRow.Delete
```

See Also   Cells, Select

DisplayAlerts Property

Property that determines whether dialog alerts will be displayed during code execution.

Description   The property can be set to False to prevent a lengthy process from halting for user response. If set to False, the assigned default action for each dialog will be taken. This property does not automatically reset when your program's execution has completed, so be sure to reset it to the appropriate value.

Syntax
[Application.]DisplayAlerts = True|False

Parameters   N/A

Returns   N/A

Immediate Window Sample
DisplayAlerts=False

See Also   Close, ScreenUpdating

FontStyle Property

Holds the style attributes of the Font object

Description   A font's style can be set by using this property. Note that the Bold and Italic properties of the Font object affect and are affected by this property. Setting the Bold property to True makes the "Bold" string appear in the FontStyle string.

Syntax
font.FontStyle = styleString

Parameters
styleString   String of styles used, separated by a space.

Returns   N/A

Immediate Window Sample
? Selection.Font.FontStyle
Selection.Font.FontStyle = "Bold"
Selection.Font.FontStyle = "Bold Italic"

See Also   Select

9

Formula Property

This property enables you to set specifications or to retrieve the formula for a range.

Description Any standard Excel formula can be entered into the Formula property. Setting the Formula property to a particular string is equivalent to typing the equal (=) sign before a formula in a cell.

Syntax
```
cell.Formula = formula
```

Parameters

formula Valid standard format formula string.

Returns N/A

Immediate Window Sample
```
ActiveCell.Formula = "=A1+10"
```

See Also ActiveCell, FormulaR1C1

FormulaR1C1 Property

Enables you to set specifications or to retrieve the formula for a range in Row and Col format.

Description Row and column format enables formulas that access cells relative to the cell that contains the formula to be easily created. For example, the Immediate Window Sample demonstrates a formula that retrieves the value from one column to the left of it and adds the number 10 to the value it finds there.

Syntax
```
range.FormulaR1C1 = formula
```

Parameters
formula   Valid formula string in row and column format.

Returns   N/A

Immediate Window Sample
```
ActiveCell.FormulaR1C1 = "=RC[-1]+10"
```

See Also   ActiveCell, Formula

HorizontalAlignment Property

Determines the horizontal alignment of an object (most often a range or style).

Description   This property can be used to set the justification of a range, style, chart title, label, and so on. The following constants determine the type of alignment: xlHAlignCenter, xlHAlignDistributed, xlHAlignJustify, xlHAlignLeft, and xlHAlignRight. For range and style objects, the following constants may also be used: xlHAlignCenterAcrossSelection, xlHAlignFill, and xlHAlignGeneral.

Syntax
```
object.HorizontalAlignment = alignVal
```

9

Parameters
alignVal   Alignment constant, including xlHAlignCenter, xlHAlignDistributed, xlHAlignJustify, xlHAlignLeft, xlHAlignRight, xlHAlignCenterAcrossSelection, xlHAlignFill, and xlHAlignGeneral.

Returns   Long type

Immediate Window Sample
```
Selection.HorizontalAlignment = xlHAlignLeft
Selection.HorizontalAlignment = xlHAlignRight
```

See Also   Select, VerticalAlignment

Insert Method

Used to insert cells into a worksheet or characters before a string.

Description   Using this method with a worksheet shifts the cells in the specified direction. In a string, the characters are inserted preceding the current string.

Syntax

```
[object.] Insert(shift)
[object.] Insert(insertString)
```

Parameters

shift   Direction to shift the existing cells. Use the constants xlShiftToRight or xlShiftDown to specify the direction.

insertString   String of characters to insert preceding current string.

Returns   N/A

Immediate Window Sample

```
Selection.Insert(xlShiftDown)
ActiveCell.EntireRow.Insert
```

See Also   ActiveSheet, Delete, Select

LineStyle Property

Sets the line style for a Border object.

Description   Excel allows several different line styles to be specified for individual parts of a border for a cell. By using this property, a subroutine could easily be made to automate the creation of a line form for reuse in Excel documents.

Syntax

```
border.LineStyle = borderType
```

Parameters

borderType   The type of border for the selected border sides. Use the following constants to specify the border style: xlContinuous, xlDash, xlDashDot, xlDashDotDot, xlDot, xlDouble, xlSlantDashDot, and xlLineStyleNone.

Returns   Variant type

Immediate Window Sample

```
Selection.Borders(xlEdgeBottom).LineStyle = xlDouble
```

See Also   ActiveSheet, Select

Move Method

Moves a sheet within a workbook.

Description   To move a sheet by using this method, you must specify the sheet either before or after which the selected sheet is to be placed. If the before parameter is specified, the after parameter should be left empty, and vice versa.

Syntax

```
sheet.Move(before,after)
```

Parameters

before   Object reference to a sheet that the specified sheet will be placed before.

after   Object reference to a sheet that the specified sheet will be placed after.

Returns   N/A

Immediate Window Sample

```
ActiveSheet.Move ,Sheets("Sheet3")
```

See Also   ActiveSheet, Close

Name Property

Holds the name of the object that can be used to programmatically reference it.

Description   The Name property holds the string of the name used to reference an object. Instead of using a numeric index with a collection, the name can be used to specify the object.

Syntax
```
object.Name = string
```

Parameters
string   Any string conforming to the standard naming conventions.

Returns   N/A

Immediate Window Sample
```
? ActiveWorkbook.Name
Sheets("Sheet1").Name = "MySheet"
ActiveSheet.Name = "MyActiveSheet"
```

See Also   ActiveSheet, Value

NumberFormat Property

Determines the display format for labels, cells, and styles.

Description   This property will specify the appearance of the value in the label or cell. Formatting characters (# / , 0) and value characters (m, d, y, hh, mm, ss) are the same as those used in the Format Cell dialog box.

Syntax
```
object.NumberFormat = stringVal
```

Parameters

stringVal   Formatting string containing codes of format to display value.

Returns   N/A

Immediate Window Sample

```
ActiveCell.Value = 12
ActiveCell.NumberFormat = "General"
ActiveCell.NumberFormat = "hh:mm:ss m/d/yy"
ActiveCell.NumberFormat = _
  "$###,##0.00_);[Blue]($###,##0.00)"
```

See Also   ActiveCell, Range

Range Object

Used to access one or more cells—the most common object used in Excel VBA programming.

Description   Most programming in Excel uses the Range object to access cell values, appearance, and operation. Ranges may be specified by using cell notation or the Cells property, or by denoting them by any named values that have been assigned.

9

Syntax   N/A

Parameters   N/A

Returns   N/A

Immediate Window Sample

```
Range("A1").Value = 10
Range("A2") = 10
Range("A3") = "Hello"
Range("A1:A8").Formula = "=Rand()"
```

See Also   ActiveCell, Cells, DisplayAlerts

ScreenUpdating Property

Toggles whether updates are displayed on the screen.

Description   Displaying updates takes a great deal of processor time. If the updates are switched off for the duration of a macro execution, the execution time may be greatly decreased. Make sure that you turn updates back on when processing is complete, because Excel does not automatically return to normal display mode.

Syntax

```
Application.ScreenUpdating = True|False
```

Parameters   N/A

Returns   N/A

Immediate Window Sample

```
Application.ScreenUpdating = False
```

See Also   DisplayAlerts

Select Method

Selects an object such as a cell, workbook, chart, or worksheet.

Description   Use the Select method to select an object, particularly a range of cells. Use the Activate method instead for a single cell. The Select method can also be used with a replace parameter to indicate that the specified object will replace the current selection.

Syntax

```
object.Select([replace])
```

Parameters

replace Optional. Boolean. If True, current selection is replaced by specified object.

Returns N/A

Immediate Window Sample
```
Sheets("Sheet3").Select
Range("A1:A8").Select
```

See Also Activate, ActiveSheet, ActiveWorkbook

Value Property

Holds a value for a particular object.

Description The Value property is used extensively within the Excel object model and is particularly useful for setting and retrieving the values of cells.

Syntax
```
object.Value = value
```

Parameters

value Dependent on the object.

Returns N/A

Immediate Window Sample
```
? ActiveCell.Value
```

See Also Name, Range, Select

9

VerticalAlignment Property

Determines the horizontal alignment of an object (most often a range or style).

Description   This property can be used to set the justification of a range, style, chart title, label, and so on. The following constants determine the type of alignment: xlVAlignBottom, xlVAlignCenter, xlVAlignDistributed, xlVAlignJustify, and xlVAlignTop.

Syntax
```
object.VerticalAlignment = alignVal
```

Parameters
alignVal   Alignment constant, including xlVAlignBottom, xlVAlignCenter, xlVAlignDistributed, xlVAlignJustify, and xlVAlignTop.

Returns   Long type

Immediate Window Sample
```
Selection.VerticalAlignment = xlVAlignBottom
Selection.VerticalAlignment = xlVAlignCenter
```

See Also   HorizontalAlignment, Select

Weight Property

Determines the weight or thickness of the border of a range.

Description   Setting the Weight property for a Border or LineFormat object will determine how the cell or range of cells appears.

Syntax
```
border.Weight = lineWeight
```

Parameters

lineWeight   Weight of the border should be one of these constants: xlHairline, xlThin, xlMedium, or xlThick.

Returns   Long type

Immediate Window Sample

```
Selection.Borders.Weight = xlMedium
```

See Also   Range, Select

9

Chapter 10
Word XP Object Model Diagrams

In some areas, the Word XP object model is not as intuitive to grasp as the other Office applications. To understand how Word can be addressed most effectively from a program, frequently record test macros of the sort of tasks that you need to automate. By examining the source code that the recorder generates, you can better understand how Word accomplishes an operation.

Word has some performance issues when progressing through a collection that contains a large number of objects. In a collection of Paragraph objects, for example, macro execution slows dramatically when advancing through a lengthy document. What may appear to execute well on the first 10 paragraphs may take exponentially longer when it reaches paragraph 200. Therefore, make sure you test the macro in real-world conditions in case optimization is required.

Word files are stored in the Documents collection as individual objects. The text itself can be accessed through the Paragraphs collection, but it is most often easier to make necessary changes to the document with selection functions. Some of the Immediate window examples demonstrate this type of functionality.

Although all of the objects in the model are shown in this chapter's object diagram, only the most useful properties and objects are detailed in the following section. For complete object and member declarations, examine the model itself in the Object Browser.

10

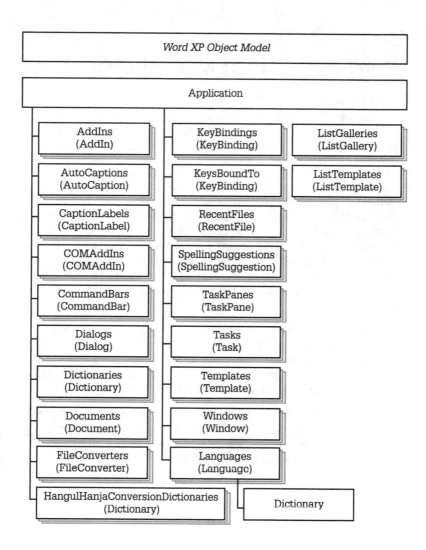

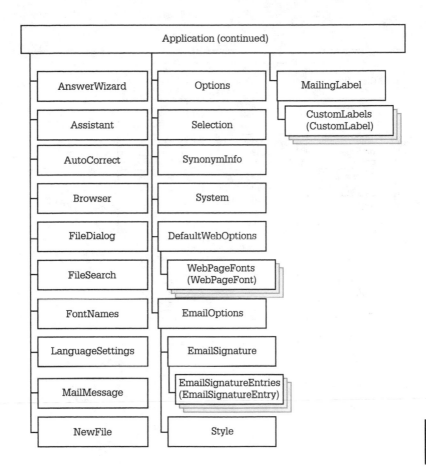

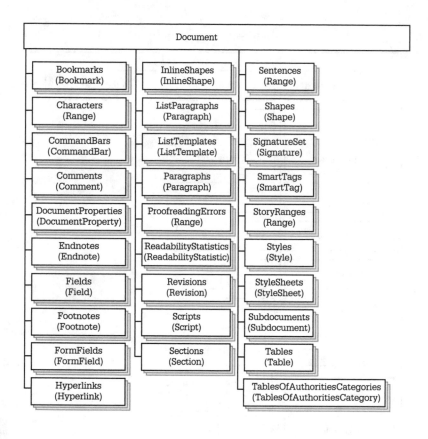

Document

Bookmarks (Bookmark)	InlineShapes (InlineShape)	Sentences (Range)
Characters (Range)	ListParagraphs (Paragraph)	Shapes (Shape)
CommandBars (CommandBar)	ListTemplates (ListTemplate)	SignatureSet (Signature)
Comments (Comment)	Paragraphs (Paragraph)	SmartTags (SmartTag)
DocumentProperties (DocumentProperty)	ProofreadingErrors (Range)	StoryRanges (Range)
Endnotes (Endnote)	ReadabilityStatistics (ReadabilityStatistic)	Styles (Style)
Fields (Field)	Revisions (Revision)	StyleSheets (StyleSheet)
Footnotes (Footnote)	Scripts (Script)	Subdocuments (Subdocument)
FormFields (FormField)	Sections (Section)	Tables (Table)
Hyperlinks (Hyperlink)		TablesOfAuthoritiesCategories (TablesOfAuthoritiesCategory)

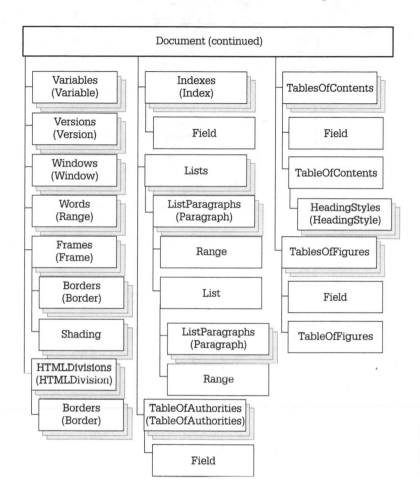

10

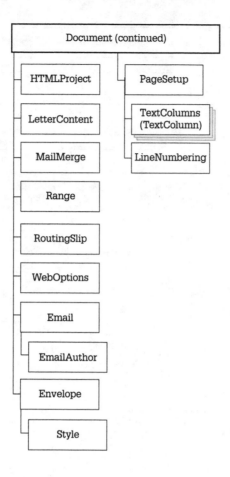

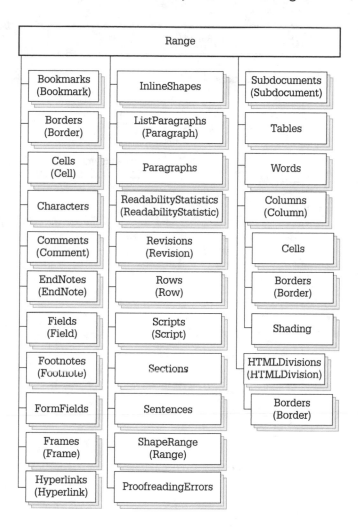

```
                              Range

  Bookmarks           InlineShapes          Subdocuments
  (Bookmark)                                (Subdocument)

  Borders             ListParagraphs        Tables
  (Border)            (Paragraph)

  Cells               Paragraphs            Words
  (Cell)

  Characters          ReadabilityStatistics Columns
                      (ReadabilityStatistic) (Column)

  Comments            Revisions             Cells
  (Comment)           (Revision)

  EndNotes            Rows                  Borders
  (EndNote)           (Row)                 (Border)

  Fields              Scripts               Shading
  (Field)             (Script)

  Footnotes           Sections              HTMLDivisions
  (Footnote)                                (HTMLDivision)

  FormFields          Sentences             Borders
                                            (Border)

  Frames              ShapeRange
  (Frame)             (Range)

  Hyperlinks          ProofreadingErrors
  (Hyperlink)
```

10

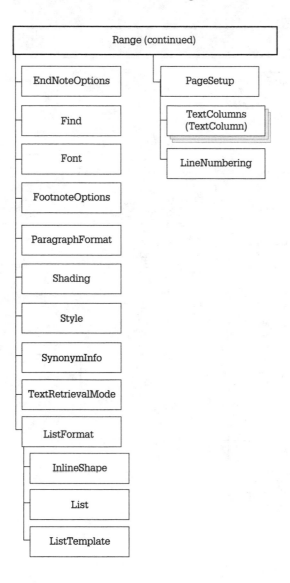

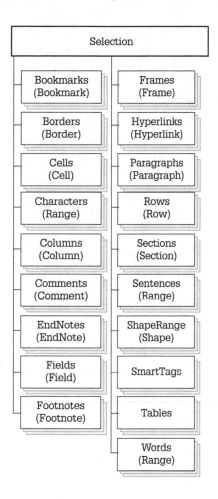

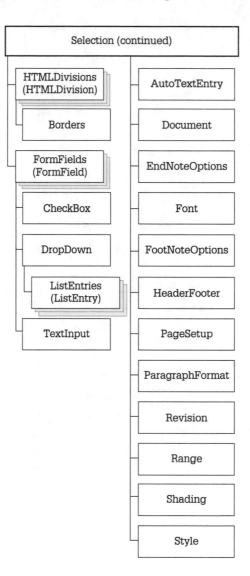

Autocorrect

AutoCorrectEntries (AutoCorrectEntry)	OtherCorrectionsExceptions (OtherCorrectionsException)
FirstLetterExceptions (FirstLetterException)	TwoInitialCapsExceptions (TwoInitialCapsException)
HangulAndAlphabetExceptions (HangulAndAlphabetException)	

10

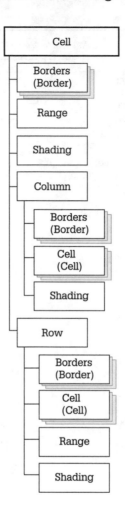

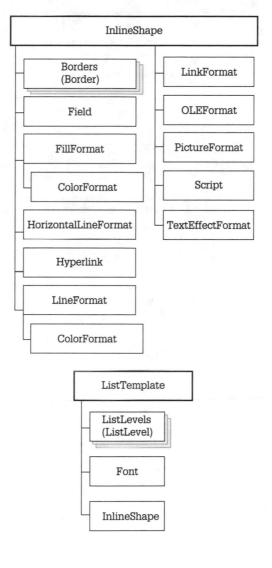

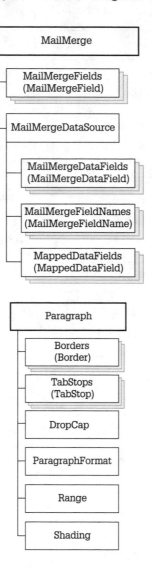

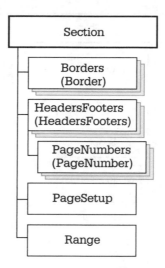

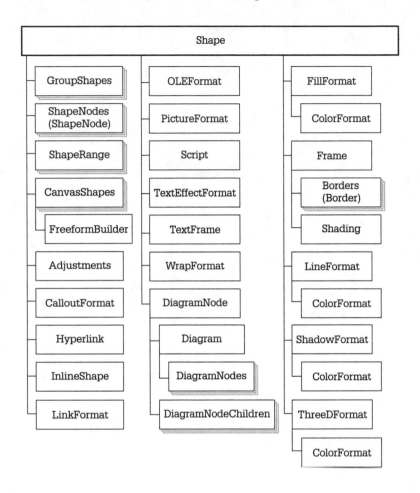

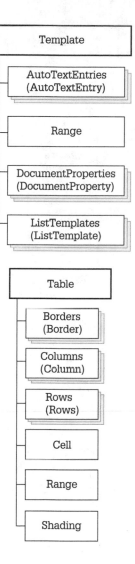

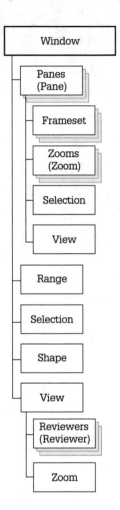

ActiveDocument Property

Holds the object reference to the current active document.

Description   This property can be used to reference the currently selected document in Word.

Syntax
`[Application.] ActiveDocument`

Parameters   N/A

Returns   Document object

Immediate Window Sample
```
? ActiveDocument.Name
Documents(1).Activate
? ActiveDocument.Name
```

See Also   Add

Add Method

Used to add an object to a particular collection.

Description   The Add method can be used, as shown in the Immediate window example, to append a new document to the current Word environment. The Add method can be used on many Word object collections, including AddIns, Bookmarks, Cells, Columns, Comments, Dictionaries, Documents, Fields, Footnotes, Frames, HeadingStyles, Hyperlinks, Indexes, Panes, Paragraphs, Rows, Sections, StyleSheets, Tables, and Windows.

10

Syntax
```
object.Add
```

Parameters   N/A

Returns   N/A

Immediate Window Sample
```
Documents.Add
```

➤ Programming Tip

The parameters accepted by the Add method vary depending on the object used. For example, when adding a new document, you can specify a template that is the basis for the new file. Check the Object Browser for the actual parameters that may be used.

See Also   ActiveDocument, Open

Alignment Property

Holds the alignment of a paragraph.

Description   The type of alignment specified within the Alignment property is held in a number of constants within the Word system. In the Immediate window example, the currently selected paragraph is set to a center alignment.

Syntax
```
object.Alignment = align
```

Parameters

align   A valid alignments constant, such as wdAlignParagraphCenter, wdAlignParagraphLeft, wdAlignParagraphRight, and so on.

Returns   N/A

Immediate Window Sample

```
Selection.ParagraphFormat.Alignment = _
   wdAlignParagraphCenter
```

See Also   Selection

ApplyBulletDefault Method

Toggles the list formatting for a specified paragraph or range.

Description   This method, when executed on normal paragraph, applies list formatting. For a paragraph that is already specified as a list, this method switches list formatting off. This method must be used on a ListFormat object of a Range object.

Syntax

```
listformat.ApplyBulletDefault
```

Parameters   N/A

Returns   N/A

Immediate Window Sample

```
Selection.Range.ListFormat.ApplyBulletDefault
ActiveDocument.Paragraphs(2).Range. _
   ListFormat.ApplyBulletDefault
```

See Also   ActiveDocument

10

Assistant Property

Accesses the animated Assistant to allow custom help for an application.

Description   The animated Assistant seems to inspire both love and hate from Office users, but programmers will find controlling the Assistant fairly easy. Animation may be set using constants such as msoAnimationSearching, msoAnimationAppear, msoAnimationGestureDown, msoAnimationIdle, msoAnimation Greeting, msoAnimationBeginSpeaking, and others. If the user has disabled use of the Assistant, setting the Visible property to True has no effect.

Syntax

```
[Application.] Assistant
```

Parameters N/A

Returns N/A

Immediate Window Sample

```
Assistant.Visible = True
Assistant.Animation = msoAnimationSearching
Assistant.Move 100, 100
```

See Also N/A

Compare Method

Sets up a file comparison and shows comparison marks on the specified document.

Description This method can activate the Microsoft Word feature that enables comparison of two documents. The filename of the document to be compared and comparison marks are automatically displayed.

Syntax

```
[Application.] Compare fileName
```

Parameters

fileName Name of the file to compare to specified document.

Returns N/A

Immediate Window Sample

```
ActiveDocument.Compare "C:\draft1.doc"
```

See Also ActiveDocument

ComputeStatistics Method

Recalculates statistics for specified range or document.

Description   This method will calculate the statistics either for the entire document or a specified range. Parameters allow the inclusion/exclusion of footnotes and endnotes and the specification of exactly the type of statistic to return.

Syntax

```
statValue = [object.] ComputeStatistics(statistic
   [,includefootnotesandendnotes] )
```

Parameters

statistic   Determines the type of statistic to be returned. Use one of these constants: wdStatisticCharacters, wdStatisticCharactersWithSpaces, wdStatisticLines, wdStatisticPages, wdStatisticParagraphs, wdStatisticFarEastCharacters, or wdStatisticWords.

includefootnotesandendnotes   Determines whether footnotes and endnotes are included. Default is set to False.

statValue   Calculated return of type specified with statistic parameter.

Returns   Long type

Immediate Window Sample

```
? ActiveDocument.ComputeStatistics(wdStatisticPages)
```

See Also   ActiveDocument

10

FirstLineIndent Property

Determines the indent of the first line of the paragraph.

Description Specified in points, this property holds the first line indent value. The property may be set for individual paragraphs, styles, or a range of paragraphs.

Syntax

```
paragraph FirstLineIndent = indentVal
```

Parameters

indentVal In points, the value to indent on the first line of the paragraph.

Returns Variant type

Immediate Window Sample

```
ActiveDocument.Paragraphs(1).FirstLineIndent = 72
ActiveDocument.Paragraphs(1).FirstLineIndent = _
   InchesToPoints(1)
```

See Also ActiveDocument, Paragraphs

Font Object

Holds all of the font formatting information for a piece of text.

Description The Font object can be set to any available font, size, and style settings that are normally available in Word. The Immediate window example changes the font of the current selection in a variety of ways.

Syntax

```
range.Font
```

Parameters N/A

Returns N/A

Immediate Window Sample

```
Selection.Font.Name = "Times New Roman"
Selection.Font.Size = 10
Selection.Font.Bold = True
Selection.Font.Italic = True
```

See Also Selection

Height Property

Holds the height of the specified object.

Description   The height of most objects may be adjusted with the Height property, including shapes, rows, columns, tasks, windows, frames, custom labels, inline shapes, and so on.

Syntax
```
object.Height = height
```

Parameters
height   Height value within the limits of the object. Value is stored as a Single type.

Returns   N/A

Immediate Window Sample
```
ActiveWindow.WindowState = wdWindowStateNormal
ActiveWindow.Height = ActiveWindow.Height / 2
```

➤ Programming Tip

By using the Width and Height properties to configure the windows, you can create a custom macro to adjust the window settings to the sizes you most commonly use.

10

See Also   Width

InsertBefore Method

Inserts text before the indicated object.

Description   The InsertBefore method may be used with either a Range or Selection to insert text into the document. The Immediate window example demonstrates inserting the word "Hello" before the first word of the first paragraph of the document.

Syntax

```
object.InsertBefore(string)
```

Parameters

string   Any valid Unicode string.

Returns   N/A

Immediate Window Sample

```
ActiveDocument.Range.Paragraphs(1).Range.Words(1). _
    InsertBefore "Hello"
```

See Also   Selection

LeftIndent Property

Determines the left indent of the specified paragraph, styles, or range of paragraphs.

Description   This property will specify the left indent of a particular paragraph, range, or style. The indent is specified in points (1 inch = approximately 72 points).

Syntax

```
paragraph.LeftIndent = leftValue
```

Parameters

leftValue   Amount in points to left-indent the paragraph.

Returns   Single type

Immediate Window Sample

```
ActiveDocument.Paragraphs(1).LeftIndent = 72
```

See Also   FirstLineIndent, RightIndent

LineSpacing Property

Holds the line spacing value of the specified paragraph, styles, or range of paragraphs.

Description   This property indicates the line spacing of a particular paragraph, range, or style. The spacing is specified in points (1 inch = approximately 72 points).

Syntax
```
paragraph.LineSpacing = lineValue
```

Parameters

lineValue   Amount in points of the line space for the paragraph.

Returns   Single type

Immediate Window Sample
```
Selection.Paragraphs.LineSpacing = 16
Selection.Paragraphs.LineSpacing = LinesToPoints(2)
```

See Also   Paragraphs

ListParagraphs Property

10

Holds the object reference to all of the numbered paragraphs within a range or document.

Description   All of the List Paragraphs contained within a document can be accessed individually through this property. The For...Each loop can be used to sequentially progress through each list paragraph. To work properly, the Immediate window example expects either a numbered or bulleted list setting for the first paragraph of the document.

Syntax
```
document.ListParagraphs
```

Parameters   N/A

Returns   N/A

Immediate Window Sample
```
Documents(1).ListParagraphs(1).Shading. _
  BackgroundPatternColorIndex = wdBlue
```

See Also   ActiveDocument, Paragraphs

MoveDown Method

Moves the selection cursor down one unit.

Description   The Move methods may be used with either a Range or Selection, and units and type of move may be defined. Movement is possible in units of lines, paragraphs, windows, or screens.

Syntax
```
object.MoveDown([,units,count [,extend]])
```

Parameters

units   Move down in the units specified by the constant wdLine, wdParagraph, wdWindow, or wdScreen.

count   Number of units to move selection.

extend   Determines whether selection is moved or extended. Use the constant wdMove or wdExtend.

Returns   N/A

Immediate Window Sample
```
Selection.MoveDown
Selection.MoveDown wdParagraph,1
Selection.MoveDown wdParagraph,1,wdExtend
```

See Also   MoveLeft, MoveRight, MoveUp

MoveLeft Method

Moves the selection cursor left one unit.

Description   The Move methods may be used with either a Range or Selection. The units and type of move may be specified, as well as whether the movement occurs in units of cells, characters, words, or sentences.

Syntax

```
object.MoveLeft([,units,count [,extend]])
```

Parameters

units   Move left in the units specified by the constant wdCell, wdCharacter, wdWord, or wdSentence.

count   Number of units to move selection.

extend   Determines whether selection is moved or extended. Use the constant wdMove or wdExtend.

Returns   N/A

Immediate Window Sample

```
Selection.MoveLeft
Selection.MoveLeft wdCharacter,1
Selection.MoveLeft wdCharacter,1,wdExtend
```

See Also   MoveDown, MoveRight, MoveUp

10

MoveRight Method

Moves the selection cursor right one unit.

Description   The Move methods may be used with either a Range or Selection, and units and type of move may be specified. Movement occurs in units of cells, characters, words, or sentences.

Syntax

`object.MoveRight([,unit,count [,extend]])`

Parameters

units Move right in the units specified by the constant wdCell, wdCharacter, wdWord, or wdSentence.

count Number of units to move selection.

extend Determines whether selection is moved or extended. Use the constant wdMove or wdExtend.

Returns N/A

Immediate Window Sample

```
Selection.MoveRight
Selection.MoveRight wdCharacter,1
Selection.MoveRight wdCharacter,1,wdExtend
```

See Also MoveDown, MoveLeft, MoveUp

MoveUp Method

Moves the current selection up one unit.

Description The Move methods may be used with either a Range or Selection, and units and type of move may be specified. Move in units of lines, paragraphs, windows, or screens.

Syntax

`object.MoveUp([,units,count [,extend]])`

Parameters

units Move up in the units specified by the constant wdLine, wdParagraph, wdWindow, or wdScreen.

count Number of units to move selection.

extend Determines whether selection is moved or extended. Use the constant wdMove or wdExtend.

Returns   N/A

Immediate Window Sample

```
Selection.MoveUp
Selection.MoveUp wdParagraph,1
Selection.MoveUp wdParagraph,1,wdExtend
```

See Also   MoveDown, MoveLeft, MoveRight

Name Property

Holds the name of the object that can be used to programmatically reference it.

Description   The Name property holds the string of the name used to reference an object. Instead of using a numeric index with a collection, the name can be used to specify the object.

Syntax

```
object.Name = string
```

Parameters

string   Any string conforming to the standard naming conventions.

Returns   N/A

Immediate Window Sample

```
? ActiveDocument.Name
```

10

➤ Programming Tip

The Name property of a document is read-only. To change the name, you must use the SaveAs method.

See Also   ActiveDocument

Open Method

Opens the specified object.

Description   This method can be used to open files through a number of objects (such as Documents or RecentFiles).

Syntax
```
object.Open(filename$)
```

Parameters

filename$ May specify the path and filename of any file Word can open.

Returns   Object type

Immediate Window Sample
```
Documents.Open "c:\mydoc.doc"
```

See Also   Add

Paragraphs Collection

Holds all of the paragraphs for a particular document.

Description   The individual objects stored in the Paragraphs collection hold all of the actual text, style, and other information for each paragraph of a document. Accessing long documents by individual paragraph objects can be a slow process.

Syntax
```
object.Paragraphs(index)
```

Parameters

index   Paragraph number to be accessed.

Returns   N/A

Immediate Window Sample

```
? ActiveDocument.Range.Paragraphs.Count
ActiveDocument.Range.Paragraphs(1).Range.Words(1) _
   ="Hello"
```

See Also   Add

RightIndent Property

Determines the right indent of the specified paragraph, styles, or range of paragraphs.

Description   This property will specify the right indent of a particular paragraph, range, or style. The indent is specified in points (1 inch = approximately 72 points).

Syntax

```
paragraph.RightIndent = rightValue
```

Parameters

rightValue   Amount in points to right-indent the paragraph.

Returns   Single type

Immediate Window Sample

```
Selection.Paragraphs.RightIndent = 72
```

See Also   FirstLineIndent, LeftIndent

10

Selection Object

Holds the range of the current selection.

Description   The Selection object provides access to the current user selection. Manipulating the Selection object also allows a document to be quickly and easily modified.

Syntax

```
[Application].Selection
```

Parameters   N/A

Returns   N/A

Immediate Window Sample
```
Selection.TypeText "Replace"
```

See Also   InsertBefore

Shading Property

Holds the reference to the Shading object used by other objects, such as paragraphs.

Description   Setting properties of the Shading object can render the background, foreground, and shading texture of objects.

Syntax
```
object.Shading
```

Parameters   N/A

Returns   N/A

Immediate Window Sample
```
Selection.Paragraphs.Shading.Texture = _
   wdTexture12Pt5Percent
Selection.Paragraphs.Shading.BackgroundPatternColorIndex _
   = wdRed
```

See Also   Selection

SpaceAfter Property

Determines the amount of space after a specified paragraph, style, or range of paragraphs.

Description   This property specifies the amount of space after a particular paragraph, range, or style. The spacing is specified in points (1 inch = approximately 72 points).

Syntax

```
paragraph.SpaceAfter = afterValue
```

Parameters

afterValue   Amount in points of space after the paragraph.

Returns   Single type

Immediate Window Sample

```
Selection.Paragraphs.SpaceAfter = 12
```

See Also   LineSpacing, SpaceBefore

SpaceBefore Property

Determines the amount of space before a specified paragraph, style, or range of paragraphs.

Description   This property specifies the amount of space before a particular paragraph, range, or style. The spacing is specified in points (1 inch = approximately 72 points).

Syntax

```
paragraph.SpaceBefore = beforeValue
```

Parameters

beforeValue   Amount in points of space before the paragraph.

Returns   Single type

Immediate Window Sample

```
Selection.Paragraphs.SpaceBefore = 12
```

See Also   LineSpacing, SpaceAfter

10

TypeBackspace Method

Backspaces at the current selection.

Description The method provides the same functionality (including across multiple selected characters) as the user pressing the BACKSPACE key.

Syntax
`object.TypeBackspace`

Parameters N/A

Returns N/A

Immediate Window Sample
`Selection.TypeBackspace`

See Also Paragraphs, Selection

TypeText Method

Enters text at the current selection.

Description Text is entered as if from the keyboard. This means that any currently selected text is automatically deleted.

Syntax
`object.TypeText string`

Parameters
string Any valid character string.

Returns N/A

Immediate Window Sample
`Selection.TypeText "Hello World"`

See Also Paragraphs, Selection, TypeBackspace

Width Property

Holds the width of the specified object.

Description   The width of most objects may be adjusted with the Width property, including shapes, rows, columns, tasks, windows, frames, custom labels, inline shapes, and so on.

Syntax

```
object.Width = width
```

Parameters

width   Width value within the limits of the object. Value is stored as a Single type.

Returns   N/A

Immediate Window Sample

```
ActiveWindow.WindowState = wdWindowStateNormal
ActiveWindow.Width = ActiveWindow.Width / 2
```

See Also   Height

10

Chapter 11
Outlook Object Model Diagrams

The customization available by programming Microsoft Outlook provides one of the most powerful incentives to use it over other Personal Information Manager (PIM) programs. The way that individuals want to interact with their personal information varies dramatically. What is comfortable for one person is tedious and foreign to another.

By programming Outlook, a custom environment can be created to handle and display everything from scheduling to notes to contacts in nearly any format. All the information contained in the Calendar, Contacts, Drafts, Inbox, Journal, Notes, Outbox, Sent Items, and Tasks folders is available for access and modification through program code. Because you can create custom user forms in the programming environment, all of this information can be provided in any manner.

Be aware that there are many security settings within Outlook, particularly related to code access to the address book. For example, if you try the Immediate window example for the Address property, you will be prompted with a security alert window. To avoid confusion, make sure that users of a program are aware of security display dialogs.

Although all of the objects in the model are shown in this chapter's object diagram, only the most useful properties and objects are detailed in the following section. For complete object and member declarations, examine the model itself in the Object Browser.

11

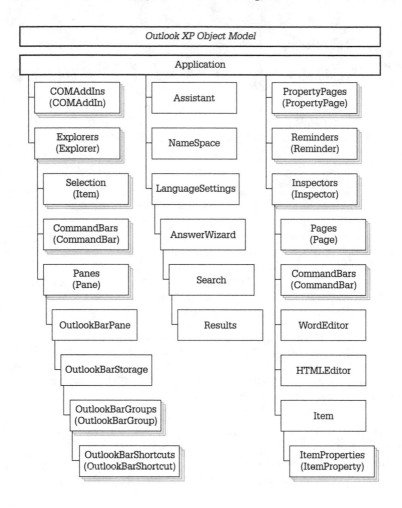

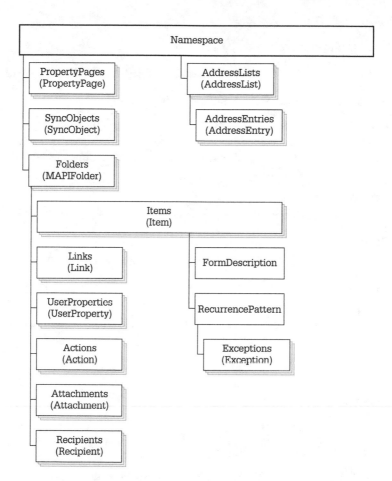

Address Property

Holds the e-mail address of the specified recipient.

Description   This property holds an e-mail address after a recipient has been added. The e-mail address is retrieved from the Address book. Use this property to determine or change the e-mail address for the mail item.

Syntax
```
recipient.Address = email
```

Parameters
email   String. Holds specified mail item e-mail address.

Returns   Variant type

Immediate Window Sample
```
Set myItem = Application.CreateItem(olMailItem)
Set myRecipient = myItem.Recipients.Add("Dan Rahmel")
MsgBox myRecipient.Name
myItem.Save
```

See Also   CreateItem

Body Property

Contains the body text of an item.

Description   This property contains the plain text (or clear text) of an item such as a mail message or a post. Change the body of the item by changing the value of this property.

Syntax
```
item.Body = text
```

Parameters
text   String. Body text of message.

Returns   String type

Immediate Window Sample

```
Set myItem = Application.CreateItem(olNoteItem)
myItem.Body = "Welcome to VB Script!"
myItem.Save
```

See Also   Address, CreateItem

ClearRecurrencePattern Method

Clears the recurrence pattern for an appointment or task.

Description   Calling this method resets the item to a single occurrence state for the specified task or appointment.

Syntax
```
appointment.ClearRecurrencePattern
```

Parameters   N/A

Returns   N/A

Immediate Window Sample
```
myItem.ClearRecurrencePattern
```

See Also   Duration

Controls Property

11

Provides access to controls stored on a modified tab.

Description   Each tab on an Outlook form can have controls such as Text Box, List Box, Check Box, Options, and so on. The Controls property provides access to the Controls collection for a tab.

Syntax
```
object.Controls
```

Parameters   N/A

Returns N/A

Immediate Window Sample
```
Set myCtls = _
  ActiveInspector.ModifiedFormPages("(P.1)").Controls
If myCtls("chkMyBox") Then MsgBox "Checked"
```

See Also GetInspector

Count Property

Returns the number of items in collection.

Description To determine the number of objects in a collection, access the Count property. Although the For...Next loop can be used with the Count property, Microsoft recommends that you use a For...Each loop to move through an object collection.

Syntax
```
collection.Count
```

Parameters N/A

Returns Long type

Immediate Window Sample
```
MsgBox GetNamespace("MAPI").Folders.Count
```

See Also GetDefaultFolder

CreateItem Method

Creates a new Outlook item.

Description The CreateItem method adds a new contact, note, or other Outlook item to the current file.

Syntax

```
Set object = Application.CreateItem(itmType)
```

Parameters

itmType   Type of new item to insert.

Returns   Object type

Immediate Window Sample

```
Set newContact = _
  Application.CreateItem(olContactItem)
newContact.Save
Set newNote = Application.CreateItem(olNoteItem)
newNote.Save
```

See Also   Controls

CreateObject Method

Creates an object reference based on the class or class ID specified.

Description   This method instantiates an OLE Automation object from the specified class or class ID.

Syntax

```
Set object = CreateObject(class)
```

Parameters

class   Class identified by string that contains either the class name or the class ID.

11

Returns   Object type

Immediate Window Sample

```
Set myObject = CreateObject("Outlook.Application")
Set nms = myObject.GetNameSpace("MAPI")
```

See Also   CreateItem

CurrentFolder Property

Determines the current folder shown in the Explorer.

Description   The CurrentFolder property holds the category of folder that is selected for the user to view.

Syntax

```
explorer.CurrentFolder = folderRef
```

Parameters

folderRef   Reference to the folder that is shown in the Explorer view.

Returns   MAPIFolder type

Immediate Window Sample

```
Set ActiveExplorer.CurrentFolder = _
  GetNameSpace("MAPI").GetDefaultFolder(olFolderCalendar)
```

See Also   GetNameSpace

CurrentUser Property

Holds the identification of the user currently logged into Outlook.

Description   Accessing the CurrentUser property provides the name of the currently logged-in user. Using the property can allow recording the name of someone who is accessing the item. If no user is currently logged into the Outlook system, the string "Unknown" is held in this property.

Syntax

```
namespace.CurrentUser
```

Parameters   N/A

Returns   N/A

Immediate Window Sample

```
Set nms = Application.GetNameSpace("MAPI")
MsgBox nms.CurrentUser
```

See Also   GetNameSpace

Display Method

Displays the specified item.

Description   Calling the Display method makes an item visible. When a new item is created, the item is invisible by default. An item can be a Contact sheet, a Meeting, an Email entry, or any other Outlook form-based object.

Syntax

```
object.Display
```

Parameters   N/A

Returns   N/A

Immediate Window Sample

```
Set newContact = _
  Application.CreateItem(olContactItem)
newContact.Display
```

See Also   CreateItem, DisplayName

DisplayName Property

11

Determines the caption below the attachment.

Description   The DisplayName property may be used to set an attachment to a piece of mail to something other than the actual filename. Thus, even if you're sending to a system using the eight-character DOS file name convention, the name on the attachment can be descriptive.

Syntax

```
attach.DisplayName = name
```

Parameters

name   String. Contains the name that will be displayed on the attachment when item is viewed.

Returns   String type

Immediate Window Sample

```
Set myItem = Application.CreateItem(olMailItem)
Set myAttachments = myItem.Attachments
Set myAttach = myAttachments.Add("C:\test.xls")
myAttach.DisplayName = "This is a test"
myItem.Display
```

See Also   Body, CreateItem

Duration Property

Determines the duration in minutes of the appointment.

Description   Sets the duration of an appointment or journal entry in minutes. This property is also used within an appointment item for the recurrence pattern.

Syntax

```
item.Duration - minutes
```

Parameters

minutes   Long. Duration in minutes.

Returns   Long type

Immediate Window Sample

```
Set myItem = _
  Application.CreateItem(olAppointmentItem)
myItem.Duration = 48 * 60 ! 2 days = 48 hrs * 60 min
myItem.Start = now
myitem.Subject = "myMeeting"
myitem.Save
```

See Also   ClearRecurrencePattern

FileAs Property

Contains the keyword string when a contact is filed.

Description   This property is automatically initialized when contact is first created. Use the property to set or retrieve the default keyword string.

Syntax
```
item.FileAs = fileStr
```

Parameters
fileStr   String. Default keyword string assigned to contact.

Returns   String type

Immediate Window Sample
```
Set myItem = Application.CreateItem(olContactItem)
myItem.FileAs = "DP artist"
myItem.Save
```

See Also   CreateItem, DisplayName

GetDefaultFolder Method

Provides a reference to one of the default folders.

Description   Complete access to the items within a folder is possible once an object reference to the folder itself is obtained.

Syntax
```
Set myObject = object.GetDefaultFolder(fnum)
```

Parameters
fnum   Contains the index number of the desired folder.

Returns   Object type

11

Immediate Window Sample
```
Set myContacts = _
  GetNameSpace("MAPI").GetDefaultFolder(olFolderContacts)
```

See Also   GetNameSpace

GetInspector Property

Provides the top-level Inspector object associated with the specified item.

Description   The Inspector is required to access many parts of the Outlook system. Code on an Item form can obtain a reference to this root object by using the GetInspector property. You can also use this property in order to compare the associated Inspector object with the Application.ActiveInspector property to determine whether they are the same.

Syntax
```
Set myObject = object.GetInspector
```

Parameters
object   Valid Item object.

Returns   Object type

Immediate Window Sample
```
Set a - myItem.GetInspector
```

See Also   CreateItem

GetNameSpace Method

Returns the object reference to the NameSpace object of the type specified.

Description   This method returns a reference to the root data source. The object can be used to retrieve information from the folders, to get user information, and to access other data sources. Currently, only the "MAPI" namespace type is supported.

Syntax

```
Set object = GetNameSpace(type)
```

Parameters

type   String. Namespace type to return object reference.

Returns   String type

Immediate Window Sample

```
Set nms = Application.GetNameSpace("MAPI")
```

See Also   CreateItem, GetDefaultFolder

Importance Property

Determines the importance of an Outlook item.

Description   This property contains the importance level (low, normal, or high) of an item. This property is available to every item type.

Syntax

```
item.Importance = level
```

Parameters

level   Long. The level can be set to one of three values: olImportanceLow (0), olImportanceNormal (1), or olImportanceHigh (2).

Returns   Long type

Immediate Window Sample

```
Set myItem = _
  Application.CreateItem(olAppointmentItem)
myItem.Importance = olImportanceHigh
myItem.Start = Now
```

11

```
myItem.Subject = "Emergency"
myItem.Save
```

See Also   CreateItem, ClearRecurrencePattern, Duration

MeetingStatus Property

Determines the meeting status of an Appointment item.

Description   The MeetingStatus property can indicate the status of a meeting and make the MeetingRequestItem available to the Appointment item.

Syntax
```
item.MeetingStatus = meetType
```

Parameters

meetType   Long. The type can be set to one of four values: olMeeting (1), olMeetingCanceled (5), olMeetingReceived (3), or olNonMeeting (0).

Returns   Long type

Immediate Window Sample
```
Set myItem = _
  Application.CreateItem(olAppointmentItem)
myItem.MeetingStatus = olMeeting
myItem.Start = Now
myItem.Save
```

See Also   CreateItem, ClearRecurrencePattern, Duration

ModifiedFormPages Property

Holds reference to the tabs in the user-modifiable tabs collection.

Description   In Outlook, all form construction occurs on the additional hidden tabs of an Item object. This property provides a reference to enable access to items on the modified pages.

Syntax

object.ModifiedFormPages

Parameters   N/A

Returns   N/A

Immediate Window Sample

Set myPages = ActiveInspector.ModifiedFormPages

See Also   CreateItem, GetInspector

ResponseState Property

Determines the status of a task request.

Description   This property can be used to quickly set or determine information on the overall status of a task request. By using this property with automated code, a routine can presort incoming tasks.

Syntax

item.ResponseState = state

Parameters

state   Long. Holds the current state of the task that is one of these values: olTaskAccept (2), olTaskAssign (1), olTaskDecline (3), or olTaskSimple (0).

Returns   Long type

Immediate Window Sample

Set myItem = Application.CreateItem(olTaskItem)
If myItem.ResponseState = 0 Then ? "Simple"

See Also   CreateItem, Save

11

Save Method

Stores any changes in the form fields to the Outlook database.

Description   Changes that occur to the Outlook fields, programmatically or through user interaction, are not automatically stored to the file. Calling the Save method will update any changes. If you don't want to save items you created without user confirmation, use the Display method instead. After an item is displayed, the user is prompted for saving before the window may be closed.

Syntax
```
object.Save
```

Parameters
object   Any valid Item object.

Returns   N/A

Immediate Window Sample
```
Set myItem = Application.CreateItem(olTaskItem)
myItem.Save
```

See Also   CreateItem, Duration, ResponseState

Sensitivity Property

Determines the sensitivity or confidentiality of an item.

Description   The Sensitivity property can be set to make an item Normal, Personal, Private, or Confidential.

Syntax
```
item.Sensitivity = value
```

Parameters
values: olConfidential (3), olNormal (0), olPersonal (1), or olPrivate (2).

Returns   Long type

Immediate Window Sample

```
Set myItem = _
   Application.CreateItem(olAppointmentItem)
myItem.Sensitivity = olConfidential
myItem.Save
```

See Also   CreateItem, ResponseState

ShowFormPage Method

Shows a specified form page.

Description   This method sets the form page to be shown by the Inspector. The Immediate window example requires a custom page tab named MyPage to exist in the item.

Syntax

```
inspector.ShowFormPage(pageName)
```

Parameters

pageName   String. Name of page to be hidden.

Returns   String type

Immediate Window Sample

```
ActiveInspector.ShowFormPage("MyPage")
```

See Also   GetInspector, ModifiedFormPages

11

UserProperties Collection

Holds all of the fields or properties added by a user.

Description   All of the normal fields are referenced by simply using the dot (.) command. However, properties/fields added by the user are stored in the UserProperties collection and must be referenced through it. The Immediate window example requires a user property named Custom1 to exist in the item.

Syntax

```
item.UserProperties(propName)
```

Parameters

propName   String. Valid property name.

Returns   Variant type

Immediate Window Sample

```
MsgBox myItem.UserProperties("Custom1").Value
```

See Also   Controls, CreateItem

Chapter 12
Internet Explorer Object Model Diagrams

In the last few years, the World Wide Web has significantly matured and the browsers used to access Web sites have advanced with it. Almost every browser is now capable of executing script code of some type. Although script languages vary, the object model for Web pages that has been widely adopted is the World Wide Web Consortium (W3C) standard. Learning to program the object model (Internet Explorer embraces the W3C standard) is a prerequisite for most intermediate-level Web developers.

Learning the model also has potential beyond implementing script code in an HTML page. Internet Explorer can be embedded into programs like any other ActiveX plug-in or OLE control. This enables you to supply a browser interface within your own programs. When the IE browser object is added to a VBA environment, you will need to use the object model to control the actions of the browser.

In the following examples, VB Script contained within <SCRIPT> </SCRIPT> tags is used to control the Web page objects. For this section, examples have been included as simple HTML source files to demonstrate the capabilities of the browser. These can be entered into any text editor (such as Notepad) and loaded for execution into Internet Explorer.

Although all of the objects in the model are shown in this chapter's object diagram, only the most useful properties and objects are detailed in the following section. For complete object and member declarations, examine the model itself in the Object Browser.

12

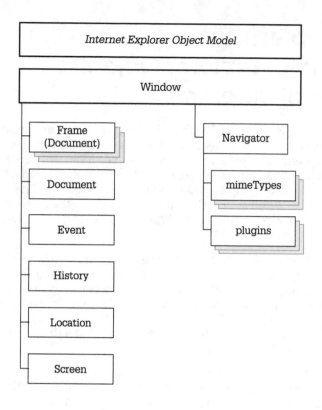

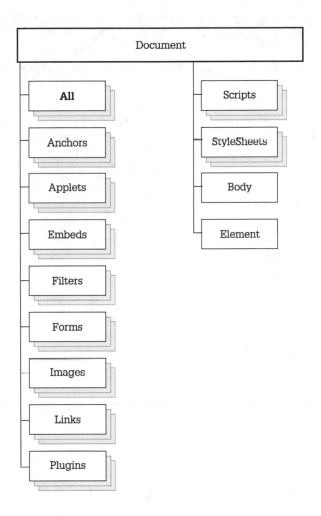

Back Method

Moves the browser back one link.

Description   Use the Back method (a Forward method is also available) to move within the History list of the current browser.

Syntax

```
History.Back
```

Parameters   N/A

Returns   N/A

HTML Code Sample

```
<HTML>
<BODY>
<FORM NAME="myForm">
    <INPUT TYPE="BUTTON" VALUE="Back"
    NAME="cmdGo">
<SCRIPT LANGUAGE = "VBScript">
  Sub cmdGo_OnClick
     History.Back
  End Sub
</SCRIPT>
</BODY>
</HTML>
```

See Also   Document

Document Object

This object is the central HTML document.

Description   The Document object holds all of the HTML, form, ActiveX, Java, and other objects for the current page. The sample code is a simple HTML page that uses VB Script and the Write method of the Document object to write text to the page text.

Syntax   N/A

Parameters   N/A

Returns N/A

HTML Code Sample

```
<HTML>
<BODY>
<SCRIPT Language = "VBScript">
<!--
    myGreeting = "Hello World!<P>"
    Document.Write myGreeting
-->
</SCRIPT>
</BODY>
</HTML>
```

See Also Back, HRef

HRef Property

The HRef property holds the currently browsed URL location.

Description A program can determine the current URL by examining this property. Setting the property changes the viewed site to the new URL.

Syntax

```
Location.HRef = string
```

Parameters

string Required. Complete URL to a location.

Returns N/A

HTML Code Sample

```
<HTML>
<BODY>
<FORM NAME="myForm">
    String: <INPUT NAME="myString" Value=""
    MAXLENGTH=50 SIZE=50>
    <INPUT TYPE="BUTTON" VALUE="GO"
      NAME="cmdGo">
<SCRIPT LANGUAGE = "VBScript">
```

12

```
Sub cmdGo_OnClick
    Dim curForm
    Set curForm = Document.Forms.Item(0)
    Location.HREF = curForm.myString.Value
End Sub
</SCRIPT>
</BODY>
</HTML>
```

➤ Programming Tip

Make sure the HRef property is set to a complete URL (that is, http://…). If the URL is incomplete, an error won't be generated. The browser will simply not move to the new location.

See Also   Back, Document

Item Method

Returns a reference to an item stored on the HTML page.

Description   The Item method is used to gain references to objects that are active on the current page. The sample code demonstrates referencing a Form object on the page and retrieving the value from the input text box.

Syntax
```
Set myObject = object.Item(refNum)
```

Parameters
refNum   The reference number of the object within the HTML page.

Returns   Object type

HTML Code Sample
```
<HTML>
<BODY>
```

```
<FORM NAME="myForm">
   String: <INPUT NAME="myString" Value=""
   MAXLENGTH=50 SIZE=50>
   <INPUT TYPE="BUTTON" VALUE="Display"
    NAME="cmdGo">
<SCRIPT LANGUAGE = "VBScript">
  Sub cmdGo_OnClick
     Dim curForm
     Set curForm = Document.Forms.Item(0)
     MsgBox "You entered: " + curForm.myString.Value
  End Sub
</SCRIPT>
</BODY>
</HTML>
```

See Also   Document, Submit

Length Property

Holds the number of items in an array.

Description   This property contains the length of several of the object arrays that contain the elements presented on an HTML page. The Length property is useful when a For...Next loop must be created to step through HTML elements.

Syntax
```
object.Length
```

Parameters   N/A

Returns   N/A

HTML Code Sample

12

```
<HTML>
<BODY>
<A HREF="teste2.htm">Link #1</A><br>
<A HREF="teste2.htm">Link #2</A><br>
<A HREF="teste2.htm">Link #3</A><br>

<FORM NAME="myForm">
   String1: <INPUT NAME="myString" Value=""
```

```
MAXLENGTH=50 SIZE=50><P>
String2: <INPUT NAME="myString2" Value=""
MAXLENGTH=50 SIZE=50><P>
<INPUT TYPE="BUTTON" VALUE="Dummy"
 NAME="cmdGo"><P>
<SCRIPT LANGUAGE = "VBScript">
Document.Write "<br># of Frames: " & frames.length
Document.Write "<br># of Links: " & _
   Document.links.length
Document.Write "<br># of Applets: " & _
   Document.applets.Length
Document.Write "<br># of Images: " & _
   Document.images.length
Document.Write "<br># of Forms: " & _
   Document.forms.length
Document.Write "<br># of Form items: " & _
   Document.Forms.Item.length
Document.Write "<br>Name of item #1: " & _
   Document.Forms.Item(0).name
Document.Write "<br># of History items: " & _
   History.length
</SCRIPT>
</BODY>
</HTML>
```

OnMouseOver Event

Activates when the user moves the mouse over the specified item.

Description   When generated, this event executes a single line of code specified in the definition of the attached element. Often, this single line of code calls a subroutine or function to execute additional lines of code. The Immediate window example demonstrates using this event with the OnMouseOut event to display one graphic when the user moves over the element (usually a highlighted button) and return it to the original graphic when the user moves out of the area.

Syntax

```
onMouseOver = scriptCode
```

Parameters

scriptCode   A single line of code written in the default language for the page.

Returns   N/A

HTML Code Sample

```
<HTML>
<BODY>

<a href=""
  onMouseOver="imageButton.src='hiliteOn.jpg'"
  onMouseOut="imageButton.src='hiliteOff.jpg'">
<img src="hiliteOff.jpg" name="imageButton"></a>

</BODY>
</HTML>
```

Submit Method

Sends the data entered into the user form.

Description   By trapping the Submit method, as shown in the sample code, the contents of submitted information can be checked. If the data is valid, calling the Submit method manually actually activates the Submit operation.

Syntax

```
object.Submit
```

Parameters   N/A

Returns   N/A

12

HTML Code Sample

```
<HTML>
<BODY>
<FORM NAME="myForm">
    String: <INPUT NAME="myString" Value=""
    MAXLENGTH=50 SIZE=50>
```

```
   <INPUT TYPE="BUTTON" VALUE="Submit"
   NAME="cmdGo">
<SCRIPT LANGUAGE = "VBScript">
  Sub cmdGo_OnClick
     Dim curForm
     Set curForm = Document.Forms.Item(0)
     If RTrim(curForm.myString.Value) = "" Then
        MsgBox "Empty", 16, "Invalid"
     Else
        MsgBox "Full", 32, "OK"
        curForm.Submit
     End If
  End Sub
</SCRIPT>
</BODY>
</HTML>
```

See Also   Document, Item

Chapter 13
Active Server Pages .NET Object Model Diagrams

Active Server Pages (ASP) is the programming environment that executes on Microsoft's Web server, Internet Information Server (IIS). ASP.NET, the newest version of ASP, contains objects that must be understood to create the most effective Web-based applications. These objects enable program code to access user input form data, to read and modify session variables, to manipulate user browser cookies, and even to determine the content of HTTP response output streams.

ASP.NET includes several changes from the earlier ASP implementation that may cause problems for existing code. The primary changes from the original ASP are

- **Change in file extensions** Instead of .ASP and .ASA for program files, ASP.NET file extensions have the letter x added (.ASPX, .ASAX) to signify .NET constructs. You may change the extension on existing .ASP files to .ASPX and, aside from modifications for compatibility, existing code will execute on the new system.

- **<% and %> delimiters can't be used for function or variable declaration** All declaration code must now be placed between <SCRIPT></SCRIPT> tags. Only declaration code requires this new approach; other code will still execute with the simpler delimiters.

- **Collections are zero-based** All collections and arrays default to a lower bound of 0 instead of the bound of 1 that was the standard in ASP.

- **All method calls require parentheses** Previously, if no value was returned by a method, the parentheses could be omitted.

- **Changes to the Request object** Five of the properties of the Request object (Form(Item), Headers(Item), Params(Item), QueryString(Item), and ServerVariables(Item)) held a reference to an array of strings. Each property now contains a reference to a NameValueCollection.

- **New language support** Under ASP, the two primary languages were VB Script and JScript. With ASP.NET, the VB Script

13

language has been eliminated and support has been added for the core .NET languages of C#, VB.NET, and JScript.

- **Single language per page**   Although multiple languages could be mixed on a single page under ASP, ASP.NET requires that only a single language type be used per page.

- **Variant data type has been eliminated**   The default data type is now Object, just as in traditional VB.NET applications.

- **Date variable type is now 8 bytes long**   Previously, a date value was stored as a 4-byte Double value. ASP.NET uses the 8-byte DateTime type.

- **Option Explicit is the default**   Explicitly declaring each variable to be used is now the default requirement.

- **Set and Let keywords have been eliminated**   Object references can now be transferred between variables with the standard equals (=) operator.

- **ByVal is default for parameters**   Parameters passed in ASP.NET use ByVal as the default, although explicit ByRef passing is still available.

- **No more default properties**   Although previously a property could be omitted if it was the default of the object (for example, myStr = txtBox), now each property must be expressed explicitly (for example, myStr = txtBox.Text).

- **Integer values are now 32 bits and Long values are 64 bits**   The size of these data types has been doubled because of the more advanced processors now available.

- **Try, Catch, and Finally error handling added**   Although the old style error handling is still supported, the advanced Try architecture that is part of the .NET is supported in Web pages.

- **Application configuration is held in text-based XML files**   The configuration information is now held in individual XML files (instead of the Registry) that act much like INI files did in previous versions of the Windows OS.

When programming ASP.NET, the most commonly used routines and data sources should be placed in the global.asax file for global access from all the pages of that application. Additionally, objects created in global.asax can remain instantiated for the duration of the user session and are not removed by garbage collection until after the completion of the session.

Although all of the objects in the model are shown in this chapter's object diagram, only the most useful properties and objects are detailed in the following section. For complete object and member declarations, examine the model itself in the Object Browser.

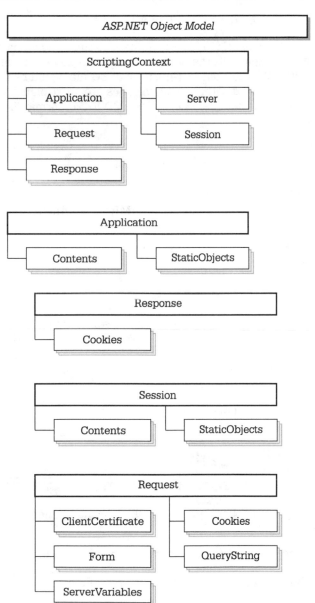

ContentType Property

Determines the MIME type to be sent to the browser.

Description   Each HTTP document sent to the browser has a document type that tells the browser how to display the incoming file. For example, the ContentType for a JPEG file would be the "image/JPEG" string. Other common types are "text/plain" and "text/HTML." The sample code writes a 3D VRML format file into the browser.

Syntax
```
responseObject.ContentType = myStr
```

Parameters
myStr   String type that defines the MIME type of the document.

Returns   N/A

Code Sample
```
Response.ContentType = "x-world/x-vrml"
Response.Write("#VRML V2.0 utf8")
Response.Write("Shape { geometry Box { size 1 1 1 } ")
Response.Write(" appearance Appearance {")
Response.Write(" # Make the box the color blue")
Response.Write(" material Material " & _
    " { diffuseColor 0 0 1 } ")
Response.Write (" } } ")
```

See Also   URLEncode, Write

Cookies Property

Holds the values of client browser cookies in the Request or Response objects.

Description   Cookies can store values in the client browser. In a *Request* object, the properties represent those stored on the browser and are read-only. In a *Response* object, the cookie collection represents the values to be written into the browser, and these properties are write-only.

Syntax
```
object.Cookies[myName] = myStr
```

Parameters
object   Either a Response or Request object.

myName   Name string of the cookie.

myStr   String value of the specified cookie.

Returns   N/A

Code Sample
```
Response.Cookies("mySingleCookie").Value = "Apple"
Response.Cookies("myMultiCookie")( "Inventor") _
    = "Ben Franklin"
Response.Cookies("myMultiCookie")( "Inventor") _
    = "Thomas Edison"
```

See Also   Form, QueryString

Expires Property

Sets the amount of time before the page expires on the client browser.

Description   This property, included in the page being sent, tells the browser when to eliminate that page from the client cache. The Expires property sets the time (in minutes) before the page expires. Setting the property to 0 makes the page expire as soon as it is received.

Syntax
```
responseObject.Expires = myNum
```

13

Parameters
myNum   Number of minutes before page expires in user cache.

Returns   N/A

Code Sample
```
Response.Expires=7*24*60  ' 7 days worth of minutes
```

See Also   WriteBlankLines

Form Property

A property of the Request object that returns submitted form data.

Description   The objects of the Form collection contain all of the values that have been passed to the ASP file from a submitted form. By addressing the properties by name, the values submitted by the user can be retrieved.

Syntax
```
requestObject.Form[myRef] = myStr
```

Parameters

myRef   Name string or index number of the specified value.

myStr   The string value of the specified form parameter.

Returns   N/A

Code Sample
```
Response.Write(Request.Form("singleFormParam") _
    & "<P>")
Response.Write(Request.Form("multiFormParam")(1) _
    & "<P>")
Response.Write(Request.Form("multiFormParam")(2) _
    & "<P>")
```

See Also   Cookies, QueryString

QueryString Property

Returns the values of the parameters passed in the URL.

Description   When a URL is passed through the HTTP protocol, it can contain encoded parameters following the question mark (?)

character. For example, the following URL would pass three parameters in the QueryString property:

```
http://www.cvisual.com/
search.asp?parm1=My&parm2=3&parm3=parameters
```

The QueryString property enables access to all these parameters. The strings in this property are read-only.

Syntax
```
requestObject.QueryString[myRef] = myStr
```

Parameters

myRef   Name string or index number of the specified value.

myStr   String value of the specified query.

Returns   N/A

Code Sample
```
Dim i as Integer
For I = 0 To Request.QueryString.Count-1
    Response.Write(i & ":" & Request.QueryString(I) _
        & "<P>")
Next
```

See Also   Cookies, Form

ScriptTimeout Property

Amount of time before script execution is aborted.

Description   This property, specified in minutes, can be used to limit the time that it takes to execute the script before the script is aborted. This property occurs in the Server object and can prevent a long query or an endless loop from stalling the user indefinitely.

13

Syntax
```
serverObject.ScriptTimeout = myVal
```

Parameters

myVal   Long value type specifying the maximum duration before timeout.

Returns   N/A

Code Sample
```
Server.ScriptTimeout = 4
```

See Also   ServerVariables

ServerVariables Property

Variables that store the state of the current server and client systems.

Description   The ServerVariables properties contain the variables stored by the server about the current client and the state of the server. Some of these variables are recorded in the server log file with each HTTP event.

The following are common server variable names:
AUTH_TYPE, CONTENT_LENGTH, CONTENT_TYPE,
GATEWAY_INTERFACE, HTTP_<HeaderName>, LOGON_USER,
PATH_INFO, PATH_TRANSLATED, QUERY_STRING,
REMOTE_ADDR, REMOTE_HOST, REQUEST_METHOD,
SCRIPT_MAP, SCRIPT_NAME, SERVER_NAME, SERVER_PORT,
SERVER_PORT_SECURE, SERVER_PROTOCOL ,
SERVER_SOFTWARE, and URL.

Syntax
```
requestObject.ServerVariables[myRef] = myVar
```

Parameters

myRef   Name string or index number of the specified value.

myVar   Variant value type of the specified server variable.

Returns   N/A

Code Sample
```
Response.Write(Request.ServerVariables("QUERY_STRING") _
    & "<P>")
```

See Also   Cookies, Form, QueryString, SessionID

SessionID Property

Holds the SessionID number of the current visitor.

Description   When a user initially accesses a Web page, a Session is created and assigned a SessionID. This SessionID value is sent to the client's browser as a cookie and stored in the SessionID property. Programs can use the SessionID to track the user and to record visit preferences. Although this value will be invalid after the session has ended, it can be used for tracking user selections without requiring user login. This property contains a read-only string.

Syntax
```
sessionObject.SessionID = myStr
```

Parameters
myStr   The string value of the ID of the Session.

Returns   String type

Code Sample
```
Response.Write("SessionID:" & Session.SessionID)
```

See Also   ServerVariables

URLEncode Method

Applies URL encoding to the passed string.

Description   This method provides URL encoding for characters such as spaces, control, or escape characters. Once converted, the resultant string can be passed as a parameter in a URL.

Syntax
```
serverObject.URLEncode(myStr)
```

Parameters
myStr   The string value to be encoded into the URL format.

13

Returns   String type

Code Sample

```
Dim myURLStr As String
myURLStr = Server.URLEncode( _
    "This is a test!! Test the & character, too.")
Response.Write(myURLStr)
```

See Also   Write

Write Method

Sends characters to the browser.

Description   This method of the Response object sends text to the browser. The text sent is actual HTML, so any paragraph, table, or other tags can be included in the Write string.

Syntax

```
responseObject.Write(myStr)
```

Parameters

myStr   The string value to send to browser.

Returns   N/A

Code Sample

```
Response.Write("Hello VB.NET Reference" & "<P>")
```

See Also   URLEncode

INDEX

392   Index

INTERNATIONAL CONTACT INFORMATION

AUSTRALIA
McGraw-Hill Book Company Australia Pty. Ltd.
TEL +61-2-9417-9899
FAX +61-2-9417-5687
http://www.mcgraw-hill.com.au
books-it_sydney@mcgraw-hill.com

CANADA
McGraw-Hill Ryerson Ltd.
TEL +905-430-5000
FAX +905-430-5020
http://www.mcgrawhill.ca

GREECE, MIDDLE EAST,
NORTHERN AFRICA
McGraw-Hill Hellas
TEL +30-1-656-0990-3-4
FAX +30-1-654-5525

MEXICO (Also serving Latin America)
McGraw-Hill Interamericana Editores S.A. de C.V.
TEL +525-117-1583
FAX +525-117-1589
http://www.mcgraw-hill.com.mx
fernando_castellanos@mcgraw-hill.com

SINGAPORE (Serving Asia)
McGraw-Hill Book Company
TEL +65-863-1580
FAX +65-862-3354
http://www.mcgraw-hill.com.sg
mghasia@mcgraw-hill.com

SOUTH AFRICA
McGraw-Hill South Africa
TEL +27-11-622-7512
FAX +27-11-622-9045
robyn_swanepoel@mcgraw-hill.com

UNITED KINGDOM & EUROPE
(Excluding Southern Europe)
McGraw-Hill Education Europe
TEL +44-1-628-502500
FAX +44-1-628-770224
http://www.mcgraw-hill.co.uk
computing_neurope@mcgraw-hill.com

ALL OTHER INQUIRIES Contact:
Osborne/McGraw-Hill
TEL +1-510-549-6600
FAX +1-510-883-7600
http://www.osborne.com
omg_international@mcgraw-hill.com